Almost Robbed
Of Everything

Almost Robbed
Of Everything

Stephen Brennan

authorHOUSE®

AuthorHouse™
1663 Liberty Drive
Bloomington, IN 47403
www.authorhouse.com
Phone: 1-800-839-8640

Published by AuthorHouse   03/09/2012

ISBN: 978-1-4670-0040-6 (sc)
ISBN: 978-1-4670-0041-3 (e)

Contents

Contents

Childhood

My first day at school I remember been handed over to a teacher who was friendly however I did not want to be left from my mum and the teacher took me by the hand and brought me to the playground where all the other children were playing ring a ring a rosy.

I sat by the side of the playground watching everyone play I remember I was unhappy and got bored so I ended up leaving, and walked home by myself where my mum was sunbathing in the back garden. My mum asked me why I was home from school so early and I replied that school was over.

Then a few minutes later there were some minders who were volunteering for the day who arrived at the house to bring me to school again for a second time.

I was unable to remember the rest of the day after that I was only four.

The early days of my childhood consisted of primary school and praying to the grotto at a young age from the main gate of the school. After school I d play in the park and play with my brother, sister and mother. I remember jumping off a small wall and climbing the lampposts that were in the park.

In the summer I spent the afternoon collecting lady birds and storing them in a match box and then release them by watching them fly everywhere. Other child hood memories were playing by the beach swimming off the pier on white rock and making sand castles by the shore collecting baby crabs in sandy cove and storing them in sand buckets with my fishing net.

There were always aunts and uncles dropping by the house and friends and neighbor s would also drop by for cups of tea and coffee.

I was close to my mum and when I was not so young we took trips into Dublin city to see the book of Kell s in Trinity college and visit the catherdral s at Christchurch and have lunch and go shopping both mum and son were happy to be spending time together.

The early years were good and I had an ok childhood teachers in primary school told me that I would get involved in drugs and at the time I thought nothing of it I was only eight years old.

Drugs arrived later on after about 12 years. When you are a kid you hear a lot of things and don t really think anything of it until your older I suppose.

I remember my granny who ended up senile and she would come visit our family home one day she repeated so much that who's house were we all in this went on for hours and I turned around to my mother and asked who's house were we in after listening to her for about three hours repeating the same sentence over and over.

My mum commented that I was as bad as my granny that she was the one senile I was always a bit dizzy and had an angelic look about me. People would comment to my mum that I was a lovely child and I received a lot of attention when I was growing up.

Growing up in Dalkey was a lot of fun there were the hills in to play in and friends of mine who lived around nearby had a lot of pets which I played with there was a tortoise that wandered around the garden also there were kittens and cats and an aviary of birds which were amusing to see flying everywhere when you started to scare them off their perches. The baby buggies were very cute.

At the back of my friends house there was a pig farm where the pigs were reared and later brought to the slaughter house the baby piglets were cute and amusing to watch however the smell of pig shit was unbearable after some time so there was only so much time you could spend with the pigs. All in all spending time with animals when you are younger is good fun.

I adopted a cat called smoky who ended up attacking the owners Christmas turkey one year and the owner decided to throw the cat out.

I rescued him and looked after him. I loved that cat and one day he came home with a black and white kitten in its mouth which it took from some litter in the neighbor hood of Dalkey. So I ended up looking after this mystery kitten however the kitten was not responding to the special bottle of milk I bought in the local pet shop and I ended up bringing sutty which I christened to my friends farm where we had a cat who just had kittens to look after otherwise he was going to die.

I left him in for six week s so he was looked after by the adopted mother cat. And after six weeks I bought him home not really knowing which kitten was mine when I dropped him off however I picked the one I thought looked like mine which I dropped off six week s previously thinking that he was the original one I had rescued earlier when my other cat brought him home one day.

Both Smokey and Sutty were doing well until my younger brother arrived on the scene the cat was discarded to the back garden. There were also chickens that took up resident in the make shift shed where the bikes were kept they made such a mess dropping their droppings all over the bikes the eggs were cool though because they were fresh however my parents had enough of their mess and eventually got rid of them.

I remember swinging from the cloths line one winters day there had been a lot of rain and the ground was all covered in muck. All of sudden the cloths line collapsed and all the cloths were on the ground my mum saw the line collapse and went mad she came running out and started shaking me for destroying her washing which she had spent hours doing with an old twin tub.

I was old enough to understand that my mother had spent a lot of time washing the cloths by a twin tub and now they d have to be washed again I was sent to my room and remember staying there for some of the day.

On night s when I was in bed I usually awoke in the middle of the night walking around my bedroom late at night this would usually happen about two or three in the morning with my hands out aimlessly trying to reach for something this went on for a couple of years and I can remember to that time because I felt like I was looking for something inside me which I can still feel like that sometimes today. Not really having found what I was looking for I ended up carrying that through all of my life it s like something that was completely out of reach for me.

Sleep walking is a very solitary thing to do and I spent a lot of time on my own. I remember in my farther s house in the country playing by the pond for hours collecting tadpoles amusing myself for hours on end or jumping about in the hay barn and collecting chickens eggs also picking mushrooms in the fields in the early hours of Autumn. After picking mushrooms in the field we would cook them with some sausages and bacon which my dad and I would have for breakfast.

Friends occasionally travelled too and we would spend most of the time in the upstairs lounge sitting by the open fire, sitting there rolling cigarettes and stealing turf from the house next door and on cold winter nights when the fire died down we would watch television.

I visited the neighbours and was popular with the old ladies who always made me tea and spoil me with cake. I loved spending time in Tipperary on the farms and playing with the sheep dogs Shep and Toby also sitting by the fire with the older people after they had milked the cows and worked all day on the farms. There was always a lot to eat and I loved having country food it was much better than what you would buy in the city. Creamier milk and different cut s of meats and home made breads and different baked cakes.

One summer on my way to the shop for sweets I was playing with matches by a ditch which I did a lot however one day the ditch took off with fire and got out of control I ran in a panic and entered the shop to buy sweets where I picked out some chocolate and crisps and walked back up the boreen to where the fire had started looking on with shock I ran to my father to tell him the bad news about the fire which had grown about 40 feet in length and there were hay barns not so far away which were at risk. I never forget running in, in a sweat thinking oh my god could somebody please control what I had started and trying to explain that it had nothing got to do with me.

My father and local neighbour for the rest of the afternoon used buckets and large containers of water to

11

keep the out of control ditch under control luckily they kept it under control which was a huge relief to me.

My dad was more relaxed when he was in the countryside with us except for this summer s afternoon where he spent the day keeping a fire under control. We could stay up later than when we were in Dublin and played by the river Shannon and spent day s swimming too. It was good fun. And later in the evening we d walk through old country roads with some derelect houses thinking in the dark that they might be haunted with a twilight spooky feeling from them.

Our trips to the country happened four or five times a year winters were cold upstairs in the lounge I always sat and slept by the open fire which I loved to watch late at night and then fall asleep on the sofa when it died down usually about 1 am watching the coals and turf turn to a deeper red imagining pictures from the smouldering coals.

My dad loved having me around because I would cook and clean parts of the house that were dirty and stock the range fire on a constant supply of fuel. Even growing up I d spend days inside on cold winters days cleaning and cooking and maybe for an hour walk around outside when the weather was bad there was not a lot to do outdoors I preferred indoors.

Trips to the country were always freer than at home where my family would spend time in the kitchen watching television. There was more space in the house in the country especially in the lounge which was half the size of the house upstairs with a cool view over looking county Clare.

I hung out with friend s at different stage s of when I was younger. There was a lot of fun growing up in Dalkey especially at Halloween dressing up and going out for apples and nuts.

I can remember when I was about 8 years of age dressing up in a vail and fairy out fit for Halloween running down the street in my element playing like a girl. I d raid my mother s wardrobe and put on her high heels and parade around the garden for hours on end amusing myself.

One time my uncle was there with his partner Gordon playing in my mothers cloths when my dad commented that he did not know what he was rearing and my uncles partner Gordon said you know exactly what you are bringing up. I was quite an effeminate child and was always putting on make up from my sister Dolores, playing with her Barbie dolls which I was a huge fan of and Adam Ant where I was drawing white lines across my face and doing my hair in different styles. It was fun and creative.

This was usually by myself and I when my sister s friends were about.

The church car park was always good fun to play tennis and hang out on long summer days playing tennis and smoking behind the church in the priests field where there were some donkeys grazing on the grass.

Myself and my friends would make swings from the trees and we were always climbing the larger trees looking out from a view from the top overlooking Dublin Bay. There were always a lot of kids hanging out in the church car park. The wall behind the tennis courts there were always tennis balls going missing and if you lost your tennis ball over the wall and went looking for it you usually ended up with someone else s tennis ball too. So you ended up with extra tennis balls after a day of playing tennis.

It was great there for smoking cigarettes out of watch from Adults hanging about the fields with a puff of smoke rising from underneath the wall and when it was time to go home all the other kids would hide their cigarette boxes in bushes and parts of broken walls around the church car park you always go half s with someone of your own age for a box of ten cigarettes back then a box cost something like 70 pence.

Also there was the Dalkey island hotel which had space invaders and asteroids games in the gaming area which we played with friends. One of the machines you could put 10 pence coins into and the box at the bottom would slightly open where you could take the money out of after you put it in. so you d end up playing all day for free.

After a busy wedding in the hotel you could go in and practically empty the machine which would pay for the drinks too. One day I was there with my friends and the guy who filled the cigarette machine accidentally left it open and left.

We all walked off one day with a black bag full of cigarettes which kept us all in free cigarette s for about a month we got away with a lot from the Dalkey island hotel.

Most of the receptionists were all models and every year there was competitions in the hotel for miss Dalkey island they should have never sold that hotel it was in a great location where there are apartments now it was a cool place to be however everything changes.

The harbour beside it was a tourist point to bring people back and forth to the island. In summer there were boats coming and going all the time it was great exploring the island and lying about the small beach. The goats on the island were wild and you could climb up to the top of the Martello tower where you could look out all over Dublin bay. In the parks locally you could fish and pick wild daffodile s and bluebells in spring and early summer. They were all growing wild under the trees and on a May morning the views were amazing over looking Dalkey Island.

I got a lot of stick growing up when I was a kid about been gay my sisters older friends gave me a hard time calling me faggot and faggot features and Stephaine and when I was out on the street in the local supermarket there were some of the rougher guys giving me a hard time too calling me a bitch and that I should go home. Some older guys in the local supermarket would ask me to suck their cocks and at the age of 8 I found this intimidating.

The effect bullying had on me was that with people giving me a hard time at times I spent time alone and became close with my mother.

Primary school was good however I remember at time s keeping to myself and on other occasions running about the schoolyard with the girls that were in my class. The playground in the schoolyard was great with sea views from where you'd play and underneath the playground was a man made rock swimming pool. Where we were always slagging about nuns, swimming there naked, however we never saw any probably just as well.

One Christmas I played one of the three wise men and loved dressing up in my costume and participating in the play. After 1st class I was transferred to the national boys school in Dalkey and entered into second class there I remember a teacher who was from Galway who was in his late twenties teaching. I found this teacher very attractive and probably became aware of my sexuality at the age of 8.

I played with my school friends in the playground different games like marbles and hopscotch I was never into football and always found myself on the pitch of the field kind of wandering aimlessly about with the teacher shouting at me to get a move on. One day however the ball was kicked to me and I scored a goal for my team that was the only time this happened,

In primary school I was on the chess team for and remember playing at a tournament there was a lot of preparation for it and after our school plays where there was preparation for the day that was coming up. Four classmates entered the tournament somewhere on the north side of the city and spent the day playing chess I won some games however I was beating by a guy from Bonnybrook who was sharp and fast at playing. It was a good day out. In second class there were rows for the guys who were the most intelligent and they consisted three rows. The first row was for the smartest the second for the in between and the last row was for people who did not have a lot of intelligence or else they did however did not use it. I was in the second row and never moved from there. This was in second class.

One day while playing marbles in the schoolyard with my friends we saw a guy drop 5 pounds on the ground. The three boys picked it up and thought about giving it back. However we decided to split it in three. Later after school the three of us bought ourselves sweets and drinks. Back then 5 pounds is probably worth 50 euro for three young kids today. While sitting outside the local shop the three of us boys were stuffing ourselves with sweets one of the boys mother s appeared and saw how much sweets we had and questioned us on where the money came from. Paul spilled the beans to his mother and told her where we got it from and later on Paul s mother reported the three of us to the school headmaster and the three of us were punished by our parents and taught a lesson.

I ended up grounded and so was one other I was pissed off that one was allowed to play after school by his parents. I was stopped my pocket money for about three weeks and had to come home early after school for two weeks. I was also stopped from going on the school outing to the zoo too.

In second class there was a school trip to France and I saved for it and was looking forward to it there was great excitement it was for ten days travelling through France the first stop over was in Paris where we spent three days I remember sharing a room with other boys and on standing outside on the balcony the view from the street was great overlooking the Parisian Streets.

We travelled by bus to Rosslare to Le Harve and then travelled by bus to Paris. Paris was very exciting and on the first night we had a lovely meal in the centre of Paris. Later on that evening we were sitting on the coach looking at women on the street dressed in expensive coats hanging out on the street. This was the first time I saw ladies of the night and had one of the older lads explain to me what they were about.

We travelled by metro through Paris and for a young boy I thought this was exciting for me however I was scared that I d be left on the metro by myself and stayed very close to one of my minders. Paris was my first experience of a big city other than Dublin I can remember London as a small child spending it with family one Christmas however I was 8 now and Paris was one city that I d remember more clearly we did all the sight seeing that was there and spent time at the Eifell tower the Notre Dame and also a day at the palace of Versailles it was a marvellous time for a boy of 8.

I remember walking around the gardens of Versailles and thinking how beautiful it all was and admiring the fountains and architecture from the gardens.

On our last night in Paris we ended up at the Sacre Cor where the view over Paris I thought was something else. Climbing all the steps to reach the top was worth it and arriving out at the top with a view over the city was amazing. I and my school friend walked around the top looking at all

17

the street artists and looking into the Salvador Dali museum at the side overlooking the night lights of Paris.

The following morning we left for a trip to Lourdes by coach and spent about 12 hours on the bus travelling through the centre of France in Paris some of us bought fireworks, we were looking forward to letting off in Lourdes unknown to the teacher s of course.

I remember we stopped off in the heart of France in a lovely French town that night and walking around a small town with a beautiful park in the centre of it. It was so peaceful and calm it was a lovely summers evening and all the flowers in the park were in full bloom.

The following day we left for Lourdes and arrived that afternoon checking into the hotel we gathered our bags and packed them into the small designed French lift. In the lift there was a small French lady who took a shine to one of the boys she started hugging and kissing him for no reason the rest of us in the lift starting laughing while Brian pushed her away.

We threw our bags in the hotel room and explored the hotel there was a lovely top floor view over Lourdes from the hotel with table s and chairs we started letting off our bangers and one boy poured firework sulphur over a table and lit a match the sulphur exploded and ended destroying the table he was later punished for it and the rest of us were warned to behave ourselves. Later that day we all ended up in the Grotto of Lourdes where there was an amazing torch light precession where our classes were giving candles and where singing in the choir we had been practicing all year and were singing to our hearts content.

One boy ended up farting into the microphone which echoed over part of the grotto. The rest of the boys started to laugh while one of the priests started to give out. Later on we all entered the baths and were dipped into the water in a small white sheet which was wrapped around your waist it was only for about three seconds and was a very calming experience, after that we were allowed to play around Lourdes and later slept in the hotel I think we were allowed stay up until about 11.30

While the rest of the volunteers spent the time sitting by the hotel bar drinking and chatting. The school trip the following day was spent by the Alps on a lake in rowing boats rowing around the lake it was very peaceful and was a nice experience. Michael Jackson s Billy jean was playing on the juke box how appropriate.

Later that day was spent browsing around Lourdes and sitting on the rooftop terrace drinking coffee and having fun one boy poured sulphur on one of the tables on the rooftop and set it alight and with that there was an explosion on the table and it was destroyed he got into trouble and was grounded from going out that night. The rest of us got away with it.

I shared a room with three others and we played snap and told ghost stories that night and tried to scare each other too. I think the explosion of fireworks earlier on scared enough of us to our rooms.

The following day we were returning to Dublin with a stop over in a hostel before the journey by boat to Rosslare. In the hostel that night supper was served and some of us played pool and played outside in the gardens. It was a warm evening and we were all so relaxed after our adventure in France.

The following morning we left by coach and boarded the ferry from La Harve to Rosslare. It was a smooth crossing and I was playing the slot machines everyone was off the ferry while I was still playing the slot machines my teacher was calling me to leave and I was still engaged in my gambling when all of a sudden I got three stars and the machine dispensed 5 pounds which I happily took from the machine later that day in Arklow I bought some presents for my family with the ones I already bought in Lourdes it was a nice win for a boy of 8.

I spent the next four years at Harold boy s school until I entered Marian college I was twelve now and did not do well at academics and was always baking cakes at home and cooking dinners. There was one guy who I became good friends with and spent Saturday afternoons in the centre of Dublin playing pool and video games with his friends we were all the same age and I remember fancying one girl called Emma who I saw for about three weeks the other time s I spent with my friends in Dalkey hanging out in the local fields smoking and playing video games in the local space arcade hall.

Secondary school for me was not really keeping me interested in my studies and I frequently copied my homework on the dart on my way into school from my classmates. I did well in Geography and English and thought I was better off in a school that was catered more for the arty type of student. Most day s I left my classmates at lunchtime and spent a lot of time on the dart travelling from Howth to Bray and browsing through the shops in town. A lot of this time was spent by myself and while my mum worked part time in the afternoons I returned home about a half an hour after she had left the house for work. Again usually by myself.

There was no one at home until about 5.30 so I had the house to myself for some hours and no one knew what I was doing. I was continously called up to the headmaster for bad behaviour and was suspended twice my mum was called in on different occasions and I was giving warning s for my bad conduct. One day the history teacher flung a chair at me because I was disrupting the class it just skimmed past my face and ended up at the end of the classroom floor I thought this was hilarious because the teacher had missed me so I was brought outside side and giving a wallop across the face and told that I was barred from the class until further notice.

I spent a lot of time on my own when I was either skipping classes and one friend Paul and myself spent our time together on the hop and having chips and tea in Jury s hotel on certain occasions when Paul stole from his father s wallet. The two of us would share pocket money and hang out in the snooker hall s along bachelor s walk. At this stage Paul was been bullied by a kid who was homophobic I also got stick but for some reason was not picked on as much as Paul was. It was terrible and Paul was a fragile child. However something was done about it and the problem was solved after about a year of this going on. Paul and myself were both gay and we were starting to hang out together in a bar on Dame Street called the underground which was in the gay district of Dublin the two of us were 14 and usually sat drinking with the rest of the crew from the snooker hall on Bachelors walk. One evening I left to buy some cigarettes and ended up in a gay bar accidently on Georges Street to buy cigarettes which when I returned I mentioned to Paul where I bought them. Paul replied to me that the George was a gay bar and the following weekend I ended up sitting downstairs with a vodka and lime wandering where all the guys were going to that walked by me.

After my vodka and lime I followed one guy to see where he was going and found myself in a gay disco bar the downstairs bar was for older guy s and while I joined some guys upstairs who all introduced themselves to me. One guy asked me how old I was and I replied 15 and the guy replied does your mother know where you are and I replied does your mother know where you are everyone laughed and I experienced my first night out in a gay bar by myself.

So over the next couple of weekends I spent time on my own going to the upstairs bar in the George joining different people and chatting to different guys I mentioned nothing to Paul and on different nights would be out by myself. I was working part time in a garage cleaning a four court and serving and stocking in a shop.

I also started going to gay clubs and spent some night s dancing and hanging out with different guys for which I ended up with on different night s. Always back at there place. by this stage I was 15.

I was always polite and happy within myself however my brothers friends did not accept me and gave me the cold shoulder bullying can stay with you from an early age however my acceptance into life was difficult and even today I'm affected that's the thing about us gay men we all went through something of that nature and we can identity ourselves in gay venues however some of them are good fun and also risky of been exposed to danger especially younger guys who are just coming out with the availability of drugs.

While I failed my exams in School I left early to do a catering course in Sallynoggin and was also bullied while I was there too. At the weekend I was working on a four court in a garage and pupils from the school would come down and try and rob what was in the garage. I tried to control the situation where I was working with my colleague whilst the crowd from Sallynoggin teck destroyed the four court and ripped open bags of coal and set off fire extinguishers I was left in a wreck and dreaded these knackers coming on a Sunday evening after the roller disco was on. And dreading what I had to face with them on Monday when I returned to my catering course.

So from an early age there was a fear mechanism built inside me almost of dread. Soon after this I was threatened by gangs from my school that I was going to be beaten up and whilst I kept this to myself withdrew into my own world where I ended up with mild depression and started to experiment with drink and smoking drugs for an escapism.

One summers night after working I walked home from the garage on West Pier along Crofton Road and passed the East Pier in Dun Laoghaire where I noticed guys cruising and walking alone I got a rush from this and while observing this kept walking and thought about what I had noticed by this stage I was 14 and the following week had drinks with friends in a bar in Dun Laoghaire and after Dutch courage I left my friends and cruised Dun Laoghaire pier I stumbling across some older guys and picked a guy out from under the arches and walked with him to the other side of the pier where we played around with each other I was in a state of excitement because I knew I was gay and thought that I wanted to experiment with my sexuality. The guy I picked was 28 and I was 14 after about 20 minutes later after having sex I left and walked to the train station to catch a dart home.

I thought about the encounter and decided to sleep and see how I felt the following day after awakening I knew I had opened something inside me from my first Gay sexual experience. I thought about my friends and how I was going to react around them and later that day met up with some and mentioned nothing after that I was cruising most weekends.

One weekend I met a guy who worked in Abracadabra on the main street of Dun Laoghaire in Dun Laoghaire Pier we kept in touch and he was living in a flat on the Sally noggin hill he was 26 and I was 14 we were seeing each other for about 6 weeks in Ben s flat when one night we were talking about my sexuality and Ben mentioned that he was in a Gay Church called Metropolitan Community Church and that the priest who ran it in Dublin could help me with my sexuality.

Ben mentioned to me that he was very good at helping young boys who were gay come to terms with their sexuality I was interested and thought that I could have guidance with my sexuality. Ben had mentioned that he had been helped with his sexuality and that he set a meeting up for me to meet this priest called Billy.

I never thought anything of it and left Ben s later that Sunday night and made an arrangement for me to meet during the week. So on a half day from school the following Wednesday I turned up at a house beside Sandy cove Dart Station and rang the bell for the address I was given for the trap I was lured into without realising it at the time.

Ben answered the door and welcomed me in and brought me into a grotty kitchen where he made me a cup of tea. I noticed that Ben looked different from the way he looked in his flat in comparison to when we were together in Sally noggin hill.

He was wearing a crucifix with formal wear the kitchen was grotty and run down Ben was not his usual friendly self to me and mentioned to me that he was on his way to work and that Billy would be along soon.

Billy s partner was sitting in the kitchen and was introduced to him his name was Jonathon and came across as very distant and camp he was a chef in a restaurant in Dalkey and I felt that although Ben was different in this flat I thought that we still liked each other however the vibe I was experiencing now was completely different.

It was my first real contact with other Gay men and I wanted so badly to connect. With that Billy walked in a priest s uniform so happy and delighted to meet me. I picked up on his chatty and friendly attitude and thought that this person was all right.

Billy said to me that I had nothing to worry about been gay and that when I was ready we could go into the other room and chat. We left the others and sat in a rundown lounge.

Billy just seemed to be so interested in me and asked me about school and how I was doing. I was sitting there in my school uniform thinking that the friendly priest who knew so much about been gay and so confident about it all I thought he had something that I could use.

Billy explained to me that there were about 12 in the congregation and that there was another guy who was 16 and that he was helping him come to terms with his sexuality and that he knew his mother and they all attended church on Talbot Street.

I was welcomed to join at a later date however I was told that I was welcome to drop around anytime and that they were moving out of this grotty hole to a three leveled house over in Monks town in a couple of weeks and that the house was free for me and that I was welcome anytime.

He made me feel more at ease this man was so friendly and interested in me after all he seemed to have my best interest at heart. (Bastard)

I left that afternoon with his phone number and was told that they drank in the Parliament bar on Parliament street and that there was a group going out the following Friday and that I should come along they drove in and there was a lift available for me. I thought this was great and I trusted this man and thought nothing of it and arranged the following Friday to meet for drinks.

Friday arrived and I met Billy in a way I looked up to this man because he was wearing a priest s uniform and he seemed so sure of himself and showy and happy.

That night we drove into town and I was introduced to another couple who were also in the car Ben was there too and Billy was full of chat and excited. We arrived into the parliament bar and Billy ordered a round of drinks for everyone and the five of us sat down and I felt comfortable and in this dark lit bar I felt at ease with a group that seemed friendly after 5 drinks we all drove home and Billy all the time was interested in me.

I was dropped to my home and slept in my bedroom that night and just thought that I had connected with a nice bunch of people and was happy that that was it. I had found a group of people who I thought I could trust.

Soon after that the cult moved into the house in Monks town and I was welcome anytime. By this stage I had bonded well with Billy and with all his knowledge and way of the world and telling me his life story about splitting up with his wife Dianne in Bournmouth after having five children explained to me that he was happy been gay now.

By this stage I was meeting up now with the group most weekends and Billy invited me over to the house and after one night out in town I spent the night with Billy.

Billy s partner was also present to and from the first meeting I did not like this man at all. That night the three of us slept in the same bed with his partner at one side of the bed Billy in the middle and me on the other side.

They started kissing and I was told I was welcome to join in if I wanted too I was drunk and was lying there thinking that I was not really interested and just wanted to sleep with that Billy put my hand on his cock and put a bottle of poppers under my nose I responded Billy s cock was huge and very erect.

With that Billy turned onto me and started kissing and slobbering all over me he tried to get me to join in with his partner however I was not interested and found him quite effeminate and cold. By this stage I had been groomed by Billy and had bonded.

I was reluctant to have sex with Billy and Billy was so persuasive he mentioned that everything was ok this stage he was under the covers giving me oral sex and every so often would come up and shove poppers under my nose. His partner had turned over at this stage and said he was going to sleep.

Billy was in his element and with his unshaven stubble was kissing me and saying everything was ok. I could smell the booze of him and although I was drugged and under the influence by this stage of poteen and poppers and with the drinks in town was out of it for a 14 year old boy.

After about an hour he had sucked me off and had also come himself I was told to relax now and go asleep we slept beside each other the following morning I awoke and left and was dropped to Salt hill dart station.

By this stage Ben had distanced himself from me and I was unhappy about this Ben explained to me that he was leaving for Brighton

There were nights out in town in Barkely Dunnes and the William Tell where I was hanging out with Paul from Castle knock. Paul was also experimenting with drugs and booze and in a way we were like two souls that were coming to terms with been gay.

Barkley Dunne s was a bikers crowd and gay too with a mix of all sorts and was one of the wildest bars in the mid

1980 s and across the street was the William tell that had the funky crowd listening to James Brown get on up and music from the 70s playing in the Georgian designed rooms full of sofas and armchairs with long table s about the rooms

Saturday nights out where a good way to relax from what I was going through and also with my part time job in the garage the effects it was all having on my development. However the threats from the crowd who were coming to the garage from school for me when I was back in school was beginning to take its toll and my self esteem was starting to take an effect on my personality.

I started to stay in bed and get depressed and unhappy about life and started to think about ending it all or running away. My mum suspected something was wrong and one day asked me what was going on so I explained what was happening to me in School for some reason I mentioned nothing about the abuse. My mum reported the situation to my Vice Principle and there was an agreement for me to leave school early 15 minutes before everyone else.

By this stage I was been sexually abused by the head of this so called church I thought I could trust in the so called metropolitan community church and with all this going on I withdrew totally further into drink and drugs parties one night stands and gay saunas. For some reason Kim Wildes Keep me hanging on comes to my mind as in the video of her standing alone singing with the darkness which is surrounding her of what one person did to her especially the lyrics get out get out of my life.

Men spoiled me and also preyed on me however it was not all bad there were nice guys too however there was a lot of exposure to older guys and by this stage I was 15 and with the bullying and feeling s of not been excepted into society

I felt that the only way I could cope with it was to cruise in cruise areas.

It was an escapism from a life of hell also into another life of darkness. I passed my exams in catering college. I left and started working in a restaurant in Dalkey where I ended up practically running the kitchen. Amazingly with what was going on.

I did well there and my friends would drop in it was a relaxed athmosphere and I assisted the baker too that was there making different cakes ice creams and preparing dough prepping toppings for pizzas and serving food on the restaurant floor.

Soon after starting I was working some weeks up to 65 hours a week and was hiring staff and generally running part of the kitchen there was a good crew of staff and I was in with most of them. Bono would drop in for coffee or Neil Jordan would drop in too for pizza and there was the ladies morning who would take over the restaurant for meetings and social groups.

There was also the Bohemian crowd who hung out in the evenings high on drugs and I usually ended up with a glass of wine chatting to some. While I was working in the kitchen there was an order for a round of drinks to be taken from staff and someone was sent into the club bar for a tray of drinks to be bought into the side of the restaurant by one of the bar staff and by the end of a night most of us were well on our way. We were always listening to Grace Jones and Simply red, Sade s smooth operator and some Abba with Frank Sinatra too. Then after closing on Fridays and Saturday on certain night s we sat down and have some caraffs of wine and pizza and sit chatting till the early hours of the morning. It was a cool job to have and was out and about after work with colleagues in different bars around Dalkey village.

I was also hanging out in gay bars in town and dancing in Horray Henries and Mynskies nightclub which later became the legendary shaft in the 1990 s. Unfortunately sexual abuse was going on in my life and did not really think it would have such a detrimental effect on my life until I turned 23.

I worked for about 14 months at Kellermann's and later ran to London to get away from my abuser and the aftermath of been bullied in school and feeling generally not accepted into this world. I suppose looking back I ran from my heart.

Over in London I worked on a night shift cooking for 25 staff and worked by myself I was there for three months and did not socialize with anyone except my cousin and Aunt where we sat in the garden near Twickenham drinking Malibus and coke on gorgeous sunny afternoons in one of the hottest summers on record for the late 1980s in London.;

There were trips to Rich mound and one night pickups in Central London bars where I would pick up guys and spend Saturday night s with guys in different parts of London. There were also trips into Earl s court where I spent night s dancing in Bromptons and chatting and drinking with different guys.

There was a bar called the Colherne where one night I walked into one evening and thought it was too hardcore and crazy I took one look around and saw guys in leather and skinheads with tattoos and piercing s. I couldn't handle it and left and caught the tube to Hounslow where I was living in a flat over a hair salon with my cousin Michelle.

I did not stay in London long and did not get caught up in the London Gay Scene until another 4 years later in my life.

The crowd I was in touch with in Dublin was notorious and involved with drugs and rent boys and prostitution. There was a guy called Barry I met before I ran to London who called me up to see how I was doing. Barry was besotted with me and worked for a prostitute in Dublin babysitting her children.

Barry called one day to say he was coming to London to see me and wanted me to hang out with him while he was there. I was looking forward to seeing Barry and planned some time off to hang out with him.

We spent a night in Bromptons in Earls Court and although Barry was fucked up from drink and drugs and insecure from his parents dying while he was in his early teenage years I enjoyed his company.

Barry was staying in a relations flat in Kilburn and I travelled by tube across London to see Barry. Barry was sitting in this bedsit delighted to see me and we walked through Kilburn to the tube station and ended up in a bar in Victoria drinking. Barry was leaving that evening for Dublin by bus and waived goodbye to me from Victoria bus station asking me to keep in touch it was a Sunday evening and I later ended up in a bar off charring cross road drinking alone. After a beer or two I left and walked up charring cross Road to Compton s in Soho and had some more drinks there was a group of guy s there which I joined and one came onto me however I was not interested I thought they were pretty messy and after that I left and walked to Picadilly tube station and bought a ticket and walked to the picadilly line and waited for my tube to Hounslow east. The journey down flew with the effects of booze and I sat there with a pair of sunglasses on.

After arriving into my flat Michelle had been with a guy who she met whilst living two doors down from us. They had spent Saturday night together and most of Sunday The two of us sat there exchanging what had gone on over the weekend and watched television and then had an early night in.

My aunt would drop by and sit by the window with me watching everyone go by and comment on the handsome guys. My aunt commented to me that it was all happening here and we both laughed.

Blessington Street

By the summer of 1988 I returned to Dublin for my sisters 21 st and stayed with Barry in Blessington Street where most of the house was gay also there were drug addicts coming and going on a continual basis.

I attended my sisters 21st and to my parents disappointment because I was not staying with them in Dalkey. There was a night of dancing and drinking in a venue in a hotel in Dun Laoghaire and it was a fantastic weekend.

I returned to Blessington Street and thought this was all so amusing and entertaining and never experienced this sort of life. Before and whilst on a weekend of continuous drinking and partying the following Monday was sitting in a bar on O Connell Street coming down from the weekend.

I had to catch a flight in two hours and decided to stay in Dublin. Barry had become emotional about me leaving and persuaded me to stay in Dublin that I could move in with him rent free in Dublin.

I was attracted to the party lifestyle and free and easy way of living so decided there and then in the Gresham hotel to stay I was in a drink and drug haze and on a sunny summers day decided to stay all the crowd decided to go out and celebrate and ended up in the George dancing and drinking. Later that evening we ended up in Blessington Street.

I did not really know what I was getting into and just saw the attraction of a party life style and got caught up in the midst of it all.

The house I was living in was full of all different characters coming and going most were on the dole and also on the game. One of my neighbours was a prostitute and used to do a punter in his 70s Barry was working for a lady who was working in a brothel and the other guy upstairs was also working for a prostitute around the corner I was fascinated by all the carry on and settled into the house sure it was a drink and drug haze in a house of bed sit s in rent free with a constant supply of booze and parties.

There was a brothel next door beside where I was now living and I used to sit there watching the clients come and go in. On certain time s I noticed men picking up the courage to go down the stairs and after standing outside hesitating to go in and on different occasions banged on the window behind curtains whilst they were on their way down I was always amused by their reaction of fright and then watch them walk quickly away.

There were constant night s out and endless nights of clubbing. By this stage I started work in a garage around on Dorset Street where I worked three night s a week

Sex between Barry and me was not great and I was looking elsewhere for one night stands with different guys. By this stage I was 17 and was experimenting with different guys.

Never really settling with anyone. Barry was drinking himself into oblivion most night s and I was out and about having a good time. Most people thought about me with Barry and that what was I doing with a guy who was in such a mess and I suppose since been gang raped at 16 and sexually abused before that for 2 years I was on a serious self destruct streak myself And just wanted to get out of my head.

Leaving night clubs I started charging guys for sex on different night s when I was low on money and sold myself on the quays in a notorious pick up area which was used by older men who drove around in cars. The procedure was walk around Burgh Quay and find a reasonable good looking driver who was usually married and most of the time I was usually sucked off in the front of a car further on down Sir John Roger son Quay. Then I was dropped off to where I was picked up on Burgh Quay and then home to my bed sit in Blessington Street. I remember talking to a guy at the door once who used to drop by to see someone in one of the flats. I was chatting to him about Super Tramp the logical song and how the lyrics were good we both agreed.

The house was mad there was a couple in the back flat who were from Kildare and both knackers who had not got two pennies to rub together. They continuously drank and argued. Samantha was yapping all day long henpecking her partner I stayed well away from her because she was mad and her partner was always shouting at her. They had not got two brain cells to rub between them I never knew what became of them. They never went out only to shop for food and go to the off licence when they were drinking they were quiet and then when the booze ran out they were screaming at each other.

I used the money for food and towards cloths. And usually for going out the following night while Barry was collecting rent for the landlord with both of us living rent free there was plenty to go around.

I was out shopping a lot and two friend s of Barry s were dropping around for dope sessions and then we d all take off to a house in Castlenock for more drink and drugs. Watching

34

videos of guys from Thailand getting stoned off there heads from the golden triangle and then watching Disney cartoons. There was a constant supply of duty free because the lady of the house was flying back and forth to London for stock ups. Tigh was interested in my music collection so I brought it along and on these night s Tigh would take his missus by the hand and dance together they had something between them it was love and five children he was a dope dealer who hardly strung two word s together and she was a prostitute who was earning 1000 pound s a week which was a lot of money in the late 1980's they originally lived in Ballymun and somehow managed to get out of their high rise flat and land themselves a house in a private estate in Castlenock good on them I thought at least they seemed happy together. They always danced to Kylies Tears on my Pillow.

After about a year. Myself and Barry moved to Nelson Street and we were given a free hand on doing up our flat which we shopped for and picked up carpets furniture and kitchen fittings picked out spotlights and a television and curtains and blinds. The works.

This flat was rent free too because Barry was working for the landlord collecting rent for the two houses that he owned, There were constant coming s and goings to Nelson Street and I was hanging out with another middle class guy from Omagh.

I helped Chad because he d go out in drag in Dublin to Horray Henries and when he returned to his partner unfortunately got beaten up. I consoled Chad and looked after him when he was in these traumatic states both lads knew deep down that we wanted to have a better life for ourselves. My family wanted me home and also Chads family wanted Chad home Chad used to go around the house singing Shirly Bassey songs and camp it up.

35

When I first met Chad I thought the state of him his face was covered in spots with bleached blond hair and his face was pasted with white foundation and bad make up. However the two of us became close and good friend s to each other as we resided in Nelson Street. We would take trips to the launderette in Phibsboro where we would do our laundry and go to the pub for drinks while it was been washed in the washing machine and then later run around to throw it in a tumble dryer and sit there drinking coffee waiting for it to dry. What a life.

It was the best launderette in Phibsboro and usually there was a crowd of us there once a week and because we were gay got to know some of the women who worked there too I suppose we did not have to be gay to know other women. They were two ladies who were in there mid 50s.

One day I started experimenting with one of the washing machines they were computerised and realised that if you selected a 30 degree wash without a pre wash the machine would start for free. All you had do was select the 30 degree button there was a selection from 30 to 90 you cHose one of them and then selected pre wash or no pre wash however on the 30 without pre wash which was the only one that it worked on you got a free wash so we all started using this when we arrived pretending that we put in money.

After about month of doing this Adam told one of the ladies that was working there to the woman s delight she must have thought I was sent to her in her prayers because straight away she was doing service washes on drop in by customers and not writing them in the book she was earning more than she ever earned in her life.

She asked me how did i figure it out and I told her that I was just messing with a machine one day and discovered it. She was made up the other lady was rumored to have paid off part of her mortguage in no time and the other lady had paid off all her debts.

She started socialising with us and going out on the town. I had a soft spot for her because her husband was a alcoholic who only left the house on his dole day and drank himself stupid for two days. Mary was good crack and always up for a laugh and on certain nights would accompany us to the George bar on Georges street.

However after a year of this the owner of the laundrette noticed because one of the guys had his cloths in a machine early one morning and whist the machine was washing the owner emptied it for cash and discovered that there was nothing in it and thought how was this possible.

Margaret was questioned about this however played dumb and let on that this was the first time that this had happened. Both ladies were kept on and were lucky they were not caught. However there scheme lasted a year and I and the crew in Nelson Street had free washing for about a year. Also free coffee too. I remember one of the women there working one afternoon in her element singing to Charlenes never been to me on a sunny afternoon in a Phibsboro launderette.

One day my dad and older brother tried to bring me out of this situation but I refused. Whilst sitting in a bar on Dorset Street one sunny afternoon my Dad and brother arrived in unexpectedly to try and bring me home.

I ran and whilst running down Fredrick Street held onto railings whilst my dad and brother tired to talk reason to me. They bought me to St Michaels Hospital where they had me tested for drugs while waiting for the results to come through wandered what was going on.

I explained to the doctor that I was gay and living with a guy in the city centre of Dublin and that my family did not know about my sexuality and that I was experimenting with my new found freedom.

The doctor was very understanding and we decided to keep our conversation to ourselves. I spent that night with my family and later returned to the house in Nelson Street.

At the time I did not really see the trouble that was lying ahead with all this and just lived rent free and basically lived it up. There was always a party and I cooked meals for my landlord and different guys that were about. There was a constant stream of people coming and going.

Months would go by where I did not see my family for months on end and would see my sister in town for drinks and meet up for coffee and chats. The house was crazy and across the street was two brother s who were also gay. I suppose when your young and gay you just want your freedom with other gay guys to explore yourself and surround yourself with gay guys.

The police had been around with a photograph of a guy who was murdered inquiring did anyone see his where about s. By this stage I was living with Barry and everyone in the house was either gay or on the dole. There was also a couple in the attic flat they were living together in artistic bliss.

The older one was a dodgy art dealer who was living with a younger lad and the older gentleman paid for most of the drinks when we were all out together, one would draw social welfare on a certain day and was brought out for a night on the town to the Parliament on Parliament street, and then onto to a club. One night the duke box was playing Damien let s do the time warp and Chad was giving it loads and about 10 of us sat around the bar upstairs drinking and singing, I had left the garage and was now working at shop on O Connell Street where I was working across from a notorious pick up area which were the toilets on O Connell Street were.

I befriended a rent boy called James who I started hanging out with. James was a mindful of information to me about the carryon s that was happening just outside were I was working from. There were allsorts married men, granddads, older gay guys and old queens to hustlers who stood at burger king to men who picked up on their lunch hour to guy s who cruised after work.

A lot of the guys were customers in the shop they would come in for cigarettes and drinks. Whilst taking a break from cruising. When the security guard was on his break I had to stand at the door to check for dodgy customers and usually saw what was going on from just across the road.

I never got involved I thought it was to seedy for me however what i was getting up to at night was enough and kept my work life separate. However James contacted HIV and back then in the late 1980 s was a relatively new disease to contract. However it had been on the news since the early 1980 s to me. I was there for James and helped him in his early stages of contacting it.

James was drinking his head off and I joined him on nights out in town for two young gay guy s I suppose 10 pints was a lot usually starting off in my flat with take away beers and then off to the George for the last two hours and then off to night club, and usually stopping off for a cruise on Burgh Quay, and then home. I was not selling myself every night I was out and thank god never fell into it on a permanent basis.

I remember one prostitute who contacted AID s and was still selling himself on Burg Quay and the last time I saw her she was wearing a wig and light cloths on a freezing night wasting away and almost blind.

I had been introduced to her by Barry before and god love her she had no one to help her and she was almost out casted by the gay community. I never saw her after that night she must have died better off when you are in that state I suppose she was also on drugs to and was an alcoholic.

On other days there were poker sessions in my flat with a couple upstairs Patrica was a nurse and Bob was a builder, the four of us sat around in the afternoon playing poker and drinking coffee. I won and usually took the money and usually ended up in the pub for the early evening.

The other tenants that lived in Nelson Street were a straight couple and above Adam s and every weekcnd they had us around for drinks usually a bottle of Vodka and cheap beers. There just seemed to be constant stream of trips to the off licence and sitting around each others flat drinking and chatting and getting trashed.

My flat was the nicest in the building and was always spotless and tidy. I knew that I was only there temporarily because I was not attracted to Barry sexually and knew I had to move on away from this crazy ness.

Barry was an alcoholic who constantly drank and was always in a mess. I knew that I was on a slippery slope and supposingly because I had been brutally raped had settled with Barry something that I did not want. However the rent was free and I enjoyed all the drama about this crazy house on Nelson Street.

Chad and myself were close and paired off together and looked out for each other, Because the house was central to all kinds popped in and in a way Barry was entertaining and funny. He was an insecure alcoholic and was always terrified that I would leave him. Our sex life was terrible and I dreaded having sex with Barry because I did not find him attractive. I suppose when you have been sexually abused you don t really think much about yourself because you have been robbed of your healthy experimental years of good healthy sex experiences. That and from the age of 14 to almost 17

So I kept Barry at bay most of the time usually Barry drank himself into oblivion and when Barry passed out I left and ended up in a club in town drinking and dancing and having fun. There were other hot guys who were interested in me however i never really made the connection and on and off had one night stands.

There was arguing with Barry about my fleeting moments and I mentioned to Barry take it or leave it. Barry did not have a choice because i had the upper hand in our relationship it was definitely not love as far as I was concerned I had been robbed of this from the time I was been raped.

I never really thought about it however was always out and about and became close to a guy who used to drop around from Santry who was over from London and invited me to come over and hang out with him I was attracted to Mr Santry and arranged a trip to London and stayed with my Aunt who was around when I was living there.

So two weeks later I flew to London and hung out with Mr Santry who was living in Camberwell we hung out in bars in Vauxhall and after drinks left to return to Mr Santrys flat where we slept together sex was on and off and I thought that Mr Santry was not exactly getting into the vibe so decided to fall asleep. It was dark when we arrived and earlier on in Soho when we hooked up just had one drink in Soho and then Mr Santry ushered me out and wanted to drink in Camberwell I wanted to stay in Soho however fancied the arse of Mr Santry so decided to do what he wanted to do. Mr Santry was delighted that I was over and he suggested to me that we would have a weekend in London clubbing and hanging out having fun. I was looking forward to the week ahead and the following morning decided to leave some cloths in Mr Santrys which was on the Wednesday morning and left for my Aunts in West London.

Mr Santry joined me after work that evening and we had some food in a pub in Hounslow and later slept together in my Aunts the following day which was Thursday I ended up lending Mr Santry some cash out of my holiday money and was to receive it again on Friday when we were going clubbing on the Friday.

Mr Santry ignored my calls on Friday so I thought fuck him and arranged with a guy I knew in Brighton to stay with and caught a train to Brighton and spent the weekend in Brighton drinking my head off I was giving free drinks from Mark in a bar on Stein Street and saw my fist ever male stripper who was rubbing body oil over him and dancing on a small stage to Donna Summers hot stuff.

Mark was happy to see me and also a familiar face from Dublin and introduced me to his new boyfriend Paddy who he was living with. Later that night I picked up a guy I was attracted to and had drunken sex till the early hours of the morning and returned to the bar on Stein Street for the day drinking and chatting to the locals explaining to them what had happened with Mr Santry.

They advised me to give him a wide birth and I agreed. Later that night I ended up in a club in Brighton and felt like a fish out of water so left and stayed with the guy I had been with the night before.

On Sunday Paddy walked me to my bus and we kissed and hugged Paddy was a sweetheart and I invited him to Dublin and told him that I would be a good guide for him we were both attracted to each other however he was with Mark and I did not want to rock the boat.

I jumped on my bus to London and was happy with my trip to Brighton I had made up for a shit time with Mr Santry and enjoyed Brighton seeing Mark and Paddy and the handsome stranger I had spent two night s with in a seaside bedsit Georgian house.

Returning to London I stopped off in Earls Court and spent the night drinking and dancing in a club in Earls court and thought about my belongings that Mr Santry had and planned to turn up at his job and demand to see him.

Earlier in the week I had walked Mr Santry to his work place one morning after spending our first night together. So on Monday I arrived at reception and asked for him there was a message to his extension number and 5 minutes later this blond haired lady arrived down to see if there was a package for Mr Long and whilst been told no she checked me out and left.

I knew she had been sent by Mr Santry and decided to leave and wait outside in the grounds of where he worked after been told that he had left for the day. It was just approaching 5 and I knew he was still at work.

So hiding behind a tree just at 5 pm I spotted Mr Santry leaving the front of the building looking out to see if I was anywhere to be seen and while thinking that he was in the clear he left the building. I walked up behind him and said thanks for fucking up my trip and told him how let down I felt. I noticed that he was wearing a pair of shoes I had left in his flat and said to him on the bus nice shoes.

We walked to his flat and I said by the way I ended up in Brighton with friends for the weekend and had a great time and hope that Mr Santry had had a shite weekend and that if I knew that this scenario was going to happen than I would not have bothered coming over to London I cleared my belongings from his flat and duty free cigarettes which Mr Santry had helped himself to and then asked for my shoes he was wearing. I was fucked if he was going to have them. So with some of my belonging I walked out and turned around to Mr Santry and said that if this was the way he treated his friends that he was going to end up alone and told him I never wanted to see him again.

Walking through the street s of Camberwell I dumped the shoes in a bin and jumped on a bus to central London and caught a tube to Hounslow and spent the night in with my Aunt. It was Monday now and I was flying home on Tuesday to Dublin.

I thanked my aunt for having me over and that night had an early night and flew home to Dublin to Barry.

By this stage Barry had been evicted by the landlord and I was alone in Nelson Street everyone was inquisitive to me about my trip to London and I filled them in on what had happened.

Apparently Barry had been pocketing the rent collection money that he was supposed to be lodging into an account and this was going on for about four months over the last year Barry was in a constant oblivion from booze and I never questioned where the money came from.

I was working and Barry was working on a building site part time and we were living rent free so there was a lot of disposable income anyway. However Barry was fiddling the rent book too and drinking himself further into an abyss I was certainly not going down with him and just did my own thing anyway.

Our relationship was dead as far as I was concerned because one night Barry got the deep fat fryer and threatened to throw it all over the sitting room floor in a drunken rage and the only way I was able to stop him was by decking him in the head. I had never hit Barry before however on this occasion thought that this was the only alternative to avoiding a carpet full of fat and a room destroyed with an over turned deep fat fryer.

So while I had to contend with a flat by myself now and rent to pay I pondered on what I was going to do everything had changed now, and so my first night back in Dublin I was to see the landlord and tell him that I had nothing to do with it all which was true because this was the first I had heard of it.

On Thursday I saw the landlord and agreed to move to a smaller flat back into Blessington Street where I settled into a cosy bed sit alone.

Barry was in touch with me and I did not want to know however he would arrive on my doorstep drunk and nowhere to stay so I agreed for him to sleep on the floor.

His sister was calling to me saying that his family did not want anything to do with him and that I was all that he had. I explained to his sister that I was having none of it and that I was not family and she would have to deal with him so the problem was passed around. For about 6 months Barry was in a mess from his lifestyle and by the age of 29 it had taken it's toll.

I cooked for him when he turned up and one day Barry left with my dole money and fucked off to the George and drank it all. When I arrived in and demanded my money and Barry sat there locked saying to me come join him for a drink

I told Barry to fuck off and left and ended up behind with my rent for a month.

By this stage Barry was living back in the family home and on dole day turn up in the George pissed and tried to join the rest of us who this stage we just ignored him and carried on with our own party.

The house in Blessington was a dangerous environment the first flat was smashed up one night and another week one of the neighbours was slashed in the face with a stanly knife and I ended up bringing him to A and E where he ended up with 36 stitches and about 2 years of therapy. The guy never was right after that.

By this stage I knew I was living in a hell hole however was working in a newsagents on O Connell Street with an employer who had just been discharged from St John of Gods the two of us ended up good friends and had some night s out in clubs in Dublin.

After work we usually ended up in a bar having drinks. She had just split up from her husband and we had some good chats about life. Her ex husband was Greek and she was just out from hospital for having a nervous breakdown. It was terrible how booze can affect a person. I ended up working there for about a year and a half and eventually left and got myself a job in Trinity college where I was working as a catering assistant.

Gay Influence

Adam had a great gay influence growing up with his uncle Albert and his partner Gordon they were great together and gave Adam a lot of time when Adam was younger.

Adam can remember from the age of three the bond he had with his uncle and boyfriend when they stayed over in the family house he was crying when they left after one weekend without saying goodbye Adam was asleep when they left its funny the bond you can have with people as a child and then with what life can do to you in Adams thirties he is a bit of a recluse that s life though.

Also been gay has a lot to do with it too. Depends on what life style you pick from been a recovering addict, from sex, drugs. And alcohol can take its toll and there are side effects from it too apart from damaging you nervous system you can also be prone to depression.

All is in this book and Adam is learning to survive day by day now from all that has happened. Recovery teaches you that it's a day at time. Coming off drink in Dublin is hard because of the culture of socialising in bars however as you get older you grow out of certain parts of life and change that's what it is all about I suppose.

Still living in Dalkey is good though and walking about this heritage village is nice to do you can get lost in nature as apposed to sex drugs and night clubs half way around the world.

Recovering from sexual abuse is hard there are many acute ways of surviving from it one it is so damaging to one self esteem and you can avoid it for years in Adams case it was nearly twenty years now he is in therapy now for almost two years there has been a lot that has passed and now drug free and sober and dealing with a sex addiction and having good friends and a supportive and stable family helps a lot however credit to Adam too for putting in so much effort to get to where he is today it has not been easy however in some aspects of his life it has been easy.

A lot of men spoiled Adam and having two lovely gay uncles were a bonus. So where is this leading to this book Adam can type at 5 am and think who knows his mum does not want him to do anything with it however Adam thinks that maybe it could become a film with a good soundtrack and also a book.

I hope this book has helped other gay men who have had similar experiences here to recover and stay healthy in the abuse they have suffered however that is what is part of some life. Adam often thinks of other people he has known who have not survived abuse and have taken their lives however support is out there and there is help at hand. It is not a walk in the park and at times its seems as if nothing is going right but that s life and all survivors of abuse can maintain a somewhat reasonably satisfying life from where giving enough time you can grow from the damages that have been done healing is very important and giving the right environment and encouragement can be done.

There is a lot of support from a twelve step program and the people that are in tHose rooms there is a lot on offer and they are not to be sneezed at I don t go to enough of tHose meeting s however because I can still isolate today from people I am still healing from past hurts and am probably doing 50 % of what I am capable of doing however I have got all the time in the world and so what if I am still on the dole in another two years time and I don t have a proper job it s the quality of life that counts and the people that matter to you are the ones that matter and the ones that don t matter well just don t matter. Loving one self and taking good care of yourself is what matters and been there for your family even when you feel like you don't want to.

Life is a struggle and also to be enjoyed and if you stay true to yourself and have hopes and dreams that s cool. I always remember in a video I saw of a gay erotic artist called Tom of finland that if you are anyway different don t give up because of that keep going and give yourself time to heal it s very important to have the space to do that and fuck so what if you don't have that perfect job its not all its cracked up to be money does not make you happier however it does help

I always remember a lady saying to me in a hospice I worked in that love goes out the window when poverty comes in the door she was funny and at 50 years of age was very with it an ex airline hostess. I reckon she saw it all maybe a bit like me yet there is still a lot to see and experience it's a day at a time and I can sit here in bed coming to the end of another winter typing under the duvet thinking its good I am comfortable content warm and loved.

London And Inter Railing Around Europe

Whilst Working in a Diner in Blackrock Adam took a six week trip around Europe for his 21 st birthday and started off in London where he was staying with his uncles he flew over on a Friday night and caught the tube to some family in Hounslow to say hello. In a bar in Hounslow Adam was asking his cousin's partner did he know where he could get some E Roger did not know and Adam was mentioning that he was going to a club in Brixton called the Fridge and thought that he probably score one there. He had never tried one and thought that it probably be cool to see what all the hype was about.

So Adam left the bar in Hounslow and ended up in a club in Charring Cross on a Friday night drinking and checking out the talent. After heaven closed his caught the nightbus back to Blackheath and slept in the upstairs room above his uncles on the middle floor.

The following evening which was Saturday he had dinner and drinks with his Uncles and caught an over ground train from Blackheath and changed onto the tube at Charring Cross. From Charring Cross he changed lines to Brixton and walked up the high street to the Fridge and stood in the que to gain entry. There were lot of people in the que and there was a hostess drag queen ushering people in the door. There were some beefy black bouncers standing outside who were huge and Adam thought you do not fuck with these guys.

He paid a tenner in and left his coat in the cloakroom and wandered around the club it was an old theatre converted into a nightclub with a large dance floor and stage at the end. The place was packed and Adam asked this guy did he know where he could buy an E. The first guy he asked did not know so Adam asked another guy who led him by the hand to the D J box where he nodded at a dealer and approached him and asked him what did he have the guy mentioned that he had some snowballs and Adam bought one.

After that he ordered a beer and moved towards the dance floor that was starting to build up he was casually dancing and with that popped an e and waited for the effect to take place. There were about 2000 other guys there and the stage was full of people dancing.

With that all of a sudden the stage was cleared and Rose Royce came out on stage singing I am wishing on a star with a pink cadilac behind her by this stage Adam had come up on his E and was looking at the handsome hunks manouovering about Rose Royce it was pretty awesome Adam loved that song and was not expecting this to happen. While she was singing at one stage she was looking at Adam and smiling Adam was swaying slowly back and forth and after she finished some strippers up above started dancing to the good men giving it up. All of a sudden there was a build up around the club and with that there was a huge amount of dry ice pumped onto the dance floor with lasers shining through the floor and with that everyone just took off.

While dancing for some time all of a sudden there was this amazing amount of balloons released from the ceiling

51

and were popping down on everyone s head. So with everyone dancing and all these balloons popping up and down for about an hour it was something else the lasers were opening up and projecting almost like a cloud of purple and green and after some time the balloons disappeared. The effect of e and all this happening was amazing to Adam and he felt for the first time in his life that he belonged somewhere and was part of something that was good.

There were nice guy s everywhere and the atmosphere was great with that the balloons disappeared and Adam thought were they really there at all and was thinking was he hallucinating. It was one of the best nights of his life an opened a door to his life that he had never imagined he spent the night drinking and dancing and having a ball at the tender age of 21.

Thinking on the dance floor about nightclubs and what was in store for him for the next six weeks was mind blowing for Adam and thought that if the clubs in London where like this what did the rest of Europe have to offer. There were older guys there too who looked fabulous and fit and sexy too. So in a haze till six A M, Adam spent the night in style and decadence. Fabulous. Where had he been all his life he thought.

There was not much conversation with anyone that night which did not really bother Adam the E was enough to take in and with such a circus club Adam was not really interested in chatting the music was excellent and that s all Adam was interested in.

Later that morning when it finished a lot of the guys stood outside cruising and chatting Adam ended up in Mc Donalds at 6 am for breakfast and came down from his night and later caught the tube into central London for the changeover at Blackheath and collapsed into bed about 9 am Sunday morning.

Everything changed for Adam after that his whole attitude towards life and what he was going to do in the future. After sleeping he left the house and walked into Greenwich to the market and bought some presents for his uncles he was leaving on Tuesday to travel down to a mate in Taunton. So for the remainder of the weekend he relaxed and chilled and prepared himself for the trip to Taunton. Thinking about his night in Brixton and the rave scene Adam thought yeah I can more of that and thought about his trip to Taunton.

Tuesday morning Adam left his uncles and caught a train from Blackheath into the city of London where he jumped onto a train to Taunton and sat there comfortably looking out the window. After arriving in Taunton Adam phoned his mate Chris to say he had arrived. Chris was happy to hear from Adam and mentioned that he would be there in an hour to meet Adam.

While waiting for Chris Adam explored the town of Taunton walking down the main street he liked the look of this town and was looking forward to relaxing with Chris. Chris s dads partner used to go out with the drummer of pink floyd and they shared a nice 18th century stone thatched roof cottage in the middle of Devin. Chris had mentioned to Adam that his father grew hash plants in the back garden and that they would be smoking some of them whilst Adam was staying.

Adam thought that was cool and whilst Chris was working Adam would be spending some time with his dad during the day, After walking around Taunton Chris arrived and picked Adam up they greeted each other with a hug and jumped into the four wheel drive and drove through Taunton until they were in the middle of the countryside driving up and down small country roads they arrived into this lovely stone thatched roof cottage with dogs running and barking.

Whistle Adam was showed to his room upstairs Chris prepared some hash to smoke. It was late in the evening by this stage and both lads chatted about what they were going to do. Adam s dad mentioned that they should visit stone Henge and Glastonbury and that if it was sunny that the beach was not too far away Adam thought that that was nice and was looking forward to the next couple of days. The house was very country and had a good vibe to it. Later that night all said goodnight and slept till morning.

Chris's girlfriend was staying to and later that day took a trip to a housing trust in summerset and spent the day walking around this lovely stately home where they took in some beautiful gardens and lakes. The sun was shining and we all walked about for three hours. Chris s dad suggested that we go to a local Devon bar and try the local cider.

Adam thought this was a marvelous idea and whilst sitting in this lovely Devon garden sat there and had dinner with some local Devon cider we had three drinks and the effect was quite strong so sitting there surrounded by gorgeous plants with the sun going down and talking to the locals was wonderful.

Later that night we ended up home and had some joints. Adam s dad was chatting about Pink Floyd and Woodstock and how he loved living in Devon. Whilst chatting a bat flew into the kitchen and was flying about in a panic so after about 15 minutes we managed to usher it out. And we sat about drinking wine and talking about Dublin and the history between Ireland and England.

The following day we all took off for Glastonbury and had some tea in a traditional English tea house and later walked up to a tor hill and sat there with some hippys looking out onto the English countryside it was quite magical and with the sun setting was quite special. Later that evening Chris cooked and we sat around the kitchen table drinking red wine and with Chris s brother too. Chris s dad was asking Adam questions about where he was going to visit in Europe, Adam was mentioning that he knew someone in Brussels and that that was where he was starting off and that he wanted to see Amsterdam and Munich and parts of Eastern Europe and that he was hoping to Spend a week on Mykonos. And also see the Acropolos.

Chris s dad suggested for Adam s final day in Devon that we should spend the day at stone henge and after if it was sunny we could end up at the beach. Adam thought this was a nice day to spend the last day with some of Chris s family and was looking forward to it.

Later on before it got dark Chris brought Adam to the back of the barn where they entered a doorway that was padded unlocked it into a fine amount of hash plants where the two lads looked at each other and smiled. Later that evening we smoked some hash and slept. Later that night Adam had an out of body experience where he felt his body rising and moving around the bedroom. It was almost like as if there was a presence in the room and whilst Adam slept awoke at 5 in the morning in this Tudor style room looking out the window at a very peaceful setting Adam was having a lovely time and thought how special this time had been.

Whilst thinking about next couple of weeks was looking forward to what was coming up and thought so far so good.

On his last day in Devon we all drove to stone henge and whilst Chris s dad Jerome was explaining about the gathering of the summer solstice and on how that there was a huge gathering of people there Adam thought wow and whilst looking at the stones was in awe on how they got there so many years ago. After about and hour Chris was dropped to work and Adam and his dad drove to the bank and bought some food for the beach we drove down some country roads and arrived almost to a cliff side road which brought you down to the beach where we set up deckchairs relaxed over lunch with some red wine and smoked some home grown hash and comfortably chilled for the rest of the afternoon.

Chris s dad was happy that Chris had a friend in Dublin like Adam and wished him well for the next 4 weeks. Later that evening when the sun disappeared they drove to the house where they ended up later in a local bar for drinks.

The next day Chris s dad drove Adam to the train station where Adam caught a train to central London and jumped on a train to Folkston where he caught the ferry to Belgium he arrived at Bruge and spent the evening walking about the harbour he stopped off at a café to have some dinner and walked about the harbour admiring the yachts and enjoying the sunny evening.

Later that night Adam slept at the train station and jumped on a train to Brussels and met his contact who he knew through a friend of his in Dublin. On arriving at the train station in Brussels Adam was aware that it was six am and walked about the station with a crowd of shady characters hanging about. He stopped at a café and orded a café crème and sat there drinking it and checking his map for a hostel to stay in and while dawn approached he caught a bus to the hostel and checked in. Whilst asleep for some hours after that he met his contact in Brussels in a café called the Grand Café Michael arrived and both guys greeted each other and sat having coffee in the rush hour of Brussels. Earlier on that day Adam explored the city and ended up in a park which had a palace at the end of it.

Later on both lads had drinks at a gay bar and later ended up in another bar just down from one of Brussels attractions called the little pissoure which they ended up at looking at this statue pissing into the pond it was small and cute and later that night Adam said goodnight to Michael and walked back to his hostel where he stopped off at a bar for another beer he was thinking about his time in Brussels and London and Devon all was good however he was on his own in a strange city so decided to go to bed.

The following day he checked out of the hostel and took a bus to central station and looked at the board and saw a train leaving for Amsterdam in twenty minutes and jumped on. Three hours later he arrived in Amsterdam and was looking forward to his day s there and hanging out in cafes smoking dope and checking out Amsterdam s famous Gay Scene.

He caught a tram to his hostel and checked into a room that was sleeping six. After sitting in a café down the street he took off for a café and sat there smoking a joint and later ended up strolling about the city checking out shops and walking about the canals. Later on he caught a tram to his hostel and slept for some hours and showered and threw on a pair of jeans and hit some bars just off Central Train Station on arriving in one bar thought it was very small and ended up walking into another which he liked and sat beside a London couple drinking and chatting. They ended up in the cock ring and had more beers and later that evening the lad s left Adam to his own devices.

Adam cruised around the Cock ring and was in the dark room he could hear someone urinating on another person however was unable to see them. There were two rooms and Adam was going back and forth he ended up with this guy who was cruising in the bar earlier on. He invited Adam home and Adam agreed. They left the Cock ring and drove to his Apartment which was an hour and a half drive out of Amsterdam. Whilst driving the Dutch guy and Adam chatted and Adam was thinking that he was quite vulnerable and realised the risk he was taking.

However when they arrived at the Dutch guy s apartment they had drinks and ended up in bed sex was good and the following morning the Dutch lad brought Adam breakfast in bed Adam thought this was lovely and after breakfast they had sex. Later that morning Adam was dropped to the station and the Dutch lad asked Adam to keep in touch that if he was in Amsterdam again to look him up and said sure.

That day Adam spent some time in a café off the red light district smoking joints and remembered how uneasy he felt after smoking it and later had some drinks in a Gay café just off from where he was staying he stumbled across a market and browsed about. Later that night he ended up in an old palace nightclub with the London couple dancing and drinking, there were go go dancers on a balcony dancing and the club took off. He stayed till about 4 am and whilst outside afterwards did not know his whereabouts. He met some Dominican republicans who he started chatting to and they walked him back to where he was staying whilst walking back they offered Adam drugs and Adam turned them down on their offer. The two lads were friendly and Adam felt safe enough in their company. After saying goodnight Adam slept till the following afternoon and by this stage it was Sunday.

Adam spent the afternoon with the London couple exploring the city they were leaving later that night so we all had dinner in a restaurant that was Chinese. Later Adam ended up in a funky gay area drinking and chatting to some locals. Afterwards he ended up in a kind of loft nightclub dancing however it was not very busy so ended up in the all night sauna just off where he was staying. The sauna was huge and Adam explored the mazes of rooms on the top floor where he was fascinated with the guy s there who were doing bongs and a lot were stoned. Most of the guys were in their cubicles sitting up naked waiting for someone to come in and join them for sex and to do some drugs.

Adam was cautious of all this and spent about an hour walking about these mazes and taking it all in. Later he sat in a Jacuzzi and a handsome older man sat beside him and tried to have sex Adam was not in the mood and turned him down. After that he left the sauna where everyone was in the locker room this queen came in and said twenty past seven again and everyone laughed.

Outside on the street there was a guy there on his bike cycling beside Adam as he walked to his hostel trying to pick him up Adam was not interested and turned into his hostel where he ended up in bed. There was a woman and her son staying in the room where Adam was sleeping and she had a dose of diarrhoea and while Adam was trying to sleep the poor woman was on the toilet running back and forth to the bathroom for about three hours Adam was trying to sleep and was quite stoned the smell in the room was horrible and whilst lying in bed Adam thought would she ever stop going to the fucking toilet it was unbearable you could hear her bowl movements and all Adam wanted was to sleep.

Later that day Adam awoke still in a toxic haze and in the room of six one of the lads lockers was broken into at this stage Adam was paranoid and thought he was suspect for breaking into the locker and had breakfast with the guy who had his wallet stolen there was conversation about what he was going to do about the situation with his money taken and all Adam thought at this stage was that he wanted to leave and sit on a train for some time to his next destination.

So after breakfast he caught a tram to central station and boarded a train to Munich and fell asleep.

He ended up chatting to a choreographer from New York and they had some beers she got off at some stop and Adam arrived in Munich about 8 am Tuesday morning. So after inquiring at information he jumped on a bus to the hostel that was recommended to him and met up with some guys from Newzealand, Australia and Denmark. Later on that night we had drinks in some beer halls in Munich and had dinner with some German ladies who were singing and dancing at our table.

After ordering another round of drinks our waiter brought the pitchers of beers over and on complaining about the heads on the beer he threw us out, I suppose he was highly insulted and thought who were we, only tourists.

So after that we left and walked back to the hostel chatting and laughing, After one night in Munich Adam spent the following day by train travelling to Prague and whilst travelling through the chequisavakia countryside with another lonesome traveller we chatted about Jim Morrison and the doors drugs taking drugs and how he died at such a young age. Later on that afternoon Adam checked into a hostel in Prague whilst travelling by train and tram to his hostel Adam noticed how poor the area was and on entering his hostel realised that it was an old hospital converted into a hostel the feel of the hostel felt like death and Adam thought to himself that he was going to spend as little as time there as possible. He met his roommate and they decided to explore Prague together, Jeff was from Australia and thought Adam was on drugs because he kept saying that the craic was good in Dublin, Adam explained to him that he was talking about fun and that the word was used as slang for fun, Adam and Jeff caught a train to the centre of Prague and walked through the centre of Prague admiring the beautiful architecture. They walked across Charles Bridge and thought how beautiful it was and how calm the river looked.

After spotting a restaurant beside the river they had dinner there chatting about Dublin and Ireland in general. After a couple bottles of wine Jeff decided to call it a night and Adam left him and ended up in an old bunker which was converted into a nightclub.

There was a show on which consisted of a guy dressed in a white sheet with his face painted white and he was dancing around in a strange way. After that Adam left and caught a taxi to his hostel and slept in this ere hostel Jeff was already asleep and later that morning they had breakfast downstairs.

After breakfast they ended up on the underground and somehow lost each other so Adam explored Prague by himself and walked up a hill side to a tower which overlooked the city. The view from atop was really picturesque and on top of the hill was a park and a café however it was a cold day and misty from raining and after spending some time up there Adam jumped in a cable car and returned to the ground.

He ended up having caviar in a restaurant for starters and wild boar in a pink sauce for main course and later returned to his hostel for an afternoon snooze. After sleeping for some hours Adam ventured out and later had some drinks in a bar in the city. He met some people who knew a colleague of Adam s and thought that it was a small world.

The bar was an Irish bar and some of the clientele were from Dublin. After that Adam left and jumped into a taxi and later slept till dawn. The following day he caught the underground to central station and travelled to Venice where he spent the night at the station waiting for a train to Brindisi.

In Venice train station there were a lot of poor people hanging around and by the time he arrived it was about two in the morning and waited until six am for his connection to South Italy. The atmosphere there was very dark and Adam was thinking about the war in Bosnia and thought that some of the people there were refugees and had nowhere else to go. One woman who stood out in particular looked about 50 and she was with her daughter they had some large bags and were dressed very shabby. Adam felt sorry for them and thought that they had nowhere else to go.

After putting his head down he later woke up and had coffee and later about 6 30 caught his train to South Italy the train was packed so he took one of the only seats on the train which was beside a family who looked like they were out for the day there was a Italian lady with her grandchildren who smiled at Adam and she asked Adam did he speak German and Adam replied no then she tired speaking to him in Italian and after that she realised that they both were unable to communicate with each other.

Every so often she would look over and smile and she had a little pooch on her lap. Later that afternoon herself and her family got off and said goodbye and smiled. After about 12 hours travelling by train Adam arrived a Brindise and walked into a tourist office and changed some travellers cheques into cash.

From there he left and had Dinner in a restaurant and found himself with about two hours for his ferry to Athens. He met an English guy called Ben who he spent the night chatting to on the overnight ferry. Ben was also travelling to Athens too. And had an address for a hostel where they decided was a good place to stay. After sleeping on deck later that morning Adam awoke to a beautiful sunrise and noticed how the coastline of Greece looked so inviting Ben was asleep on a bench beside Adam and both lads Admired the Sunrise. The first port of call was Corfu where the ferry stopped off and Adam stood at the side of the ferry admiring the view.

After travelling by some of the Greek Islands later on that day they arrived at a port just outside Athens.

Athen s and Mykonos.

Adam stopped off at Paros and caught a bus to the other side of the Island to a small fishing village Nauousa and found a small b and b where he dropped his bags. After hiring a moped he drove around the Island and stopped off at a beach where he sat in the sun for some time. Late that evening he had some dinner and late sat beside the harbour watching the sunset listening to sitting on the dock of the bay.

After dusk he had some drinks in a club and chatted to some guys from Athens who were holidaying for a couple of days. After saying goodbye Adam drove around Paros and later came off his moped and almost hit a tree. His leg was grazed and was lucky that it was a minor accident.

The following morning he caught the ferry to Mykonos and while stopping at the port found a lady who was advertising some rooms. They drove up a hill and from the hilltop you could see over part of Mykonos. The view was lovely and Adam s room was nice. There was a balcony there which was very peaceful and from the calm summers evening Adam thought sweet.

After relaxing for some time Adam left and decided to venture into the town, and ended up hiring a moped for the following 7 days. The town was picture postcard and very relaxed, he phoned Ireland and spoke to his Dad and told him everything was alright. Later that evening he sat in a café chatting to some guy from England and had drinks in a square chatting to some guys from Canada they were leaving the following morning and recommended some place for Adam to visit. It was a gorgeous summer s evening and a nice start to the week ahead on this Island.

Later Adam cruised around the harbour and met a Spanish guy called Hose they chatted and later returned to Hose s Apartment where they had sex and decided to meet the following day to go to the beach. Hose was in his late 30 s and well built and handsome. He worked in an art Gallery in Madrid and Adam thought it was a good start to his first day on Mykonos. Later that night he said goodnight to Hose and drove up the hillside to his room and fell asleep,

The following day he met Hose and they drove to the beach where they spent the day sunbathing and swimming later that evening they had tea in a café beside a gym where they sat admiring the guys going in and out. Adam and Hose got on well and after tea they drove to Adam s room and later had sex.

Hose arranged for them to meet later that night and ended up clubbing at a club beside the harbour. It was a wonderful night and Adam got very drunk and passed out. He later awoke alone in a daze thinking that he was in a train station somewhere in Europe and thought that he was waiting for a train. Then he came to his senses and remembered where he was so with the staff cleaning up after the night before Adam left and found his moped and drove to his room and packed his beach bag and drove to the beach.

He spent the day sunbathing and walked the cliff beside the beach and just admired the view. It was hot and sunny and there were guys cruising around.

Adam met a French waiter and they had sex and chatted the waiter was from France and was working in a posh restaurant in London after that he returned to the beach and had lunch overlooking the beach. It was so relaxing and peaceful. So for the afternoon Adam sunbathed and dosed off.

After that he drove to his room and watched the sun set from his balcony. It was gorgeous and started to get dark. Later that evening he had drinks in the local square and met Hose. Hose was asking Adam was he enjoying himself and Adam replied that he was having a marvellous time. He introduced Adam to some of his friends and they later walked the pier and sat looking at the moon and reflection in the water. Hose thought Adam was interesting and deep and liked been around him. Adam liked Hose and found him handsome and gentle.

Later that night they slept beside each other back in Hose s room and the following morning had breakfast on the balcony. Hose was leaving in a couple of days and wanted to make the most of his time with Adam. So after breakfast they arranged to meet later that evening,

Adam spent the day browsing around the town and sat in a café having coffee by the harbour, he later snoozed in his room and thought that life could not be any better he was having a wonderful time and enjoyed his time with Hose he was very gentle and about 15 years older than Adam.

On Hose s last night Adam met Paul a Dj from Sydney they were standing by the side of the square and started chatting to each other. Paul thought Adam was from Germany and Adam explained that he was Irish. Paul wanted Adam however Adam did not find him attractive. Paul introduced Adam to his friends and mentioned that they all sunbathed together during the day on super paradise and invited Adam along the following day. Adam was delighted because Hose was leaving and thought that he was going to miss him.

So while Adam and Hose had drinks they said there farewell s to each other and hugged and kissed. It was a lovely couple of days and Adam thought that he was going to miss him. They did not keep in touch Hose had a partner back in Spain and Adam thought that the last couple of days where something to remember.

Paul and Adam met the following day on the beach and swam together Paul introduced Adam to his friends and later that evening they all had dinner in a garden restaurant there were 8 of us. Two guys from Belgian, a couple from London, a nurse from Scotland and a nurse from London, who were camping beside the beach, Paul from Sydney and Adam from Dublin.

Later after sunbathing and chatting Adam and Paul drove up the Cliffside from the beach and stopped off in a supermarket. Adam was checking out the bottles of Ouzo and was thinking did they all taste the same so while there was no one around Adam opened a bottle and took a sip to see if it was the one he wanted. Paul was laughing and thought Adam was hilarious and commented that he never seen anything like it before,

Paul and Adam got on very well as friends and Paul was telling Adam about his flat mate Steve who collected Barbie dolls. Adam was chatting about the London Gay Scene to Paul and both lads agreed that it was fantastic. After the supermarket they sat on a hillside overlooking Mykonos town watching the sunset. It was marvellous and later that evening all met up for dinner.

Paul was explaining to everyone his pick up of a shop assistant in the town earlier on that evening. He was trying on a pair of jeans and the shop assistant entered the dressing room and checked Paul out.

The shop assistant asked Paul did he need a different size and Paul mentioned that they were fine. Whilst looking around the shop with no one else there the shop assistant said to Paul did he want some fun. Paul said yes and with that the shop was closed. They had sex in the changing room and Paul left with his new pair of Jeans. We all thought this was hilarious and everyone was in full holiday mode. There was a pelican walking about casually and cats too. Later on we all ended up in a café by the sea drinking Irish Coffees and chatting. The front of the bar was filled with cocktails and fruit and by the windows the sea waves were splashing up onto the windows the moon was shining and all in all this Island was just wonderful.

One of the guys from London was explaining about the night before how he was giving a guy head and the sun was coming up. The bin men were collecting rubbish and did not even bat an eyelid. He was dressed in linen and thought about his suit and how expensive it was with him down on his knees not caring about his linen suit.

Later that evening Adam and Paul ended the night in an Irish bar dancing and drinking beer.

The following day they hung around the town and sat by a square chatting about nightclubs in Sydney. They ordered fruit with Greek natural yoghurt and sat in the hazy sunshine. Paul commented to Adam that he had a lovely personality and Adam complemented Paul on his friendliness.

Later that evening they all met up for dinner and drinks and browsed the local shops. Paul asked Adam to keep in touch because he was leaving in two days and after their evening they drove along the coast and took some photographs together and Paul tried to kiss Adam. Adam did not take Paul up on his advances and explained that he liked him as a friend. Paul was disappointed however did not try to show it.

Later that night Adam slept alone and awoke with a bug and a dose of the runs. He spent the day in bed trying to recover and missed the boys on the beach. Later that evening he stayed in his room and caught up with boys the following day feeling sick. Paul flew out that evening and both boys exchanged numbers and promised to keep in touch.

Adam was leaving the following day and had drinks that evening in the local square and sat in a café by the pier thinking that he did not want this time to end. He had an amazing time and thought about his trip home to Dublin and how long it would take him. Three days he thought would do it at a steady pace and a stop off in Paris along the way would be a nice way to finish up.

However he was still sick and the wind s on the Island were starting to pick up the ferry s were cancelled for the next 6 hours so he spent the wait curled up in a ball with some stomach cramps. Finally the boat arrived and everyone boarded after some delay. Adam got on deck and settled on a bench he was still sick and by this stage he just wanted a bed.

He thought about Athens and the hostel he stayed in and decided after the 6 hours of ferry crossing that he would check into the hostel. He arrived and while was not able to hold any food down had a youghurt and a pear and later threw it up he had caught some bug and spent two day s in bed in a hostel in Athens trying to recover.

There was a music festival on outside with the music blaring and Adam was curled up in a ball running to the toilet and getting sick. After two day s he felt better and caught the underground to the port and jumped on a ferry to Brindisi. From Brindisi he had to wait 12 hours for a train out of there to Turin because there was a train strike.

By this stage Adam was walking around Brindisi with his back pack thinking all he wanted to do was jump on an overnight train and sleep. So after the 12 hour wait he boarded a train to Turin and spent 18 hours on the train going at a very slow speed because the signal s were down and the train guard had to stop off at the crossing by the roads to stop the traffic for about 6 hours. Adam thought he would never get off the train because it was moving so slow and after been sick thought about his stay in Paris.

Finally after 18 hours he arrived in Turin to another train strike and everyone in the station was stranded till the following morning so he plonked himself beside the information screen and waited for the announcement of the next train to Paris.

While waiting he met a couple Roger and Sarah who were also backpacking around Europe and sat with them having sandwiches and drinking Ouzo. Later that evening they explored Turin and walked around the center stopped off for coffee and chatted about their travels. Roger and Sarah were staying in Paris and suggested that Adam stick with them for the trip to Paris.

After the 7 hour wait in Turin they boarded a train to Paris and slept in a carriage overnight to Paris. Arriving the following morning it was a metro journey to the hostel where they checked in. and that afternoon walked the streets of Paris chatting and drinking some Ouzo it was cold and the effect of the Ouzo was keeping them warm.

Later that evening we had drinks outside a café and by this stage Adam realised that his trip was coming to an end. And thought about his final journey to Dublin and was thinking about travelling though London and considering stopping off.

However he was due into work in three days so decided to take it easy. It was a Septembers late evening summer was over.

So after staying a night in Paris slept and awoke to an early morning start to travel by ferry to Folkstone. He was searched in customs and was asked where had he been in Europe after that he boarded the ferry to Folkstone and snoozed most of the way,

Back on English soil Adam thought about his final journey to Dublin and was caught in the middle of the London underground rush hour. He made it to Huston Station and caught the Holly head train out of Huston and spent the next 7 hours thinking about his wonderful time in Greece.

It was all coming to an end and Adam was thinking about work and how he was due in in two days all good things come to an end. Whilst walking into Holly head train station Adam dropped his back pack on the ground his 2 litre bottle of Ouzo hit the ground and Adam thought fuck it that it had nearly smashed and was lucky that it was still in one piece and thought he had gotten it this far and was going to enjoy it when he was home on Irish soil.

He spent the next three hours on a ferry to Dublin sitting by the window looking out to sea and was looking forward to seeing his friends and catching up with them.

He was picked up at Dun Laoghaire by his dad and drove to the house and sat there exchanging stories about his trip it was a Monday and Adam had an early night and returned to work on Tuesday night to work, he stood at the grill and thought about the weekend ahead and was looking forward to going out with his mate and drinking some Ouzo and invited him over the following Friday for a drink.

After working that week and chatting to the others in work about his travels it was a week to think back about the previous six weeks.

A few weeks later Adam was asked to share a house with some friends in the city center and Adam said sure and moved out and moved into Emmet Street to share a three bedroomed house. While on a trip to London to do drugs Adam met up with some friend s from Kensington and later was introduced to some people in the Fridge in Brixton and in a café there. That night he took some acid and e and later some speed whilst dancing on the dance floor he came up on this and with an explosion of feathers all over the dance floor Adam was flying off his head dancing with a crowd around him everyone there seemed to be off their heads and Adam was dancing with a guy from Limerick who was dancing in his underpants Adam had a pair of sunglasses on and thought that the night was hilarious however he took to many drugs and ended up on a bad trip running about trying to relax and calm down.

He ran into the powder room trying to find somewhere to chill and started looking around him there were skinheads with fans fanning themselves and the rest of the crowd were in the mirrors doing their make up by this stage Adam thought that he had nowhere to relax and stood outside the club realising that he was not in a safe place and thought how was he going to get through the night realising that he was fucked on drugs decided to return to the club and spent the night watching everyone on the dance floor.

While standing there looking at everyone Adam cruised a guy who he thought he could have sex with however was too drug fucked to go over and say hi.

There was another guy who approached him and mentioned that he could come back to his place that his mum was cool with him bringing someone home Adam looked at the guy and did not find him attractive at all and just turned to him and said no thanks mate.

By this stage Adam thought how he was going to come down from all the drugs he had taken and approached the bar and tried asking for a beer the bar man could not understand him and asked him to speak up and while Adam tried could not manage to get the words out just pointed to the red stripe beer and put up a finger to indicate that he wanted one beer. The barman looked at him and just thought that he was in a mess.

Adam paid for the beer and walked about dance floor after seeing a guy lying by the steps on his own messed up Adam thought what was he doing and tried to relax a bit more but could not settle and left and returned to the top floor of the club and just drifted through the crowd and thought he was safer just watching the crowd.

He needed to pee and ended up in the toilet with guy s standing at the urinals playing with themselves and later Adam ended up in a cubicle with a black guy who commented to Adam that he was a very sexy guy however Adam was unable to relax and left the black guy there thinking that if he had sex with someone that he feel better however the drugs where messing him up.

Later he stood beside the D j box and was watching the flashes of light s which lit up the dance floor for about four seconds and watched the expressions on everyone faces and thought that that was awesome there were mini fireworks going off from above and the track that was playing was jam and spoon right in the night.

By this stage Austin found Adam and asked him was he allright and Adam just nodded and was happy to see a familiar face.

Shortly after that they left in a taxi to Kensington and sat in the bedroom Austin produced a bottle of poppers and

Adam took some and two seconds later ran into the toilet and got sick and later fell asleep.

The following Sunday they left and caught the tube to central London coming down from the night before and later ended up in a bar in Soho drinking beer. Adam told Austin he was returning to Dublin and was cutting his trip short. He was shaken from the night before and just wanted to be home in Dublin. They were due to go clubbing later that night and Austin asked Adam was he sure and Adam said yes.

So after beers in Soho they caught the tube to Kensington and Adam packed his bag took the rest of his speed and flew down to Heatrow by tube and checked his bag onto the plane. He skated through duty free and sprayed some perfume on himself thinking it was aftershave and commented to the perfume assistant that it was a lovely fragrance she just looked at him and shortly after that Adam was airbourne to Dublin and could not wait to be home. The journey home was fast because of the speed he had taken and Adam spent the journey looking out the window looking at the light s on the wing of the plane buzzing around.

By this stage he was in Dublin landing and Adam got off the airplane and jumped on a bus to Dublin 7 walked into the house and his flatmate s asked him how come he had returned so early. They asked him how London was and did he want to join them for a joint Adam explained to them that he was tired and needed some sleep and said he explain everything later and fell asleep and later got up and mentioned that he had had a bad trip.

His flatmates were staying in however Adam had itchy feet and decided to go out and ended up in the rock garden in Temple bar where he took some acid and did not want to communicate with anyone by this stage there was lesbian there who commented to Adam that she got the impression that all Adam wanted to with life was get off his head and Adam just looked at her and said nothing.

After dancing and later riding home in a taxi Adam was looking at the taxi driver thinking that he was goodlooking however after paying him he realised that he was in his late fifties and thought about the acid he was on and what it was doing to his mind.

Inside the kitchen Adam was drinking tea and looking at an iron which was bubbling up in front of him and thought that he was definitely hallucinating and rolled himself a joint and fell asleep listening to some chill out music.

By this stage Adam was taking e in Dublin and had a crew of people around him going to all the latest clubs and after parties and his new found freedom was definitely taking off and a lot of people where coming and going from the house.

The two lads Adam was sharing with were stoned most days and Adam often awoke to a joint been handed to him and he always fell asleep stoned there were parties in the house which one of the lounges was used for like a club. The sitting room had four speakers in it and a bass pumper too that was at home while Adams social life had spiraled out of control Adam just thought that he was having the time of his life. He was hanging out in the pod and ended up in the Shaft on Ely place he was constantly in demand and people just wanted to hang out with him.

By this stage everything was in control however Adam was loosing touch with reality slowly and just did not think about his future in a way he did not really care if he was here today gone tomorrow,

He was chilling too at home however there was always drugs and alcohol which he was never really was away from he was on a rollercoaster ride and did not want too get off.

Adams friends were always around and on different night s there were different friends around. They crashed and Adam was always cooking food and been a good host.

He was about town on a mountain bike and sunbathing in Stephen s green and hanging out in cafes and always going to the best clubs it usually started on a Thursday in the kitchen nightclub which u2 had and later onto to house party after he knew some staff in a trendy clothes shops and was doing deals with one of the sales assistants for cloths and while all this was going on was juggling two jobs one three days a week and the other 4 nights a week also there were the trips to London and basically having a ball it was some trip he was on and from the outside all was well however he was out of control and didn't care.

Adam was walking about town in designer cloths and blue sunglasses and with all this happening was hanging out in the latest trendy bars. He was invited everywhere and always attended however his reality was all distorted and was travelling to London every two months for nights on the town over there too.

Whilst this was all going on Adam got offered a job in Café En Seine and took over the carvery and while working there for a week filling in for a chef that was on holidays finished on Friday and was paid cash in hand flew to London again and stayed with his friend Austin in Kensington for the weekend and they were out and about in Soho for drinks and started off in Comptons about 8 on Friday night and at closing time caught the tube to Picadilly to Brixton chatting gearing themselves up for the night ahead.

They arrived in to the fridge and paid their entry fee and later that night were dancing with spiders dropping from the ceiling onto their heads with this huge dog balloon been pushed from one side of the dance floor to the other side, in a way he did not have a care in the world the E took care of that and Adam did not really think what effect it was having on his life. Most of the guys there were on drugs and it was all kind of surreal

Adam would visit his family home and tell his mum about his stories and she told him to be careful and to look after himself. Adam was working and going to college in Cathal Brugha street training to be a chef and was not really missing to many days it was all going well.

One waitress he worked with was doing drugs too and they paired off together and partied together. They were working in an Italian restaurant in Blackrock. Later on she killed herself and suppose could not really handle life. Adam manages today however reality is not the same as his party lifestyle.

Working nights suited Adam fine and was finished work on Thursdays and was off till Monday so the weekend started with friends in the Globe on Georges street for drinks and usually ended up in a club on E and afterwards ended up at a house party one Thursday night everyone was back at a flat on the south circular road dancing to the prodigy and one girl asked was everyone on E and everyone cracked up laughing Adam was flying out to Edinburg at 8 in the morning and by this stage left in a taxi to the north circular road and as high as a kite and packed a bag realising that he had not much time to catch his plane called a taxi with no sleep jumped into the taxi they were driving through Drumcondra and the airport bus was in front of them so Adam asked the taxi driver to speed it up to the next bus stop so he could catch the airport bus because he was thinking that he could save himself some cash he paid the taxi driver and took his suitcase from the taxi and just about caught the bus and arrived at Dublin airport and boarded a plane to Prestwick in Scotland. It was a Friday morning and after having no sleep sat on the plane and dozed off after 50 minutes he left the plane and walked through the airport as high as a kite thinking about the next three days in Scotland and what he was going to do.

Adam boarded a train from Prestwick to Glasgow and cruised the train stewart who was manovering up the carriage with a trolley of refreshments he smiled at Adam and checked his ticket and after about 2 hours arrived in Glasgow early on Friday morning. The next train to Edinburgh was in two hours so Adam walked about Glasgow center looking around and checking out the architecture and had breakfast in a restaurant. It was rush hour and everyone was going to work and Adam had been awake since the night before in Dublin and had drank and drugged and still had not come down. It was a lovely Septembers morning and after about two hours boarded a train to Edinburgh and sat looking out the window at the Scottish highlands and after about two hours arrived in Edinburgh. He walked out of the train station and admired Edinburgh castle and thought that Edinburgh was a nice city.

After finding a hostel about midday checked in and collapsed onto a bed and fell asleep till the afternoon. Whistle waking up Adam checked his Spartacus and asked for directions to a gay bar and sat there at the bar sitting over a pint. There were three people in the bar one guy who looked sleazy and the barmaid and another guy Adam thought it was too early to be sitting around at a bar and asked for directions to the best shopping area and to the record stores. He spent the afternoon looking for 12' records and thought there were a lot less expensive than in Dublin bought about 50 of them and walked about a bookstore browsing at gay literature and flyers for what was on later that evening. So with his record s and flyers of what to do that evening he returned to his hostel and showered and slept. After waking about 9 Adam got dressed and ventured out into the Edinburgh night scene. He walked into a bar and ordered a drink and moved through the crowd and stood at the bar counter checking out the scene.

After about half and hour he got chatting to a guy called Brad who was wearing a baseball cap with a muscle tee shirt. They were instantly attracted to each other and Brad asked Adam where he was from and Adam explained he was here for the weekend. Brad was good looking and had a nice gentle personality. After some drinks they scored some E and sat waiting for it to have an effect. There was a dance floor downstairs and both lads started dancing and with the effect of the E there was a lot of sexual chemistry between them and Brad asked Adam did he want to spend the night with him Adam said sure and after the club was over they walked through the streets of Edinburgh and arrived at Brad s flat and had some tea.

Brad worked in a bar and was off the following day both lads were attracted to each other and started kissing after getting aroused they stripped each other and ended up in bed having oral sex and rolling around in each others arms later after coming they slept in each others arms and fell asleep.

The following morning they had breakfast and Brad walked Adam to the bus stop and they exchanged addresses and decided to keep in touch.

After returning to the hostel about 11 pm Adam walked about princess street and walked up to Edinburg castle and paid in and walked about the castle admiring the view from the castle wall it was a nice sunny afternoon and after about an hour walked through the streets of Edinburgh stumbled across a park and spent the afternoon sunbathing and watching some guys playing football. After about 2 hours he ended up in a toilet and cruised a guy at the urinal and after checking each other out both guy s left however Adam lost the cute skinhead guy who was wearing tight jeans and a bright tee shirt and walked by Edinburgh theatre and down onto the main street of Edinburgh he checked out some shops off the main street and was in a trendy cloths shop browsing through the flyers of what was on that night.

With his information on what was on Adam returned to his hostel and slept for some hours later showered and ended up in the bar he was in the night before. He got chatting to some local lads and they were saying how small Edinburgh was and that they preferred London that London had more to offer than Edinburgh for a guy that was gay. They also mentioned that Edinburgh was too small a town for someone to be anonymous and that everyone knew each other.

After spending the night chatting to a group of guys Adam left early about 2 am and said goodnight and walked back to his hostel and slept till early Sunday morning his flight was at 6 so he packed his bag and caught his train to Glasgow it was a grey day and Adam sat on the train looking out at the Scottish countryside after two hours he arrived at Glasgow and caught a train to Prestwick airport and flew home to Dublin.

That evening he spent the night with friends smoking dope and listening to music.

On Monday he returned to work and caught up with his work colleague Mary and worked the following week till the next weekend. Mary was on drugs too and Adam and Mary were both mentally intuned some of the other chefs that were there to were also on E too and the Egyptian brother and sister who were almost running the restaurant were quite judgemental of Adam.

They were from another culture and saw Adam as a party boy who was living it up. The Egyptian chef told Adam that he should grow up and while Adam prepared desserts and salads and spent his days baking bread and making ice cream got on well with the rest of the staff. Paul was gay and Adam knew him from been out and about in gay bars in Dublin and recommended Adam for a position in the restaurant. Paul was flamboyant and was always cracking jokes about absolutely fabulous sweetie darling darling sweety.

There were time s when the staff sat around on lunches chatting and eating pizza. Mary was fun and she and Adam were out on different night s clubbing in Dublin. On their days off they d spend afternoons in cafes drinking coffee and chatting about different D J s and nights that they had out in Dublin. Adam often bought wine from the restaurant and have nights in drinking in his bedroom with friends and smoking hash.

Adam was seeing Ben from London who also worked in a restaurant in Blackrock and would meet him after work and jump in a taxi and go clubbing with him.

Ben was older than Adam and lived on the South Circular Road in a Georgian style house which he let out some rooms to tenants. Bens house was designed very well and he had a lovely dog called snuggles who had a white shaggy coat and was always very playful.

Adam invited Ben home one night after the George and they saw each other for about 4 months. Ben was from Devon and had lived in London for about 15 years and had met an Irish opera singer who lived in London and they decided to buy a house in Dublin and turn it into a gay B and B.

Adam and Ben got on well and did E together and Adam would stay over with Ben and they d hang out together. Ben was an only child and his partner was from Ballinasloe.

They were together 5 years and their relationship had drifted. Ben explained to Adam that their sex life had dwindled and they had grown apart and that the house was going up for sale and Ben was moving back to London they both had enough and they decided to call it a day.

Adam enjoyed his time with Ben and they were both laid back and easy going together.

Adam bought Ben to different parties and one Star party they were at in a hair salon on Exchequer street Moby was there and it was for a girls twenty first. It was invitation only and a lot of people were trying to get in. Adam was there with his friends and Ben and Adam bought his brother too it too. It was a fantastic night and everyone spent the night dancing till about 8 am.

Whilst the sun was coming up there were builders with hard hats on working outside and looking in and laughing. One airline stewardess was asking Adam how long were himself and Ben together and Adam mentioned 4 months however Ben was going back to London and while Adam explaining this to her she mentioned that they were a nice couple and it was a pity that they were going to part.

Later on in the morning Adam left with his friends stopped off in a shop on parnell street to buy rizlas and chocolate and walked though parnell street and mountjoy square as high as kites the foursome ended in Adam s and all ended up back in Adams bed the four of them sitting up and chatting smoking joints and listening to music. After sleeping for the afternoon Brian arrived in with a tray of tea and toast for us and we sat there coming down from the night before the four of us had been partying all night and Brian bought us in a tray of tea and we sat there drinking tea and toast.

The other three left Adam in bed and ended up in the parliament on parliament street for drinks. Adam did not feel like going out and stayed and got stoned and slept till Monday morning. He skipped college and spent the rest of the afternoon pottering about the house with Brian sitting in the lounge playing with his play station and rolling joints.

The rest of the week was in work in Eddie rockets and Roccia nera in Blackrock juggling two jobs and waiting for the weekend ahead. Adam was still going out with Ben and was not looking forward to him leaving they were hanging out in the POD and taking E and partying together usually they ended up in Brian's on Monday or Tuesday watching Videos and drinking beer smoking joints and having sex.

There was a continuous amount of drink and drugs and none of it seemed to end. Whilst living in Emmet Street one evening Adam decided to stay in however Brian and his Partner arrived home with magic mushrooms with some of there friends and there was about ten of us off our heads in the space of an hour everyone took a large handful and in the space of half an hour everyone was off there heads and whilst sitting in the sitting room chatting and continuously laughing we were all so high that we needed to calm down so Adam bought a vinyl which he bought in London called calm down and take it easy because we were all so high.

At one stage the sitting room felt like we were at a slant and everyone was seeing visuals and Adam mentioned that he was about to fall out the window. So he put on Chris and James calm down and take it easy.

Whilst listening to the track one of the lads was up off the sofa manoeuvring to the guitar to the sound and all were calming down.

Whilst under some control, we all calmed down, and later everyone was walking about the house tripped out of their heads.

One of the house mates was in his room listening to chill music and Adam entered and was trying to have a conversation however by this stage we were all in our heads and trying to get some grip on our state.

Brian and his partner ended up in bed whilst Adam was in his own room listening to Sabres of paradise smokeblech and trying to relax.

Whilst everyone ended up in their rooms the rest of the guests were in the sitting room chatting continuously.

By this stage Adam was bored and asked everyone did they want some food so about 3 am he made a vegetarian curry and dished it up.

The kitchen was trashed and everyone had been in there helping themselves to food and all the units were open. Adam didn't really care and cooked around most of it all and later we all ended up in the lounge area having a curry about 4 am. The rest of the crew left about 6 and Adam and his house mates were still awake.

Whilst coming down at 7 Adam thought he could sort out life and felt so natural and in touch with his body, Adam got into bed and fell asleep and thought what a crazy night this was one night he was trying to stay away from drugs however the drugs came to him.

Adam slept till late in the afternoon and later ended up in work in Roccia Nera trying to work and kept himself in the prep area of the kitchen making ice cream and desserts and preparing different salads. Decorating them in different way s and jazzing up desserts and enjoying his creative side.

Brian asked Adam why was he a chef and Adam replied because it was trippy and he turned to his partner and said did he hear what he said.

Living in Emmet street for the best part of a year Adam completely lost touch with reality and by Christmas had withdrawn into his own world. He had left his job in Roccia nera and whilst the rest of his colleagues in Eddie Rockets were leaving for Australia Adam's world was soon to change.

His colleagues in Eddie Rockets were preparing to leave for Australia and there were new managers checking out the state of how the restaurant had been run. And were not happy with how it had been.

Charlotte was manager and Sal was supervisor and rostered all the crew that were partying together on the same shifts and had the rest of the staff working together. It worked out well however when all this changed Adam was left in limbo and when the rest of them all left Adam left too.

So then this was where he just got into drugs even further and decided that that was it and thought that he was in a no win situation and thought fuck it that he was just going to kill himself with drugs by this stage he did not really care and was definitely not looking forward to spending Christmas in reality especially how he was living his life.

He signed on the dole and was even missing to sign on and thought what was happening to him.

Whilst at home that Christmas Adam was in a drug haze in his mind and thought that he was not in a happy state and just completely lost interest in life by this stage. His work colleagues had left for Australia and with both jobs gone all was in a state.

Adam left his family home on Stephen s day and arrived to Emmet Street crying and himself and Brian sat down and got stoned again,

By this stage Adam was withdrawing from everything and was falling into a state of depression and thought that he just drink himself and drug himself to death, what was there left to live for he thought and spent the next six months unemployed and going to college as a day release chef. He was out and about in bars in Dublin and cycling about on his mountain bike.

He was having conversations with his sister Patsy in the Hairy Lemon and she was saying that Adam was burning his brains and thought that he needed to cop on. They'd walk through town and go out for dinners.

Six months passed and Adam spent time in his room doing drugs and partying at the weekend. Adam missed his colleagues big time and was left with a big gap in his life,

Concentration was a problem however Adam thought with the amount of drugs he was doing that something had to give either suicide or a drugs overdose. All was not well and the crowd he was with were doing his head in.

Most of the time was spent cruising Fairview park having sex with strangers and getting stoned. The occasional time Adam would drop home to his parents and the rest of the time was spent in night clubs off his head on E. picking up guys and bringing them home and having sex.

One guy Adam met was home from New York and thought Adam had really changed and was quite concerned for Adam and how he was falling deeper into drugs and that his reputation around Dublin was at stake Adam just did not really care. And Peter commented to Adam on how much weight he had lost and what did he really want to do with his life.

Adam just lay in bed with Peter thinking that he was unsure and Peter when leaving told Adam to take care. Adam had met Peter two years previously and they hung out for about a month.

Peter was telling stories to Adam about New York dark rooms and the mess that some of the guy s were in. He had met Mark Almound there and mentioned some other famous men. Peter thought that Adam would be well interested with all this. Adam agreed however Peter mentioned to Adam that if he got into drugs in New York that he could end up coming home in a body bag that you could really loose yourself over there and no one would know.

It had been an interesting night with Peter and Adam never saw Peter again. From what he heard he was still living in New York.

So after that Adam fell further into drugs and just got off his head. Time passed in a haze and Adam spent his day s walking through the streets of Dublin and cruising in pick up areas. A place he stop off was at Stephen s Green and on a few occasions had sex with the door man from Brown Thomas who was always cruising in Stephen s Green park.

There was hanging out in cafes in off Grafton Street and back in Emmet Street and smoking hash with Brian. There were people coming and going to the house because Brian s partner was dealing hash and there was always hash around the house. Adam hated the atmosphere and just fell further into a dark space and while people were always around and noticed that Adam was loosing the plot Adam just got stoned and spent his time afterward in bed alone.

St John Of Gods Admission And Meeting Mathew

This was ongoing for about 6 months and college was becoming less and less so. Eventually he moved home and later signed himself into St John of Gods where on arriving with his dad on one of the best summers on Irish record. Adam was brought to a psychiatric lock up ward where he spent about three weeks. On been shown into an empty room one of the nurses looked through his belongings and contents in Adam s bag.

Whilst looking in his bag the nurse confiscated Adam s nail sissors and razors. While looking at Adam Adam thought that yes she was thinking what he was thinking that he just wanted to die.

It was all so blasé to Adam. It was a gorgeous sunny evening and Adam looked out his hospital room window and admired the lovely view which looked out onto a garden and tennis court. Adam thought that he was here for the rest of his life and decided that he was never going to leave and thought that this was it.

After walking through the maximum lock up ward Adam noticed the other patients who were all in a mess and so unhappy and sedated. There were television areas and smoking areas and Adam thought that it was all so quiet.

The nurses team were in an open window office and doing there administration. Later Adam was giving some sleeping pills and tranquilizers and after some time with a doctor fell asleep. Before going to sleep Adam thought of his time in Eddie Rockets and Roccia Nera and the amount of travelling he had done now he was in a lock up ward for suicide people and thought that this was it. Soon after that he fell asleep and awoke the next morning to a lot of activity going on.

It was about ten am and Adam was asked by a nurse did he want breakfast and Adam passed. Later on he was seen by doctors after he was having a bath and they were looking at him sitting on his bed in designer tracksuit bottoms and a body to die for.

That's the thing about drugs they give you such a dillusion and false perception on life and all the highs are just in your head. The doctors suggested to Adam that he rest and they would return to see him in the morning.

It was the summer of 1995 and the hottest on record since 1976. Adam spent three months there and with the right medication over time stabilised and was visited by friends and family however was cut off from a lot of people and whilst some relations visited he thought that he was so messed up from drugs and depressed this is what the doctors were saying and recommended that Adam rest.

All Adam wanted was out of this situation and was not really interested in responding to anything so he would have breakfast and go back to bed after medication time and sleep till lunchtime after lunch it was hanging about the t v room and the day was filled with medication and waiting around for tea and visitor s in the evening.

There were a lot of visitors in the evening and Adam just sat there listening to his parents and friends.

By this stage Adam s brother and partner had a baby boy who would drop up and visit in the restaurant café down stairs most people were looking at Adam and his family and smiling at Adam s nephew and looked at Adam as if to say he has a lovely family. Adam sat there thinking that all he wanted to do was stay in bed. Three weeks in a lock up ward with other screwed patients all Adam wanted to do was sleep.

For one of the weeks that he was there in St Paul's there were fire drills where everyone had to go to the nearest fire exit and wait for the drill to be over. This went on for about five nights in a row and whilst everyone congregated there after about twenty minutes everyone went back to bed.

One guy commented that it was like hide di hoe. After all Adam had basically turned into a drug addict night club recluse. He was not mixing with many and just wanted to get more drugs to numb out and sleep.

After three weeks Adam was transferred to the freer lock up ward and spent about three weeks there playing tennis and golf and walking around the grounds, by this stage Adam explained to his family that he was sexually abused and when it had happened and that he was going through the aftermath of it all and that he was mentally in a mess. From drugs and alcohol. His dad thought that Adam was very casual about it all and addressed Adam's attitude about it all that he was all so blasé about it.

By this stage Adam did not really care much however enjoyed spending evenings with his mum and dad out at the garden chatting and Adam s parents encouraging him to get better and promising him that he would.

Adam always fell asleep after his parents visit felt more hopeful and was feeling better in himself. After three weeks in the less observed lock up ward a lot were in for drugs and alcohol too.

One evening whilst sitting in the lock up ward with this batty woman who only came alive at night she had one of the patients opening and closing windows and whilst she sat beside Adam she shouted cat sat rat Adam thought she was hilarious because she was always calling for nurse and got herself prepared as if she was going out.

However after doing herself up she go running off to bed like most patients did most where in bed by 11 30 Adam felt good by this time that he had made it through another day and usually fell asleep by 1 and dreaded the day ahead the following morning.

After breakfast he usually fell asleep for an hour and just hung around the ward after medication. He was attending occupational therapy and one day was asked to draw a picture of something on a blackboard for everyone to guess because it was his turn. He drew a marble and no one could guess it and whilst becoming more inpatient after ten minutes one lady mentioned to him that he certainly knew how to pick them. There were about twenty people there and none could guess what was drawn on the board.

Adam was so disinterested in life and on certain day s would bake the odd apple tart and just hang around the not so locked up ward watching television and been unable to concentrate on anything thinking that the television was talking to him and that the cartoons that he was watching were relating to him. Been heavily sedated Adam thought that his brain was fucked up and thought God how was he going to repair the damage that he had done to himself from Drugs.

On day s when he was in the mood Adam spent time playing tennis with other patients and while playing a game it was hard to concentrate on the score and other guy s were also in the same boat however they were not on drugs or had alcohol problems which Adam had had.#

There were afternoons out to Stillorgan for coffee s and Adam would spent time browsing the shops realising that he was completely broken down and thought about his future and where he was going to end up when all the dust had settled.

There were other patients there who Adam knew and Adam spoke briefly to them not really wanting to communicate at all. There was a nurse there who brought Adam around the grounds of St John of Gods and asked Adam what he was going to do with his life and Adam thought about going back to college when he was well to finish his exams.

Adam thought that his male nurse was very nice and enjoyed his walks with him and talking to him.

After about a month of been on the not so locked up psychiatric ward Adam was transferred to the free ward where you had your own room where you shared a room with another person. Adam was sharing with a farmer who was there for a few day s and Adam thought about having sex with him but realised that he needed some self control because he was not attracted to him however Adam s intuition was telling him to keep to himself. The farmer moved out about after a week and Adam had the room to himself.

There were day s where he spent his time in bed most weekends and Adam s dad visited one day with his brother Derek who brought Adam a letter from friends that Adam worked with in Eddie Rockets.

It was from Andre who Adam originally got a job for and they worked together side by side on the grill in Eddie Rockets cooking together and also hanging out together too in Dublin.

Adam realised how much he had lost because now his friends some of them were living in Sydney and Adam was in Psychiatric hospital in a mess. Andre was writing about the wedding he was at over in Sydney and that how wonderful life was in Australia Adam always wanted to go and thought that his life was over and that how was he going to ever fulfill his dreams.

So after Adam s visit from his Dad and younger brother Adam just reclined to bed and then in the middle of the night would go running to the nurses office to ask her for a sleeping pill to try and get through the long night thinking of the day ahead.

His nurse would suggest to Adam that he was too young for a sleeping pill and that he should try to sleep naturally.

Adam agreed and usually fell asleep about 5 in the morning and awoke at lunchtime usually drinking three cup s of coffee and having lunch and then it was out to the garden s to admire the flowers and have coffee before tea in the restaurant café.

The ironic thing was that Adam used to work in the kitchen as a commis chef 8 years ago for a month and served food in the wards to patients who were sick. Some of the patients commented to Adam that his food was good and now Adam was on the other side of the fence.

He knew some of the staff and Adam felt embarrassed to be on the other side because of the stigma that is associated with mental illness.

It was a huge loss to Adam to be in the situation that he was in. however all was not lost because he was due to be out soon and however Adam was terrified of facing the outside world again because his mind was in so much fear. His doctors were encouraging him to return to college and finish his exams however Adam was hanging out in the after ward thinking about his life and what to do. Reality bit and although Adam had received a card from his employer wishing him well and that his job was still open if he wanted it which was hopeful so Adam left St John of Gods to return to work on a part time basis and also started his second year in college as day release Chef in Cathal Brugha Street to finish his training as a chef.

So three months had passed and Adam was back in the real world again. There was only one person in college that knew Adam was in hospital and she was very supporting. By this stage Adam was living at home and out and about Again with some of his friends.

This was September now and Adam was doing well. Work was going well and so was college however Adam was only mixing with people that he knew and decided to keep it that way. His parents were happy and so were his friends. However all the crew that he had with him before had disappeared and moved on in their lives and so had Adam.

One night out Adam picked up a guy who was a model in the front lounge and Adam spent the weekend with him they hung out and had fun and this boosted Adam s confidence and realised that life was on the uptake.

It was nice four days together and both guys had had problem s with drugs and talked about it. The two of them parted after 4 days and that was that.

Adam was happy and happy that life was returning to a normal level again. Living at home was a stabling environment for Adam to be around.

Then one night Adam walked up to a guy in the George and asked him did he want to fuck and the guy in question was from Australia. He replied to Adam that he would get back to him later and Adam said that he be around.

Later that evening the Australian guy introduced himself to Adam as Mathew and that he was welcome to spend the night with Adam.

Adam was happy and both lads left the George together and walked up the quays of the river Liffey to an apartment that Mathew was staying in.

Adam commented to Mathew that he could be a killer and that he could murder Mathew in his sleep. Mathew laughed and told Adam to stop going on that they were nearly at where he was residing.

So the two lads spent the night together and exchanged numbers and hooked up the following weekend at a Traditional Irish session in a bar on Harcourt Street.

Adam was introduced to Mathew s friends and they commented to Adam that he looked stoned, Adam had smoked a joint before arriving and sat beside the lads chatting and joking.

Mathew s friends asked Adam where he was from and Adam replied Dalkey and they commented to Adam that he must be rich. Adam laughed and said it was not his property and that he was living with his parents.

Mathew asked Adam was he well off and Adam said reasonably and Mathew smiled. There was a good connection between Mathew and Adam and Adam asked Mathew about his family in Melbourne and was he from a well off family Mathew laughed and so did Adam.

After the trad Irish session we all ended up in the George dancing together and Adam spent the night with Mathew in the Harcourt Hotel on Harcourt Street. They made love and slept together naked with MTV on playing Oasis.

The following morning Adam left for work and arranged to meet Mathew later on in Tomas Reids Bar on Parliament Street. They drank a few beers and chatted about Australia and how Mathew ended up in living in London for 2 years working in a hotel in Kensington as a conference and banqueting manager. Both lads had been to different clubs in London and commented about how London was an exciting place to be for a gay man.

Originally Mathew arrived in Dublin for a two week break and got ill and needed dental treatment and had to stay on. He had met Philip in Melbourne who was originally from West Meath and they kept in touch and Philip invited Mathew to stay in Dublin. So Mathew arrived for a two week trip and however got sick here and had to stay on.

Mathew commented to Adam that he was glad that he did now and thought that both lads could have a lot of fun Adam agreed.

Later that evening both lads arranged to meet up again and after six weeks moved in together on the North Circular Road. Soon after that they flew to London and stayed in the Kensington Palace Hotel on the 7th floor with a balcony overlooking Kensington Palace.

After checking into the hotel they turned on the tele and Rose Royce was playing wishing on a star. Adam commented to Mathew that this was a sign because the first time Adam was on E was in a the Fridge in Brixton he saw her play and now that the two of them together in London Mathew kissed Adam and both lads left in a taxi to go to a bar in Earls Court where Adam suggested they have a few beers which was good on a Thursay night in London.

After about 5 drinks both guys were dancing and having fun. Both guys commented to each other about the men s toilets and that how a lot of the guy s were standing at the urinal s with their cocks hanging out semi erect and Mathew said to Adam that this happened more in London than in Dublin Adam agreed.

After dancing and sharing poppers both guys left Bromptons in Earls Court in a Taxi and arrived to Kensington to chill. They stood outside on the balcony overlooking London and arranging their itenary for the next four days.

Mathew suggested to Adam that they go see the changing of the guards and then onto Harvey Nichols for lunch and browse the designer shops on Bond Street and then onto Soho for drinks he mentioned that Sheila would like that because she had never been to London before and Adam said that would be nice for her.

This was Mathew s plan. Adam s was that on Saturday night that they go to the Fridge in Brixton and then onto Trade in Holban Hall Mathew agreed that that be cool and he mentioned that the three of us go to the Ritz for afternoon tea because Sheila would enjoy that.

So Friday morning Mathew left Adam in bed for Heatrow to pick up Shiela from the Airport and bring her back to the hotel.

Mathew commented to Adam that he was culture shocked when he first arrived in Picadilly Square and trying to navigate his way around the London underground Adam agreed that it was not an easy task.

Adam was bathing when Sheila arrived and greeted her in a towel she looked at Adam and commented to Mathew that he was gorgeous and commented that they were going to have a lot of fun in London.

So after having dinner in the restaurant we had drinks in the hotel room and left the hotel and caught the tube to Picadilly Square and had drinks in a bar in Soho.

Adam ran into some mate s that he was hanging out with before and Austin was happy to see Adam with Mathew. He asked Adam how long was he staying in London for and Adam mentioned that he was here till Tuesday Austin said brilliant and we all had a good night in Comptons in Soho.

After leaving Adam arranged to meet Austin in Brixton on Saturday night and kissed each other goodnight.

We were all on a high and ended up in the hotel about 1 am and watched television till three fell asleep in a relaxed state and awoke for breakfast the following morning and sat down stairs in the breakfast room thinking about our Saturday night ahead.

After breakfast we ended up in Kensington Market and in a local bar for some beers sitting it was quiet and chilled.

Adam phoned Austin to arrange drugs for the three of us and then and later on had dinner in a restaurant in Soho. After dinner it was drinks in the village and then after that we were on our way to Brixton by tube. We changed onto the Victoria line and arrived up onto Brixton High Street and walked up to the Fridge and met Austin inside and then dropped our drugs.

The three of us were dancing and having fun and were upstairs overlooking the dance floor. At about 4 in the morning Mathew left with Sheila and Adam stayed on dancing till about 6 with Austin.

After it was over Adam caught a taxi to Trade in Holbon and arrived at the door and ended up on the dance floor dropping another E he was as high as a kite and was chatting to different guys one lad from Devon commented to Adam that he was very handsome and Adam explained to him that he was on holiday s with his partner from Melbourne.

Adam did the rounds of Trade and ended up been approached by this sexy guy who was in his late 20 s he told Adam that out of all the guy s that were here that Adam was the most handsome guy in Trade and asked him where he was from Adam told him that he was from Dublin and Nick commented to Adam that he spoke very well.

Nick was gorgeous and both lads spent three hours chatting to each other and really enjoyed each others company.

Nick was a jeweller and very successful and also very sexy the conversation just kept flowing between them and while dancing and chatting Adam was having the time of his life.

By 12 30 Adam left and said goodbye to Nick. Nick told Adam that Mathew was a lucky guy to have Adam in his life and gave Adam his phone number and said that if he was ever in London again to have no hesitation in contacting him. They hugged each other and Nick tried to kiss Adam but Adam pulled away and told Nick that he did not want to spoil his trip in London with Mathew.

Adam walked out of Trade that morning in a state of awe it was a sunny Sunday afternoon and Adam caught the tube to Kensington and walked into the hotel and up to his room.

Mathew left a note for Adam saying that he was in the Ritz with Sheila and that he be returning about 7 Adam fell asleep for the afternoon and later on Mathew returned with Sheila.

They asked Adam how was his night and Adam said fantastic. Mathew said good and that if he was up for it that they d go out for dinner somewhere that evening.

Adam stayed in that night and while Mathew and Sheila left for dinner. Adam was on the phone to his uncle Albert and Gordon to arrange to meet up on Monday for dinner.

Adam arranged to meet after Adam s uncle finished work. About 6 on Monday evening However the following day after seeing the changing of the guards and having lunch in Harvey Nick s and browsing the boutiques on Bond Street the three of us ended up in a bar in Kensington drinking for the afternoon.

We got so pissed that we cancelled Adam s arrangement to meet Albert and Gordon and ended up in a taxi back at the hotel drinking out on the balcony. At about 7 the three of us snoozed for the early evening and got dressed and ended up at G A Y in Charring Cross Road till about three in the morning dancing.

Adam saw a hot guy in hot pants dancing and ended up in the toilet with him. However Adam panicked and told him that he was here with his partner and that it just did not feel right and left and returned to Mathew and Sheila.

They asked Adam where he disappeared to and Adam just mentioned that he was cruising around.

That night Adam felt an inner insecurity about himself that he had always felt and stood at the dance floor watching everyone have fun while he was just observing all around himself.

After G A Y finished Adam Mathew and Sheila left and ended up in Soho in a late night café drinking coffee Sheila was looking forward to Dublin and having fun in Irish Bars.

So after coffee we hailed a taxi and ended up back at the hotel. Adam was talking about different part s of his life and people that he knew in Dublin after three hours part of his sexual abuse came up and he started to panic

Sheila looked shocked and Mathew told Adam to calm down and have a bath. Sheila gave Adam a valium and Adam ran a bath and relaxed.

Mathew came in and asked Adam was he all right and Adam replied yes. Mathew got a towel and put one on the floor and told Adam to relax on the floor he wrapped Adam up in another towel and lay Adam on the floor and he cuddled in beside Adam at about 6 in the morning after lying together for about an hour Mathew took Adam for a walk through Kensington Park and while the sun was coming up on a September s morning Mathew offered Adam a life in Melbourne together.

Mathew mentioned to Adam that he wanted to take him away from drugs and told Adam that he was in love with him. And that they could have a future together. Mathew explained to Adam that life was better in Australia and after working together in a restaurant in Dublin that they were good together.

Friends of Adam s also commented to Adam that Mathew was good for Adam and other people were saying how that they be together forever.

Adam sat in Kensington park with Mathew on a park bench and agreed that if what Mathew was saying about a new life style in Australia and that it was always a dream of Adam s to go live in Australia for a year.

So that was that we returned to the hotel room and spent the night in watching films and ordered room service for tea. And Adam and Mathew slept together and cuddled up till the following morning.

The following day we checked out and caught a taxi to Liverpool Street bought crossants and coffee. We sat down on the train Adam ended up vomiting all over the next carriage the croissant was like a lump of led in his stomach Sheila asked Adam was he alright and Adam said he felt better. She smiled at Adam and Adam slept at Mathew s shoulder.

So off we were to Dublin we travelled to Stanstead Airport and checked in and boarded the plane to Dublin after an hour over England and the Irish sea we ended up on Irish soil.

We travelled by taxi to the north circular Road and left our luggage at our flat. Sheila commented on how the houses on the journey from the airport were smaller and that they must be government housing we were travelling thorough Cabra at this stage.

When we arrived at our flat she was happy with inside because she mentioned that it looked cosy and she was looking forward to exploring Dublin.

We had tea and some toast and we walked down Oxmantown Road and through Stoneybatter and from there onto the quays and into Mary Street and had tea in a café there.

Sheila commented and laughed about the cakes that were in the bakery that we were in because some were advertised as fancy s and she thought this was amusing. She mentioned that she had never seen a cake advertised before as a fancy.

After tea we ended up on O Connell Street taking photographs and Adam explained to her what the clock was doing in the Liffey River and she thought that it was funny that it was put there for the countdown of 1999-2000

After walking through town we ended up in Powerscourt Shopping Centre for coffee and sat there watching hot guy s go past. Sheila thought Dublin was a nice city and was happy that you could walk anywhere in the center of the city.

After Powerscourt we ended up in Renards and sat there for the happy hour drinking beers. Then afterwards we ended up in Little Caesars having dinner and some wine. Then it was off home to have an early night.

Adam was working the following day so he organised himself for work and then fell asleep with the fire lighting.

Sheila and Mathew were off to Guiness Storehouse the following day and doing the Viking Centre and then Adam was to hook up with them in the Front Lounge later on.

Adam worked his day in a restaurant on Dawson Street and ended up in the Front Lounge afterwards to see Mathew and Sheila.

Sheila was in Dublin for a week and it was also Easter Weekend. Adam had arranged with his parents to see them on Good Friday and travel down to Glendalough.

So on Easter Thursday we got very drunk in an Indian Restaurant on Dame Street where we ended up till about 11 30.

Then on good Friday we travelled out to Dalkey and Adam stopped off to buy flowers for his mum Sheila commented on the dart that the houses were very upmarket on the south side of Dublin and that Dalkey was a lovely town. It was a sunny day and the three of us arrived at Adam s parents.

We had tea and spoke about London and where we were staying. Sheila got on well with Adam s parents and when we left for Powerscourt Sheila took a photo of the front door where she mentioned that she was going to call the photograph the Dalkey door.

After that we drove to Glendalough and walked through the pathways along to Dan s lake and spent about 2 hours there.

Sheila walked ahead with Adam s parents full of chat while Adam was behind with Mathew.

Afterwards we ended up in a restaurant for Fish and Chips the five of us and then it was home to Dalkey.

We said goodbye to Adam s parents and Sheila thanked Adams parents for a lovely afternoon and for their hospitality and when we walked to the dart station Sheila said they were lovely and that Adam should talk to them more.

Adam agreed and on Good Friday we darted it into town and then jumped into a taxi and asked the driver to take us to the North Circular Road Park End. When we arrived in we lit a nice cosy fire and sat about chatting and drinking some wine we had bought from London.

After that we fell asleep and awoke Easter Saturday Adam was working and Mathew was showing Sheila around

Dublin. Later that night we ended up clubbing at the Pod on Harcourt Street on E and then it was home.

On Easter Sunday we opened our Easter Eggs and had some breakfast. We ended up in the Front Lounge for the afternoon and sat with some of Mathew s friends for the afternoon afterwards we ended up out for dinner and then home to bed we were quite tired and happy to be free together.

On Bank Holiday Monday Sheila left for Galway by herself and was so looking forward to going to the west of Ireland Adam was explaining to Sheila about the Stone Walls over in the West of Ireland and that as soon as you saw them you knew you were there and about how they were all built by hand in the early 1900's that that was what a lot of farmers did all day when they were not farming.

Sheila was excited to see Green Fields that that s how a lot of people related to Ireland. Mathew and Adam spent Bank holiday Monday together and had some lunch in the barge Bar beside Portobello. And later that evening Adam and Mathew sat in with some wine and rolled a few joints and watched television and made love

Sheila returned after two night s in Galway and was delighted with herself she had met a guy over there and he had shown her around Galway they had sex in a field and he wanted to meet her in London because her Journey home to Sydney was via London.

She was so happy about Galway and was excited about meeting Mr Galway in London he had booked a flight with Sheila flying into Heatrow he was flying into Stanstead and they were to meet at Liverpool street.

Sheila had thanked the two of us for giving her such a good time and she said that she d always remember her stay in Ireland.

The following day we had a good bye breakfast and Sheila left in a cab for Dublin Airport we hugged and kissed her and she was all excited about meeting Mr Galway in London because otherwise she was on her own in London for one night before she left Heatrow for Sydney.

The story afterwards was that Sheila ended up almost missing her flight and that she had to run for the plane and boarded as the last passenger she delayed everyone who was sitting there when she walked thought the Isle of the Aircraft everyone looked at her and this is who held us up.

She was blessed because when she arrived at liver pool street Mr Galway was still waiting after about 50 minutes of been late. Sheila arrived to platform 5 in a panic to see Mr Galway standing there with a bunch Flowers they apparently had a fantastic evening together and the following day Sheila flew home to Sydney.

Mathew and Adam were falling in love and spent a lot of time together on day trips about Dublin and hanging out in different clubs and bars in Dublin.

Adam was attending Cathal Brugha Street and working part time Mathew was working full time. Life was great for the two of us. We were good for each other and always up for new adventures together.

Mathew mentioned to Adam that when we were over in Australia that we could visit Sheila in Sydney and that we should start saving for it. We were leaving in nine months time Adam agreed and so with that the two of us opened a joint Bank Account and decided that Mathew take care of finances.

The agreement was that because Mathew earned more than Adam that Adam pay his share of rent shop for Grocery s look after that end of things and have about 100 pound s to spend a week and the rest was to go toward s saving Adam agreed and Mathew was to do the same and save the rest of his earnings.

Adam had looked after Mathew in Dublin with a job in Fitzers on Dawson Street he was working behind the bar and doing very well after a month they gave him a rise because he had so much experience and Mathew was happy.

We bought a travel guide on India and sat in bed reading about where we were going to go our plan was to spend a month in India and two weeks in Goa. Taking in the Taj Mahal and then onto Bombay and catch a ferry to Goa.

We sat in bed on nights off reading about different places to visit and thought about our future together in Australia. Mathew often commented about on certain occasions how home sick he was and that at times he wished that he was back in Melborne just for one night.

Adam did not understand Mathew s pining to be home and because he was high on drugs Mathew too that life was going to be good for the two of us.

Mathew hung out with his friends at the week end while Adam saw his and later in the night we'd hook up and take E and go clubbing to the POD, George and Shaft.

During the week we would end up in Frank Ryan's on Queen Street and then walk home about 12 am and sleep in each others arms. For Christmas Mathew Spent his time down in West Meath and Adam spent his time with his family in Dalkey.

They were about a week apart and on Christmas day spent about an hour chatting on the telephone. Mathew was explaining to Adam that he was chatting to his parents and was told how much he was missed and that they were delighted that he was with a nice guy in Dublin.

Adam s mum would meet Mathew for lunch in town and they got on well together. It was funny because on the second week we were together Adam bought Mathew home early one morning and while asleep in Adam's room Adam s mum walked in to see the two of us in bed.

She gave out to Adam and apologised to Mathew because Adam was told not to have casual flings back in the house. Little did she know she be staying with Mathew s parents in Melbourne 14 Months later.

So later that morning Adam left for work with Mathew and stood at the end of the platform in Dalkey and Adam s mum was on the same train to standing at the other end of the platform too.

So Valentines day was approaching and Mathew had booked a table in a top restaurant on South William Street where the two of us were looking forward to our first Valentine s day together.

On valentine s day we exchanged cards and left for work later that evening we shared a fabulous meal together and ended up in the George Adam got so drunk that he blacked out and awoke to having a threesome with two guys in a sauna off Dame Street all that was going through his mind was fuck what had happened and felt so guilty about Mathew.

So at about 3 Am Adam left and arrived home to a cold Mathew Adam just stripped off and fell asleep so out of it beside Mathew he felt horrible and Mathew would not turn into Adam.

The following day Mathew awoke and asked Adam what had happened and Adam explained to Mathew that one minute he remembers been in the George and the next after trying to recollect his hours in a blackout told Mathew that he came out of his blackout in the Gym Sauna.

Mathew told Adam that he left Adam to go to the bar and that when he returned saw a single flower in the corner and Adam gone. He was very disappointed and so was Adam.

This was a regular occurrance with Adam disappearing and Mathew was quite open minded and thought that Adam would grow out of it.

As time moved on between them doing drugs together and partying out for dinners and keeping a relationship going. Mathew and Adam were allright. Apart from Adam s sexcapades Mathew was no angel either all was well.

One night out Mathew bought a psychiatric nurse home for a threesome and Adam sat downstairs listening to music and smoking dope Mathew was in bed with the guy he pulled and after about three quarters of an hour Adam joined in. Mathew got jealous and ended up kicking Adam in the noise Adam was furious and told Mathew that he could not handle the situation and that what the fuck was he doing.

Adam nearly fell over the Mezinina and then Adam knelled up in bed and nearly ended up giving Mathew a box however held back and left upset and crying. On leaving the flat Adam kicked in the glass door on leaving there was a crash of glass everywhere and the psychiatric nurse shouted that you guys are crazy.

Adam shouted to Mathew that he should count himself lucky that it was either him or the door and that he decided that it was the door instead.

So Adam hailed a taxi about 4 30 in the morning to friends who were living at Croke Park End of the North Circular Road however his friends were not in so it was another drive back to the flat. Adam arrived in to a messed up flat with no Mathew the psychiatric nurse was well gone and Mathew was downstairs with our neighbour.

She knocked on Adam s door and asked could she come in she told Adam that Mathew was sitting with her on the sofa very upset and would Adam go down to him. Adam arrived in and Mathew stood up and apologised to Adam and asked him to forgive him. Later that morning they fell asleep, and awoke to each other saying, that if they were going to have a future together that this should never happen again.

So on Adam went with his fleeting moments keeping them separate from Mathew.

Summer was approaching and we travelled to Sligo and cheked into a hotel just off O Connell Street we had tea in the dining room and left to browse through the streets of Sligo we had drinks in different bars and then we ended up back at the hotel.

At about 1130 a disco started down stairs and Adam sat in bed with Mathew and decided to check it out. Mathew stayed in and Adam got dressed and ended up downstairs drinking Malibus and coke and chatted to the best looking couple there who were from Derry.

Adam asked them about cloths shops in Belfast and what was good in Derry.

After dancing till about 2 30 Adam left and joined Mathew in bed the following morning we had breakfast and drove through Donegal talking about the meaning of life and about where do we go after this life Mathew said who knows.

We passed a police car along a mountainous road and with some sheep the cop waived at us and we stopped shortly afterward and took photos of each other standing in a stream. Donegal was so peaceful and later that afternoon we checked into a b and b in Burton Port.

We had a twin room with a view over the sea it was so picturesque and after showering and making love we ended up in a bar for a drink. From there we had bar food in another bar Mathew had Steak Diane and Adam had fish and chips.

Afterwards we slept in separate bed s because they were too small for two and the following day we drove to

Derry. Mathew was praised by the landlady for been such a nice friendly chap and we drove and arrived in Derry where we had lunch in a small Market Style alleyway which the restaurant overlooked.

It was a sunny day and we browsed the shops where Adam bought Ray Band Sunglasses got a hair cut and Mathew bought a watch.

Later we drove to Belfast and approached from West Antrim to a view over Belfast where we drove around Belfast looking for a hotel. After checking out some we drove up to the Europa Hotel parked our car and were greeted by door staff who took our luggage and parked our car.

We checked in for two nights and arrived up to the 8th floor to a small but compact room which was all done out in white. Adam told Mathew that it was the most bombed out hotel in Europe when the troubles were on and Mathew commented oh god.

After showering and throwing trainers, jeans and tee shirts on we browsed the shopping area and bought some tee shirts and chatted to the sales assistants in a trendy fashionable shop. Adam asked her where did she recommend to go out to that was open late and she recommended Thomson s Garage which was open till about three Adam thanked her and left with Mathew.

After dropping our bags back at the Europa we ended up in the Parliament Bar and ordered two beers Adam recognised some lads there who were down in Dublin and said hello and sat with Mathew at a table by themselves.

After two beers we walked to the Europa Hotel and fell asleep for an hour and made inquiries about a reservation in the Dining Room where we sat down to a five course meal. Back at the hotel we ended up having dinner it was five courses and Adam spoke to the attendant in the toilet he was about 14 and Adam said fair play to him for doing his job. He was polishing men shoes and had a stand of aftershave which he bought and charged for. Good on him Adam thought.

We ended up having Chaterbriand for main course and then we ended up in a gay bar in Belfast.

We paid the bouncer cash to get in and sat there looking around at the guy s in the bar and commented to each other that they were on edge because of the troubles and how different two hours in another country was in comparison to Dublin.

After dinner we walked to Thompson s Garage and paid another bouncer cash for entry we ended up drinking and dancing and by the end of the night some Belfast lad thought Mathew was English which Adam stepped in and told them that he was his Australian mate form Melbourne otherwise they were going to have a go at him and Adam was quick to realise that the situation could have been nasty.

Mathew left in a panic to see a guy outside with blood on his face there was an argument outside with a RUC Black Maria and Mathew was in a panic. He told Adam that he had never seen this before and was scared and Adam told him to calm down and try and relax.

Mathew said relax are you fucking serious and that what planet was Adam from because he almost got his head kicked in and that it was time to get fucking out of there. So on arriving at the Europa hotel we passed the que on the door for people to gain entry and ended up sitting in the residents bar drinking Baileys.

At about 4 in the morning we left and joined two ladies at the lift they commented to us that we were very handsome together and that we were wasted on been gay. They asked us where we were from and were amazed that Mathew was from Australia and Adam from Dublin.

The two of us crashed that night and checked out the following day and drove to catch the ferry to Scotland where we travelled to Stranair listening to Boy George playing D j on BBC radio.

After three hours driving through Scotland we arrived in Edinburgh and ended up on the road that is full of B and B s eventually we found one late Friday night and checked in.

We threw our bags on the bed showered and headed out into the night. It was cool because Adam had been to Edinburgh before and knew where to go so we ended up in CC Blooms and danced till three in the morning together Adam was looking out for the guy he met before however did not see him Mathew said to Adam what was he like expecting to meet someone he spent time with about a year ago.

So we left when it was over and took a taxi to our B and B and ended up arguing with the taxi driver over a 5 sterling note which was bank of England and not Bank of Scotland Adam told the driver that it was all the same to him that it was cash and so what if it was English and not Scottish we almost threw it at him in the end as if to say he had no other choice of excepting it and that he was too patriotic.

So after that we slept in late and ended up on Saturday having lunch in a gorgeous Georgian Building where most of Edinburgh high Society were. The food was great and the room was high ceilings and well spaced out.

After lunch we did a tour of Edinburgh Castle and looked out from every lookout point it was a lovely sunny day and we ended up doing the Royal Mile and then onto to a park to Sunbath together. After about an hour we bussed it back to the b and b and fell asleep till about 9 and got ourselves ready for Saturday night in Edinburgh we were off to Taste and by 11 30 we were in the door.

Adam scored E and the two of us dropped it and waited to come up after 15 minutes and proceeded to the dance floor where we ended up dancing by the end of the night Adam was on the small stage almost directing everyone on the dance floor Underworld s Born slippy was the last track to be played and Mathew commented to Adam that he looked amazing up on stage and was trying to catch Adam's attention however Adam was so wrapped up in the atmosphere did not notice Mathew we laughed about that and ended up back in the B an B having wild sex it went on for about 2 hours and later we collapsed into each others arms just as the sun was coming up.

It was Sunday and we were leaving for Belfast on Monday so we ended up driving through the Scottish highlands and ended up in Sterling Mathew was so delighted to be in Scotland and seeing Scottish Castles he never thought this would ever happen because when he was in Dublin on his trip originally he was only staying for two weeks and because he got sick he had to stay.

We ended up at the foot of the Scottish Highlands for tea late Sunday after noon having Haggis and enjoying our new dish. Mathew was saying to Adam how good we were together and thought if this was the start for us then what did the rest of our lives have in store Adam agreed and they toasted to their future.

After lunch we drove through Queen Elizabeth Park and stopped off beside a lake sitting in the car with the window open thinking of our trip back to Dublin and the wonderful time we had in Scotland and Northern Ireland together. So later that evening back in Belfast it was late we drove to Bangor in County Down and checked into the Slieve Donard

Hotel and spent another two day s there walking the beach and swimming together in the hotel pool having dinners and making love.

Adam had phoned into work to say he had an overseas funeral to go to and was delayed in London with family and was expected back on Friday he had asked a mate of his to call into to say he was returning and got him to apologise on his behalf however the message that was sent was misread and Adam got fired.

However on returning to Dublin there was a tax rebate in the post which set Adam up for a month financially which gave him breathing space to find another job.

He started soon at the Boulevard Café and fitted into his position well and his Head Chef was gay which was cool there was a nice vibe there and all was going well with the staff he was working with.

Adam and Mathew were in good fit states considering the amount they were drinking and drug s we were doing together. It was not all excess on day s off that s the thing with addiction it'll grip you eventually and by this stage of Adam s life it was not really a problem or else Adam didn't think so anyway.

So three months into the boulevard Café and Mathew working at Fitzers on Dawson Street all was on track for Australia.

We had booked for the end of September and decided to make the most of our time left in Dublin. Together we saved and started making plans for Melbourne and what we were going to do when we arrived.

We decided to take the first two weeks off and when arriving to travel around and relax from jet lag. Mathew was going to look up friends and decide that they would hang out in St Kilda which was on the beach and travel on the

Great Ocean Road we had watched Point Break with Keanu Rives and Adam thought the scene at the end was awesome where he disappears into the stormy waters and was looking forward to standing on Bells Beach. So we had some fantastic days out in Dublin together when we were off and night s down in Frank Ryan s bar on Queen Street as well as clubbing together.

The rent was cheap on our flat so we had a lot of disposable income because we both worked in Restaurants and were eating there when working.

Adam s second year in college was over and he decided to leave because Australia was now coming up. Mathew was counting down the day s and so was Adam too because he was living out his dream of going to Australia and now he was in love it was all just a rollercoaster ride.

So summer passed fast and by September Adam left work and was saying goodbye to his friends. He had a going away party in the Front Lounge with Mathew s friends too. There night was a big success and later on in the evening one of them said to Adam that he was going to miss Dublin and Adam nodded in a knowing nod. Little did he know what was in store for him just a few months ahead.

So on we partied in Renards and we were doing coke in the toilets and drinking too. People were coming and going and friends of Adam s were saying to Mathew to look after Adam in Australia and Mathew looked at Adam and smiled there were Bon Voyage cards and wishes of good luck messages and to take care.

So on the last night in Dublin, Adam and Mathew stayed with friends and that was it.

The following day we flew to London via Malaysia and then onto Melbourne.

Leaving Dublin And Flying To Melbourne

The night before Australia was with a gathering of friends and some family in a restaurant on Dawson Street we all shared food and wine and ended up in Renard s for a night of drinks and clubbing where afterwards ended up back on the north circular road in the Flat that Mathew and Adam shared.

Adam was playing house music and with five others was dancing around the flat saying to the rest of the crew that he should have had a foam party. The others were starting to clear the apartment out with the rest of the belongings that were in the flat. The large bay window was open and Mathew with the two others started throwing pots, cutlery and frying pans out of the window everyone was laughing and with the neighbours below trying to access the flat from the outside garden were livid because a frying pan flew past Brian which he later tried to kick the door of the flat in.

Then all of a sudden the landlady was inside the flat trying to turn the stereo off and all of a sudden the five of us were looking at each other in a silence saying to ourselves how did she gain entry, with that Adam pushed her away from the sound system and while the music was turned off the landlady was shouting at Mathew to get everyone out of the flat. So we rounded up the last of our belongings and left the flat about 5 in the morning it took us about 30 minutes to gather the sound system up with some bar bells and some bedclothes and called a taxi which later we had to call another one to take our belongings down to the other end of the north circular road.

The rest of the neighbours were standing at the front door in disbelief and one was shouting at the lads faggots Mathew shouted back to get a life and called him a down on luck alcoholic the rest of us were in hysterics and just in the mood to continue partying which we later all collapsed in a flat about a mile away about 7 am.

Later that afternoon the four of us had lunch in a bar in Phibsboro before been picked up by Adam s parents to travel to the airport. Adam vomited all over the floor before leaving. The drink was too much. The partying was non stop and there was a long journey ahead for both Mathew and Adam. On jumping into the car Adams parents commented on the stench of booze from both lads and commented on how there night must have been some going away party it was.

Dublin Airport

After arriving to the Airport Adam said his goodbyes to his parents and left them in tears. There was an announcement over the intercom for Adam to pick up a courtesy phone it was his friends from Eddie Rockets wishing him a good trip and to arrive safely.

Both lads borded the plane for Heathrow and were upgraded to first class due to different seating arrangements.

The flight was smooth and it was a clear blue sky on approaching London you could see most of the London landmarks when queuing to land at Heatrow, Kensington Palace, Buckingham palace and Hyde park it was a fabulous sunny day and on a clear day from air London looks great.

On landing at the airport the lady next to Adam asked had he far to go and replied laughing ~Melbourne but stopping of in Malaysia, both guys were excited. They waited in Heatrow for some time and waited to board the plane for Kuala Lumpar. Mathew commented that you could always spot the gay guys at airports and both lads cruised a couple on the same flight. Adam had never been on a long haul flight before and was amused by a hostess running around and organising everything.

There was a steward in the lads section who smiled at us when we sat down and he introduced himself to us and told us that he d be looking after us for the trip to Kuala Lumpar. Adam thought he was friendly. Both lads had seats beside the exit and sat beside this lady who was not very friendly,

They relaxed together and Mathew was explaining to Adam what Asia was like. Adam had never been to the Southern Hemisphere before and was all excited to be travelling there. Now that he was sitting on the plane. They took off and were airborne in a few minutes. Soon they ordered some drinks from the handsome steward. Adam got drunk while Mathew slept. The air Stewart was laughing at the amount of drink Adam consumed the poor guy was running back and forth all flight long. When Mathew awoke Adam was locked with the effects of the altitude and all the alcohol in his system from the non stop partying. It had gone on for years.

When young your body can handle more until you reach a certain age. On spending 13 hours on the flight to K L the plane landed and the steward asked the lads was this there first time in Asia Mathew commented that he had been before and that it was Adam s first time in Asia. The air Steward produced a bottle of Champagne as a welcome gesture to Asia. Adam asked him for a list of clubs to visit which he came up willingly and winked at the boys and told them to have a good time.

So with a bottle of champagne in one hand and a list of clubs in another hand both lads left the flight. They checked into their hotel and popped the champagne against the window on the 17th floor of the hotel. With that there was an amazing crash of thunder and flash of lightening both boys jumped back with fright and excitement. They poured the overflowing champagne and toasted to their future. Adam couldn't wait to see Asia.

Kuala Lumpar.

On arriving from the airport Adam noticed how everything was so green and was surprised at that. K L has one of the tallest buildings in the world and Adam was overwhelmed on how big the structures were. Both lads finished there drinks and roamed the city to look around. They were the tallest on the street and were given some funny looks by the locals. They stopped off at the night market and bought sunglasses and designer tee shirts. Everything was so cheap and both lads ended up in Kenturkey Fried Chicken in K L Mathew commented that here they were in Asia and how the fuck did they end up in Kenturkey Fried Chicken.

Later that evening they returned to the hotel and showered and got ready for a night on the town.

They ended up at blue boy for the drag show and Adam had never before seen a proper drag show the show was really part of Asia culture and professional. It was pocahontis from

Disneyland cartoons dressed up like a doll and singing some Walt Disney song she was brilliant or he was brilliant.

Adam had never seen a drag show like it and Mathew commented that he was to see plenty more in Melbourne because that was part of the culture of Melbourne. Later that night after talking to some locals Adam was told that KL guys only talk to white guys if they approach them first he explained that westerners had a tendency to be standoffish. One guy mentioned to the lads that if they were around for one of his days off that he would take him to the jungle and beaches that were not to far from K L unfortunately both lads were leaving in two days so were not able to take the guy up on his offer.

Some guys were drinking this strange exotic drink Adam asked what it was they told him it was Grava. Adam approached the bar to order this. He was told it was called graveyard and ordered two both lads drank and danced the night away in KL.

On returning to the hotel there were pimps touting for business with prostitutes down an alley way from the hotel. Adam was curious to see what they were like and were there any guys Mathew moved Adam into the hotel and both lads slept in each others arms for the rest of the morning.

The following day was a tour of KL pretty boring really because it consisted of a tour bus dropping you to local batik shops which consisted of handbags. Adam commented that if he ever did drag that he d come back because the handbags were so cheap. There was an interesting ending into the tour of some caves at the hills that were filled with Monkeys. There were also some religious carvings of half man half animal interesting to look at. There was plenty of steps to climb and at the top of the cave were monkeys were you could feed them with nuts. On entering the caves Mathew pointed to

Adam two monkeys fucking and a boy who was annoying the monkeys all of a sudden the monkeys attacked the boy and the boy ran out of the caves screaming after shaking off some of the monkeys that had attacked him. He deserved it he was pretending to feed them and then taken the food away from them. The monkeys were pissed off they were aggressive. I suppose us humans evolved from them. On part of the tour Adam and Mathew stopped off at a putter factory to see some putter that was on display.

On arriving both lads noticed that there were staff there that looked as if they were on slave labor there was a fat bastard there with a huge diamond ring buying some putter and inquiring how old it was. Mathew made some comment on that he probably had some kid sucking his cock in his hotel room. The type that is rich abuses the less fortunate and makes money from the poor. Adam was egging him on and let the proprieter know that they were not really interested in what was going on at this factory. Adam remembered that all of the staff were from third world countries.

Later on they passed some chanty towns in the area. The guide pointed out to the people living in these appalling conditions explained that most of the people living there were nomads with no fixed address and were deported from Malaysia on a regular basis only to be later found in these appalling conditions some time later again. Adam thought how unfairly divided the world is and thought of the fat bastard getting rich on the less fortunate both lads enjoyed the fact that they had made him squirm.

Later that day both lads were transferred to a smaller bus to be returned to the hotel. On entering the bus some lady that was on the plane from another hotel asked the lads how they were. Adam replied that he was hot and had drank a lot and the smell of dried fish was getting to him.

Later that night both lads took off for some clubbing on their last night in Kuala Lumpar and saw some amazing sights on the way to a club out side the town. The local boys were all over them and were offering them money for sex. Both lads were very flattered and declined their offer and thought it was a very funny experience their stay in KL was coming to an end. They both sat by the swimming pool at around 4 am chatting about their trip to Australia. On returning to the hotel they both ordered breakfast at around 5.15 AM the breakfast that arrived was shit so they ended up at the breakfast buffet around 6.00 A M chatting and all excited about Mathew meeting his family and bringing Adam home to Australia. Mathew cracked some joke about not having real milk in Australia because of the heat and Adam commented on how he could not be serious and that was he for real. Yeah right.

At the breakfast table Mathews tooth fell out and Adam thought it was funny but asked Mathew was he alright Mathew replied that the alcohol in his system would take care of it. Both lads returned to the hotel room for some wild sex and later looking around the hotel room realised that how much the hotel room was trashed it was a mess. Cloths, sheets, bottles, and ashtrays scattered everywhere around the room.

Later that morning they fell asleep in each others arms for some time. It was around 7.00 at this stage of the day and after some sleep awoke at 12.00 to do some shopping K L style. Adam was running around all the shops and by the end of it all both lads were in a state running late and had to pack for the plane for their final journey into Australia. By the time they returned to the hotel they were questioned about the mini bar and state of the room. On vacating the room there was a jacket that both lads were unsure where it came from. The hotel porter asked the lads could he keep it and Adam signed some hotel form to consent for the porter to keep the jacket he was thrilled and thanked ~Mathew and Adam for his jacket.

They both made the bus after panic buying in KL Adam was unreal around the shopping centers and Mathew made some comment around how he d swear that Adam had never been to a shopping center before. On the flight leaving soon Adam had a shop assistant weighing out silver chains and asking how much they were in the end Adam did not purchase them anyway.

They made the hotel bus and flight on time and did another spot of shopping at the airport for Mathew s family. Finally they were at the gateway to Australia.

On boarding the plane Mathew was all excited because he had not been home in over two years and was delighted that Adam was coming home with him. Mathew had commented on how his mum had mentioned to him at the Airport in Melbourne when leaving that she hoped that he would meet someone nice and yes he did.

Little did both dudes know what was in store for them at a later date down under the shit was to hit the fan big time.

The flight to Melbourne took 13 hours and both lads watched some comedy shows most of the flight were in hysterics of laughter and on flying into Melbourne Airport, Adam and Mathew were chatting to the airline stewardess she was asking the lads was it their first time to visit Australia and Mathew explained to her that himself and Adam were setting up life in Australia.

Arriving in Melbourne

On leaving the airport after some time with customs, Adam had entered on a holiday visa it was valid for three months, and was cleared by emigration. There had been a sniffer dog going through all the baggage and Adam was slightly panicked in case there had been some hash lying in the luggage that they were unaware of. It would have been a shame to have been busted over some small amount of hash. However they were escorted through customs to be greeted by Mathew s family at the airport entrance. His parents were delighted to see Mathew after all this time and happy to meet Adam.

The journey to Mathew s parents was early on a Spring morning about 5 am Mathew s mother was asking them how they had met and which countries had Mathew visited. Mathew replied that they had met in a bar in Dublin and that Adam had given Mathew a fabulous time in Dublin. That they had travelled through the north of Ireland visited Donegal and Derry also Belfast and spent some time in Scotland. She was happy to have Mathew home and explained that she had prepared a room for them and that they were having breakfast at home. She told the lads that they could stay with them for as long as they wanted until they had enough money to move out. Which was great.

The lads spent the morning chatting about their adventures together. Mathew's mother asked Adam had he ever been to Australia before and Adam replied no that it was one of his dreams to come to Australia. She welcomed Adam with open arms later that morning Mathew and Adam slept while Mathew s parents left the house for work.

Both lads were tired from the travelling and there drinking constantly for about a fortnight meeting different friends for drinks and partying. Also with been jet lagged they needed to rest. Later that day Adam prepared a meal on Mathew s parent s return Adam used his culinary skills and prepared Roast Lamb with pumpkin mash and roast potatoes. His parent s arrived home and after the meal mentioned to Adam that he d have no problem finding a job in a restaurant in Melbourne.

Later that night Mathew bought Adam on a tour of the city center and suggested to Adam where they should live. Adam was impressed with Melbourne and liked what he saw.

Adam told Mathew about a DJ from Sydney that he had met on a holiday in Mykonos about 10 years ago and heard the last time he was in touch with him that he was now living in Melbourne. Later that night Adam met him unexpectantly in a gay bar in Melbourne. Adam approached Paul and asked him was his name Paul, Paul replied yes and asked Adam who he was and where was he from.

Adam wound him up about meeting him at a party some weeks previously and asked him had he forgotten. Adam asked him about his trip overseas to Mykonos and did he have a good time at this stage Paul was puzzled and asked Adam who he was.

Adam explained who he was and Paul was surprised to see Adam again after all these years. They exchanged numbers and Mathew mentioned to Adam what was he like bumping into someone from Melbourne after all it was Mathew s town and if anyone should have met someone it should have been Mathew. After all it was the other side of the world.

The lads finished there drinks and drove home. They slept in the spare bedroom and later that morning awoke to find they had the house to themselves.

Adam had a shower and enjoyed using the exotic fruit shampoo which was new to him there was a calming feeling to the bathroom which was done out in a lovely dark blue and old style shower.

Both lads chatted about where they were going to live and set themselves up with jobs. That day Mathew bought Adam to the four seasons Hotel where Mathew used to work. He introduced Adam to some of his ex colleagues and they sat in the upstairs restaurant overlooking part of the city having some lunch,

After lunch they walked about the city and caught a tram to St Kilda and spent the day browsing about the shops and sitting in a café watching a film crew filming a soap. Mathew explained to Adam who the Actor was and that he had been out of the serious return to Eden which Adam loved.

St Kilda is a suburb in Melbourne where all the artists hang and is full of trendy people hang out it is very chilled and has a fun park which is right beside the beach.

For three weeks both lads hung out and Mathew caught up with his friends Adam liked his friends and they spent time having dinners and drinking lovely Australian wine.

After three weeks the lads moved into a one bedroomed house in Richmound the location was great it was one stop from the center of Melbourne and close to where the boys were to hangout. Adam found work in a motel in St Kilda cooking breakfasts two morning s and dinner three nights a week. It did not feel like work to Adam because he was off five night s a week and on the first week ended up out with his colleague for a drink and met another chef in the prince of Wales bar in St Kilda where they exchanged numbers. Bruce lived beside the Prince of Wales and invited Adam around for drinks during the week.

Adam spent his time working, going to drag shows, clubbing, swimming and dining in restaurants he loved the different foods the restaurant s had to offer and learnt a lot about different foods. Meanwhile Mathew was working in Crown Casino as floor manager so both lads settled into Melbourne life quite well.

On day s off Mathew brought Adam to the great ocean road and they d drive around the ocean for hours spending time in small towns along the way stopping off for drinks and food. Adam loved it all and settled in and became friends with Bruce and also was in contact with Paul.

Bruce was in contact with Adam and would pop down to the Motel Adam was working in and they walk the pier of St Kilda smoking grass and chatting away, they also were having an affair and would end up in Bruce s apartment preparing bongs and listening to house music and having sex. Adam was loving Melbourne. He was hanging out in all the right places and was enjoying his new lifestyle.

However one night out with Bruce on a drink and drugs binge Adam met his work mate about 3 am in St Kilda she commented on how out of it Adam was and hoped he be alright for work at the Motel which was in four hours time, Adam spent the next four hours puking and doing bongs and slept late beside Bruce. He phoned into work and told them he d not be in because he was to hung over and knew that was the end of his job at the Motel. He did not return. Adam and Bruce were spending time together swimming and drinking in bars doing drugs and clubbing too. Adam introduced Mathew to Bruce and just pretended that he was a friend and let on that nothing was going on between the two of them, Bruce was inquiring about Adam s visa and that he wanted him to stay for as long as possible. Adam agreed he was having a ball and found another job in South Yarra in a trendy café.

He settled into it well and enjoyed cooking new dishes and was having knock off drinks at the end of the night and hitting all the best bars for the drag shows. Mathew was on a three week rota of nights, day s, and afternoons, which gave Adam time to spend with Bruce.

The drag queens loved Adam and took him out on the town clubbing. One night Adam asked the drag queen behind the bar for a beer and she replied honey with an accent like that you can have whatever you like.

The Melbourne cup was approaching and Adam was still at the café in South Yarra. He was rostered to work the Melbourne cup weekend however Adam thought there was no way he was missing one of the best weekend s in Melbourne so phoned in sick. He explained to the staff that he was down on the great ocean road and their car had broken down and would have to spend the night there until it was repaired the following day this gave Adam three day s to party and celebrate the Melbourne cup.

It was Thursday and Adam was drinking and drugging. The big event was on Monday so this gave Adam freedom for the rest of the weekend. They ended up in a club on the Friday night where a fight broke out and Mathew commented to Adam about where he had taken him Adam brushed it off and suggested they leave and go on elsewhere.

Mathew wanted to go home so Adam said goodbye to Bruce and his sister and spent the night with Mathew. They un-winded with a few joints and some wine and later that morning slept together it was nice for the two of them to be off and spending time together. With Mathew s hours and Adam s hours they were not seeing each other as often as they wanted,

On the Saturday after they jumped into a taxi and spent the day sunbathing by Prahan pool. It was cool and Adam s first time there Mathew commented to Adam that there time together was getting better and better Mathew picked up on Adam s vibe and Adam agreed, After the pool they had dinner and returned to the house and relaxed with each other. On Sunday it was cup eve and the whole city was in full swing. They ended up in the three faces night club dancing on drugs and drinking the local beer of Victoria. Adam ran into Paul and Paul was asking Adam was he enjoying his time in Melbourne Adam replied that he was having a ball and kept running to the toilet to do more speed. The music was dance house and the two lads were in the middle of the floor having a ball Jamiriquai space cow boy was playing. Later on about 4 am Adam used the phone at reception to phone a friend and was on the phone for about an hour chatting constantly about how great Melbourne was.

At about 6 am Mathew and Adam left three faces and jumped into a taxi and arrived home and fell asleep about 7 am. They awoke at 11 and caught a train to flemmington racecourse for the Melbourne cup dressed in suits. Later on Adam had arranged to meet a lady called Annie. While entering the racecourse Adam and Mathew bought some sparkling wine and drank from it with champagne glasses they placed bet s on the first race and won. Which was a good start to the day.

Mathew and Adam met Annie by the rose bush she had tickets for a reserved section where we all ended up having drinks Mathew preferred to see the races at the front of the racecourse so both lads spent an hour in the reserved section and said goodbye to Annie and her friends.

On the Melbourne cup itself just before the start of the race this guy approached Adam and asked him what horse did Adam have his money on Adam replied that he was betting on the Irish Horse called Oscar Schindler and the guy replied that he should have his money on Saintly and that that was the horse which was going to win, By this stage everyone was in flying form and when the horse race took off everyone cheered.

Adam thought it was weird that this guy had approached him at the last minute to say this and however decided to keep his faith in the Irish horse Oscar Schindler he had been giving great media attention over the past week and Adam was sticking to him.

The atmosphere was electric by the time the horses were running up to the finish line and the winner of the Melbourne cup that year was Saintly and with that the guy came running over to Adam and mentioned that he had just one 4 thousand Australian Dollars Adam just looked at him in disbelief and congratulated him on his winnings Mathew was looking on to also in disbelief.

On leaving the racecourse both lads caught the train to the center of the city where they ended up in an Irish bar drinking and Adam commented to Mathew that he felt weak. Mathew questioned Adam s drink and drugging behaviour and suggested to Adam that he do something about it. Adam said he d take care of it and cut down. He had locked himself out of the house on several occasions and on other night s was spending his night s around at Bruce s returning several days later.

The strip on Commercial Road holds some of Melbourne's best Gay bars. There was one bar Adam loved which was called Virgin Mary's with a roof top bar overlooking the city. It had the best drag shows Adam had ever experienced. Adam usually ended up there on Sundays to end his weekend. The music was funky house and they sold gorgeous 5 dollar cocktails which Adam was buying by the double.

All the staff were dressed in tight leather shorts and some of the bar staff were wearing harnesses, the barmaid went around sweeping the floor in a white fluffy bra with white fluffy knickers. When Mathew was off he was usually there with Adam and when he was working Bruce and his sister would meet ~Adam there to catch up on what was happening,

There was one drag queen who stood out she called herself Miss Candy who was a big girl who wore a pink Sequinned dress she stood on the bar running back and forth handing out free shots of booze. Adam thought she was amazing. Her favourite songs were Charlene never been to me, Shirly Bassey this is my life and I know I ll never love this way again. She was always telling the crowd to drink more because everyone would look better.

One Sunday afternoon on a sunny day in Melbourne Missy Candy was singing Shirly Basseys This is my life she walked out of the bar onto the street and onto a Tram that was passing by she got on and started singing out the window with the whole pub singing and clapping while everyone on the tram was cracking up laughing. She really knew how to create an atmosphere and was always introducing new talent of drag queens to the bar.

There was another drag queen from Perth who she introduced one afternoon and she got up on the bar and starting singing into a dildo I will I will I will. She was hilarious and everyone was laughing.

After the show the rest of the bar would spend the rest of Sunday evening dancing the crowd knew how to party and the atmosphere for a Sunday evening was electric.

On other days Adam spent his time at Prahan pool where there was a big gay turnout. Everyone spent the day sunning themselves and posing. Adams first time there with Mathew, Mathew commented on how Melbourne just got better and better Adam agreed both lads were having a good time and were in love too.

St Kilda was another area which is cool to hang out in. There s a mixed Gay bar there called the Prince of Wales were half of it is Gay and the other half is rockers. On a Monday night they sold dollar pots of beer and the bar was always very busy.

There was this lady who came in with a parrot on her shoulder and she d stand with the parrot. The bar man served beer and stood behind the bar with a hand mirror brushing his hair. Another character was a Marie from New Zealand who had the chop (sex change) She walked into the bar one night six foot four built well with a Diana ross wig and a large pair of stilettos on. She started talking to Adam.

Adam was inquisitive about the operation and was curious to see. She called herself Star. Star told Adam about her operation and mentioned that she had a lot of support from her family home in New Zealand. Star worked in the city at computers and told Adam that she found him handsome. Adam asked Star would she mind showing Adam her operation, Star agreed to and with that they were in the mens cubicle with Star lifting her dress Adam saw where the base of the Penis was cut off and there was this whole with pubic hair growing around Adam told her it was horrible her face dropped. Adam thought about her not been able to feel the sensation of sex.

She was highly insulted. Adam was too high to care and laughed it off. They left the cubicle and returned to their drinks. Adam was lying on her boobs and the two of them were dancing to the music. A few weeks later Adam was with Mathew coming from a bar and saw star standing at the red light district with some other ladies of the night. So much for her computer job in the city Adam thought. There are so many screwed up people in the world Adam thought. Mathew was enjoying showing Adam around his town. Mathew loved the side of Dublin he experienced with Adam and Adam was enjoying his experience with Mathew in Melbourne. Both lads bounced off the others energy.

Falling into depts of Madness

Adam was starting to loose the plot. Mathew He was always mentioning that he could end up loosing his sanity for good if he did not slow down.

Prior to this Adam had spent three 3 months in a psychiatric hospital in Dublin 2 years previously. There was a strain on the relationship. He started slowly to loose the plot but was also keeping it together. It started with a lapse in concentration and in a haze of doing too much grass. Changing jobs and drinking and partying too much.

Mathew was always on his case about losing the plot for good and maybe never been able to return to a normal life. Mathew wanted stability which Adam had never really considered before. However Adam was becoming very reclusive seeing doctors, becoming paranoid and withdrawing from life. Dialling telephone numbers was a problem Adam would forget the number and then hang up. His Australian dream was turning into a nightmare by this stage Adam was out of work and sleeping a lot drinking cups of tea and coffee and smoking a lot of cigarettes.

What was to happen to Adam was to rock his and Mathew s world. Adam started seeing a doctor for depression. He was loosing contact with reality and spent most of his time in bed. The rabbit that both lads bought disappeared a couple of weeks previously it was last seen sitting beside a cat at the side of the house. Adam thought about returning to Dublin however thought he was not in a fit state to do so. He only left the house for milk and cigarettes and when the phone rang he left the answering machine to pick up all the calls. Friends of Mathew were calling around and Adam would briefly chat to them and refused to go out. If he was not in bed he was on the sofa or sitting out in the garden. He thought about jumping on a train to Perth however decided that that was not the solution. Mathew thought Adam was going through a faze and thought Adam would snap out of it soon.

Mathew kept saying to Adam to snap out of it because a mate of Adam s was flying in with the Corrs to do a tour and that he would be meeting them soon. Adam was totally oblivious to it all and withdrew even further. By this stage Adam lost a lot of weight and was asleep all day and awake all night. Mathew was working in a restaurant while Adam contemplated suicide.

Adam's mate flew in to Melbourne and arranged for the lads and two friends to be on the guest list. Adam decided to make an effort at this stage Adam was running to the doctor for prescription after prescription and was popping tran quilisers to calm him down. It was a sunny Sunday when Adam s mate arrived and Adam was sitting on the sofa drinking beer. Both lads were delighted to see each other and Adam showed Mark around the house Mark thought that the house was from the outside looked like the Sullivans and both lads laughed.

Adam took mark to St Kilda where they sat in a restaurant talking about Marks relationship in Dublin with a guy he was seeing. Adam was explaining to Mark about his situation and Mark thought that Adam should chill out. Mark organised Adam and Mathew and two mates of Mathew s onto the guest list of the Corrs and all attended and had a ball. Mathew was pleased that he had some friends on the guest list for a big Irish band in his home town.

Adam and Mathew enjoyed the concert and ended up back stage for drinks with some relations of Mark's also. They was a free bar which Adam filled his bag with some beer and later that evening ended up in the Hyatt hotel for late drinks where the Corrs were staying. Adam was withdrawn and just sat there occasionally adding to the conversation while the rest of the party talked.

On leaving the hotel Andrea Corr asked about Mark's friends Mark introduced us and there was a brief chat. Mark mentioned to Andrea that Adam and Mark had seen each other for some months in Dublin and Andrea made some comment that she thought we were nice. After saying goodbye to Andrea Adam and Mark were in Mark's hotel room were Mark gave Adam some hash. It was enough for a few joints Adam was happy to smoke it because he had not smoked any hash since he had left for Australia. Adam and Mark kissed and said goodbye to each other it was about 6 am on a Tuesday morning the next time Adam was to see Mark was in a psychiatric hospital in Dublin.

Mathew s mother had become quite concerned with Adam and invited him to stay with her in Mathew's family home Adam refused. thinking he'd be fine in the house in the city. Mathew was working trying to keep everything afloat and trying to keep the relationship alive. Adam occassionally left the house for a cycle and would return with no energy, he was aware about how unfit he had become however was on heavy doses of medication. By this stage Adam had become a prisoner in his own head.

New years eve was approaching and Mathew and Adam had organised tickets for a rave down on the docks of the city. Adam drank a bottle of champagne to take the edge off things and became quite in the festive mood. Mathew s spirit was lifted and both lads took a taxi to St Kilda to join a party with some of Mathew s work mates.

On arriving at the flat they were greeted by the hostess in a pink sequinned dress with blond hair she looked like a star. Drugs were passed around and money exchanged. Adam and Mathew did some speed and were handed some punch. Later on leaving the party they both did some e and left the party loaded into a taxi and asked the driver to take them to the docks.

Beside the taxi on the freeway was another car with some of the crowd from the party the guy driving it was wearing a toga and everyone was waving at each other and shouting.

On arriving at the docks and entering the building which looked out onto a spectacular view of the skylight of Melbourne the party was starting to kick off. Both lads got tattoos done Adam got a Celtic band on his arm. For a while they danced and then stood outside on the balcony chatting to some couple. The view was amazing and with that it was approaching midnight.

Inside there was a stage show of women dancing and singing it was all kind of of surreal due to the drugs medication champagne and beer. It was an amazing high and also a blur, at midnight fireworks went off and everyone cheered both Mathew and Adam kissed and hugged and walked outside and chatted, Mathew was saying to Adam that he could recover and that they had a good future together Adam agreed. They spent about an hour chatting and then danced inside the dance party before they knew it it was 4 am and both lads were tired so decided to leave.

The journey home was very funny walking through the streets of Melbourne in their club gear. Mathew was wearing a purple hugging top with black jeans. Adam had on a silver velvet top with pvc pants which he had bought in London. On arriving at the train Adam chatted to the cops Adam got a kick out of chatting to the police when he was high. He was admiring their uniforms tight leather pants and lovely blue shirts which they looked very sexy in. Adam was asking them did they enjoy their night which they replied yes, The Melbourne police guided the lads to their train and wished them well.

Adam and Mathew boarded the train to Richmond and got off at Richmond. Adam spent the morning chatting to his family and wishing his friends a happy new year. Later on both lads made love and when Adam came down he started searching the house for some acid that he thought he had not taken. Mathew kept saying that he had used it all and to come back to bed and get some sleep. The next following day on new years day both lads left the house for something to eat all Adam wanted to do was curl up in a ball at home watching some films. They later returned and Adam spent the day in bed while Mathew watched television. It was new years day of 1997.

Before Adam s addiction was out of control Mathew s and Adam's life looking from the outside in was looking good. Both lads thought they had found each others soul mate. Especially that they were from the other side of the word.

Adam returned to withdrawing from life only leaving the house when Mathew was off work and becoming more difficult as time moved on. Mathew insisted on them going out on his days off. One day Adam was to meet Mathew in the city to go see a film which Adam reluctantly left the house to meet Mathew.

Adam had not been out in some days so popped some pills before he left just so he could relax. The journey into the city was quiet and Adam got lost around the streets of Melbourne. Adam was walking in a trance of about 2 hours not really knowing where he was.

Eventually he found a train station and returned to the house to find Mathew sitting on the sofa in tears. To this Adam realised how much their dream had shattered. Mathew told Adam about how their lives had changed and thought that Adam did not even love him anymore,

Adam returned to bed and Mathew ended up in some bar in the city, By this stage Adam hated his life and wanted to die he thought a lot about suicide and the nightmares of the pedophile who abused him were constantly in his head. There were constant visits to doctors by this stage Adam was paranoid about everything and had stopped watching television and even listening to the radio because he thought they were talking about him,

Eventually he thought that there were hidden cameras in the house and they were recording his every move. On one of his many visits to the doctor. Adam told the doctor that he thought that there were people watching his every move the doctor replied that that sounds scary. Adam started to laugh and she prescribed him more anti depressants and told him to take care.

By this state Adam was thinking about the disastrous and negative situations in the world the starving children all over the world. Children who are abused, organised crime, prostitution, paedophilia, the IRA, drug dealers, Adam thought his mind could be read and that his every move was becoming possessed by the devil. Adam had lost contact with his family in Ireland and his friends in Australia had long gone. He wanted to die and did not care about anything anymore. He spent his day asleep and his night s awake smoking cigarettes like a crazy lunatic, The nightmares of been sexually abused by the so called priest of Metropolitan Community Church were in his head constantly and Adam could not get them out. Mathew s parents became very concerned. Mathew came home from work to find Adam sitting in the house in a daze and a complete mess. Mathew would ask Adam what had he done all day and Adam s reply was nothing and just stared into space, Adam spent hours on the floor in a ball then transfer onto the sofa and from there into bed. All he was able to manage was to take his pills and make cups of tea and smoke.

That was it it was a nightmare for him and in a complete black space. Adam became a spaced out junkie. His Australian dream had turned into a nightmare. Mathew would spend hours with Adam in bed he mentioned that if Adam was in bed that he was going to spend time in bed too. Mathew would hold Adam and both lad s had really entered a dark space in their lives. Adam thought about Mathew and thought what he was feeling and how he was going to snap out of this state. By this stage Adam had lost a lot of weight and had become almost anorexic. Sleeping under three duvets while outside it was about 16 degrees. Adam thought about winter and was dreading how he was going to survive. They would lye there together with Mathew supporting Adam and to give Adam some reassurance.

Mathew was in contact with Adam s family home in Dublin saying that Adam was in a mess and he did not know what to do. Adam had totally withdrawn. Colleagues from Mathew s work dropped by Adam just sat with this lovely couple not saying much and just wanting them to leave. They asked to have a look around the garden which Adam loved watering and attending by this stage it was starting to grow wild.

This situation went on for months with Adam seeing psychiatrists but not co operating with anything that was recommended. Mathew was doing all the cooking after retuning form work telling Adam how disappointed he was with everything and saying how he was trying to keep a brave face on when he was in work.

Mentioning all the time how that if Adam got himself sorted out that they could still have a nice life together.

Soon after that Adam was admitted to a psychiatric hospital in Melbourne where he hit rock bottom. Adam s parents were travelling over for a trip that had been arranged some months before when Adam was in a reasonable state his brother Craig was also coming too.

Adam was dreading them coming because of the state he was in however he was also looking forward to seeing them in an uncanny way because he needed to get out of this state. On a conversation on the phone with his dad Adam explained that he was on a drug called largactal which is a drug for serious disturbed people. Adam s dad asked him to spell the drug which he was unable to do. Adam s dad mentioned that he really was in a state. And told Adam that if he knew that this was all going on that he would have cancelled the trip and to what were they coming to at all.

Adam was not mixing with the other patients on the ward and spent all his time in bed sedated and paranoid. The hospital staff had faxes through from Dublin from St John of Gods so they could treat him with the right medication. Adam was fucked up big time and had lost his sanity completely. He spent his time running from the hospital to the house back and forth. At this stage he was sure Mathew wanted him out and thought that he was going to end up on the street. In hindsight Adam thought that that was where he belonged.

There were day s when Adam was out of it completely and Mathew would talk to the doctors about some solution that they could come up with. By this stage Adam parents and brother were due to fly in. Adam was not looking forward to seeing them in the state he was in. By this stage Adam was smoking his brains out and staring at the ground the doctors recall him doing this for ten hours a day. There were people passing by him and Adam thought that they had come to see this freak.

Anytime the telephone rang Adam thought it was for him and spent a lot of time running to the phone only to realise that the call was for someone else.

By this stage Adam thought that the hospital had been opened especially for him by this stage Adam had a crisis emergency team looking after him. However Adam thought everyone was out to get him and that psychics were reading his every thought and that it was all been broadcast on television.

Mad fucking shit thinking he was possessed by the devil. By this stage Adam was conscious about midday and midnight and checked his watch exactly by these times this was when he did most of his sleeping. Mathew came in with cigarettes and cloths for Adam and on day s Adam did not want to see him at all. Then one day a lady appeared to Adam dressed in a priest s uniform which Adam did not take to at all. Aware of the crucifix around her neck Adam was aware that he was drawing himself away from it and thought of the exorcist at this stage he thought that if he was possessed by the devil that this lady could help him.

They were in this small room with Adam sitting and the lady standing. Adam asked her had she any spirits after she took an injection of blood and she looked at him in an understanding manner and opened the cabinet to take hold of a bottle. She applied some of it to some cotton wool and rubbed it onto Adam s arm she smiled and so did Adam it was a strange situation however the two looked at each other in an understanding manner.

On certain days Mathew would come visit and say to Adam who was he today and who would he be tomorrow saying that he think he'd call him Joshua tomorrow. The nurse which Adam thought was an actress from prisoner cell block H kept saying to Adam that soon he'll be running out of cigarettes and that she had never really met anyone quite like him. She was carrying around this huge handbag and always appeared in the café next door when Adam was in there trying to get away from his crazy life. Adam thought that he was on every magazine in Australia and that the media were on the same plane as his parents reporting up to date coverage of the situation.

How crazy it all had become. Mathew would take Adam from the hospital for dinners and drives. Mathew's mother would visit and take a look at the state Adam was in and Adam saw tears in her eyes when she left. Adam was only having meals seeing visitors and Mathew by day and some of his family by evening. The scary part was that everyone thought that Adam would not snap out of this and that he be in hospital for the rest of his life. Adam thought he was dying and came up with a diagnosis of schizophrenia,

There was definitely a drug induced psychosis which Adam reckons also triggered schizophrenia. The visits were ongoing and one day a patient roared at him that one day he d burn in hell. Adam thought he saw the guys face on a tram who roared at him in the hospital in the city of Melbourne while out with Mathew one day whilst having his haircut. Completely paranoid, Maybe he was to Adam he had caused a lot of mayhem whilst he was in Melbourne.

Everytime Adam and Mathew met the doctors Mathew mentioned that Adam still thought that there were cameras in the house. The nurse who was Irish commented to Adam that he must come to her house and defrost her fridge. This just added to Adam s suspicion because thats what they had done when at home earlier on Adam laughed.

It was all to mad really. Adam's brother and parents were due to arrive any day now. The days in hospital consisted of long periods in bed, smoking and staring at the ground running to the house and then returning to the ward for heavy doses of medication. Adam was like a baby at this stage and depended on everyone around him. All Adam wanted at this stage was to be home in Dublin however he was in no fit state to travel. Nothing was making him happy and many nights wandered around the hall in a tranquillised state screaming at the nurses that he wanted to go home. All the doctors could do was keep giving Adam medication to calm him down. Everyone was in a state of awe. Adam was a like zombie.

Adams parents flew in and arrived at the hospital where they saw Adam in bed when they came into his room. Adam was not happy to see his parent s in the state he was in. They were very concerned and worried for Adam. Imagine their situation where you go to the other side of the world only to find a loved one in a psychiatric hospital diagnosed with schizophrenia. Some holiday for Adams parents. On day s Adam was out with his parents and brother where he was like a zombie Adam felt terrible that he had fucked up their holiday which added to his depression.

On day at Flemington racecourse Adam spoke to his mum about his situation and she replied that they were unable to bring him home. That he was too sick to travel and questioned Adam s life with Mathew everyone was saying what about Mathew. By this stage Adam did not know what to do.

Adam's mum mentioned that if Adam did not pull out of this that he would spend the rest of his life in a psychiatric hospital. Adam was even more depressed and realised the damage that he had caused everyone.

Easter 1997

Easter was approaching and everyone was planning a trip to Mathew s parents beach house for the holidays.

One afternoon some of the family were out in a speedboat and Adam and Mathew were on the back of the boat been pulled around by a ring it was good fun when they got out of the water Adam s body temperature dropped and while sitting in the beach house Adam was shivering and Mathew s mum commented that Adam was literally shivering to death. And commented on how unbelieveable he was. So much for drink and drugs,

Adam drank his way through the holidays and tried to get into good spirits spending afternoons in bed and trying to be as sociable as possible. One afternoon Adam and his dad walked around the estate and spoke about Adam s future. Adam explained that he wanted to return to Dublin thinking that he could give it a go there and make a better recovery in his home surroundings. His father agreed and told Adam that when he was in a better state of mind and that the doctors thought he was fit to travel that that would be the best outcome all round.

Later on Easter weekend they took a trip to the 12 apostles down on the Great Ocean Road. They are very impressive and stunning to see 12 rocks huge across from the cliffs and standing in the ocean.

Later Adam's parents took a trip to the gold coast with his brother. They made the most of a bad situation meanwhile

Adam returned to hospital. By this stage Adam was feeling better in himself his family had given him hope. Mathew was keeping everything afloat and the situation Adam was in seemed to becoming more manageable. With the medication Adam was on and the help from his team of doctors all was starting to stabalise Adam was still in a bad state however from his situation some months ago it was becoming better for him. He was no way out of the worst of it however having his family around really helped him and gave him hope.

There was days he left the hospital and walked about the park across from the hospital and was chatting to some of the other guys in the hospital and playing pool he was still on heavy medication and thought about his parents and brother on the Gold coast and hoped they were having a good time and not worrying too much about Adam.

When Adam s mum first saw Adam she was in tears. Destroyed by drugs and mentally traumatised by sexual abuse there was a lot to deal with. Also there was the lads future to consider and if and when where they going to settle and which country this was going to be in.

When Adam s family returned from the gold coast everyone went out to a restaurant on the last weekend of their trip. It was their final meal before returning to Dublin Adam s birthday was approaching and the week after it was his mums. It was a bleak experience for all after the meal Adam s brother wanted to go clubbing and Mathew told him that he d take him to a club that was gay. Adam s brother wanted to go to a straight club Adam felt guilty about not been in a position to give his brother a good send off and in the end everyone left the restaurant and went home.

Adam returned to the house with Mathew and the following day drove to the airport to say goodbye to his parents and brother. Adam's mother was in tears saying goodbye to Adam and asked him to co operate with the doctors about his condition, It was heartbreaking to see Adam s mum leaving Melbourne departures in tears with his dad s arm around her. Where was it all going to end,

The lads drove to the house in Richmound to talk about their future together. Adam wanted to return to Dublin thinking that he d make a better recovery at home with his family and friends. Later that day they contacted the estate agents and left the house three weeks later to move in with Mathews parents. The house was cleared and everything was put into storage. The team Adam had at the hospital wished him the best and mentioned to him not to waste his potential. The time spent in Mathews parents was all a bit of a blur.

Mathew finished up at the restaurant he was in and said his goodbyes and organised everything for the trip to Dublin.

On the morning of leaving both lads sat in the kitchen to have breakfast. Mathews mother commented to Adam about the way he was dressed they were off to Paris for a stopover for two nights before returning to Dublin. Adam was wearing a pair of tatty jeans and worn shoes and looked like a tramp mentally ill she commented fancy going to Paris dressed like that. That was the last thing Adam remembered that morning. There were no goodbyes and farewells which Adam remembered he was sedated and brought to the airport in a blackout checking in and boarding the plane and going through security was all in a blackout. He remembers nothing. Later that morning Adam woke up beside Mathew on the flight asking where he was there was no one else on the plane Mathew brought Adam through all this and replied that he was taking him home to Ireland.

Adam s state of health was serious and did not remember taking off or landing at Jarkarta. They changed planes for Singapore and had three hours to wait at the airport. While walking through Jarkarta airport Adam s nose started pumping blood Adam was in a state and Mathew took his tee shirt off to give to Adam for his nose. Mathew mentioned that he'd give Adam the cloths off his back if he had too.

They found a bar and Adam got drunk it was the only way he could get through this nightmare it was easy to do because of all the medication he was on. The time passed quickly at Jarkarta. Adam was paranoid about the people around him.

Remembering nothing about boarding the flight to Singapore Adam awoke again on the plane asking Mathew where were they now. Mathew mentioned to Adam that they were on the way to Singapore and that they have to spend a couple of hours in Singapore airport and that on no occasion was Adam to leave Mathew s side. On landing at Singapore they left the plane and walked through the airport and sat in the smoking room it was hot and humid that was all Adam remembers no conciseness of time the next Adam remembers was looking out the window of the plane at a flashing light which Adam thought was an ambulance waiting to take him to hospital and panicking.

Mathew was trying to calm him down explaining that they were in the air. Adam was still convinced that they were still on the runway and was pacing the aisles of the aircraft looking at the fire exits with the stewards looking at him in a state of disbelief. All that was going through Adams head was that he was going to be locked up in a psychiatric hospital somewhere in Singapore he was in a panic.

Mathew took out some tranquillizers and told Adam to take them that they d calm him down and to have tea and some food so he could relax. By this stage Adam was barely able to hold a cup in his hand s the nerves were completely gone. Mathew was looking at Adam in disbelief thinking how had he come to this state. That s what drugs and drink can do to a person there are people in hospitals all around the world who are completely depended on the public health services and mental health services for the rest of their lives because of alcohol and drug related illnesses. It's a sad state of affairs to be reduced to something that you can only imagine happening to someone else.

The flight to Paris was endless and arriving to Paris there were army guys everywhere due to some important Government Official. Adam was looking at the gun s they had he thought they were out to kill him. The guards were looking at Adam, Adam thought about the state of his health and realized how ill looking he must have looked. On leaving the airport they found the car hire they were looking for and put the bags in the boot of the car.

Mathew asked Adam to look at the map for the right route and Adam s brain was so fucked up that he was unable to make any sense of it. So with Mathew with one hand on the steering wheel and the other on the map started driving on the motorway. Eventually they were lost and had to stop the car and try and find the right road out of the airport. After some time they were on the motorway for Paris. It was a freezing foggy morning some change from Melbourne's warmer climate.

It had been Mathew s dream for both lads to go to Paris which Mathew arranged in the travel agents. On the day they were there the travel agent was asking them when did they want to leave Adam blurted as soon as possible and she looked at him surprisingly and booked them onto the next available flight out of Melbourne with a stop over in Paris.

It was Mathew s dream to be in Paris however with his partner psychotic it was all too fucked up to comprehend.

Mathew was flying on the motorway with Adam in toe what was going through Mathew's head no one will know travelling gives you a high and with his partner completely deranged it was all too much, By this stage they were flying down the streets of Paris not really knowing where they were going Mathew was pointing to Adam on the map that that's where there going Adam was in bits trying to navigate his way around the map Mathew was trying to concentrate on the roads of Paris and driving on the other side of the road eventually they stopped the car and starting screaming at each other on calming down they realised that the only way they were going to find the hotel was to hail a taxi so they abandoned the car in the middle of Paris Mathew was looking at the Eifel tower in the distance and stopped a guard to ask him exactly where they were in Paris so when they were leaving they knew where to collect the car from.

They found the hotel and checked in Adam thought that the guys sitting in the hotel reception area were a film crew and still thought that the media were onto him. Both lads were exhausted.

The hotel room was very quiet and peaceful which Adam needed he phoned home and talked to his mum. She commented that they should have a quiet night in and have a good night s sleep.

Adam remembered how cold it was and put on a heavy jumper if he was cold in Australia by the end of the summer he was now freezing in Paris.

By the end of summer in Australia he was sleeping under three duvets and growing hairs where he had never had hairs before.

Now in Paris Mathew and Adam ventured out for the afternoon after Mathew did all the checking in at the hotel. On walking down the chanse lise people were staring at the two of them. Adam was in hysterics and panic and thought that everyone there had come out to see him he was clutching a bag which he bought in Jarkarta airport and thinking that he needed it just so he had something to hold onto. When your going through a szhizophernic episode and drug induced psychosis your lucky you can walk. Mathew thought Adam had some sort of direction in Paris because he was there on another two occaisions Adam had none he did not have a clue where he was going.

Everyone advised Adam to stay in Melbourne to sort out his problems however Adam insisted taking the trip home and Mathew was advised that on no account was he to leave Adam's side. By the time they arrived at the metro the lads were trying to organize a ticket to use the metro Adams brain was fried from all the drugs and medication he was on and was trying to remember how to use his French he had learned at school. By this stage he was in a state and thought fuck it Mathew was in the same mood too and cancelled their metro ride and ended up lost in Paris again.

Mathew wanted to see the river seine and decided that they find a certain bridge where they stopped and took some photographs Adam remembers a photographer taking photos beside the river Seine and by this stage he didn't give a shit if it was for him or not.

Late that day they found a restaurant down a quiet side street of Paris, where they sat in the restaurant having fillet steak together with a bottle of French wine.

After dinner they ended up in a café by the hotel Adam remembers the French waiter s attitude because Adam thought he was thinking that Adam was wasting his life Adam could not wait to get out of there and ended up in the hotel it was 7 pm and both guys had a crazy day in Paris. Adam suggested to Mathew that he should venture out to the bars for some beer that he would be fine in the hotel alone. Mathew commented that he must be joking that there was no way he was letting Adam out of his sight. That he had gotten him this far and had no intentions of leaving his side. So Adam took some pills and fell asleep till the morning where they had breakfast and left the hotel in a taxi where they collected the abandoned car and packed their luggage into the back and drove to the airport for the grand finale arrival to Dublin.

Finally on checking everything in and leaving the car where it was picked up they boarded the plane for Dublin. All Adam remembered was Mathew saying something about his dream to Paris was not what he expected Adam commented that there would be other time s and that not to worry about it. That's all that Adam remember s about the trip to Dublin just that the captain was announcing they were landing soon.

Adam looked out the window and took one look at the grey Irish sky and saw the towers of Ballymun and turned to Mathew and said that de did not want to be in Dublin. Mathew turned to Adam in hysterics and roared what are you fucking like they both cracked up laughing and then the plane landed.

They arrived out at arrivals with Adam s dad waiting. Adam thought about the state he was in and the drive to Dalkey was Mathew chatting to Adam s dad with Adam sitting in the car saying nothing.

They arrived out to Dalkey and had breakfast with the family and Adam slept till the following day, Mathew ended up in town with Adam's sister and brother. The day after that Adam was admitted into St John of Gods.

He spent six weeks there and was finally making progress and Mathew had set up an apartment for the two of them to move into when Adam was released. It was hard for Adam to see his family and friend s in the state he was in because 9 months ago he had left Dublin a different person. Adam liked to party however it had all taken its toll he took it to the complete max.

After spending some time with the other patients in hospital the majority were in for drink and drug related illnesses. One asked Adam what did he get up to in Australia and did he manage to save some buck s for the trip home Adam cracked up laughing and another commented that you must be joking,

Mathew would visit everyday and tell him he loved him and was looking forward to him coming out and how he was doing setting everything up for when he was released. Adam looked forward to that day and was indecisive on weather he was going to move home or live with Mathew. In his head he was like a fucking nomad and did not know where he was in his head.

He did not know weather he was coming or going. Being locked up in a lock up ward with other suicidal patients, waving to Mathew like a baby with Adam's sister was hard for Mathew. Mathew thought what was becoming of Adam, and when was he going to snap out of all this.

One weekend while Adam had leave Mathew and Adam were back at the apartment. The doctors told Mathew that Adam was not to leave Mathews side. Mathew was talking to Adam about their relationship that they were like two brothers. Mathew was trying to explain to Adam that they were lovers and that Mathew wanted sex. Sex between the two had been non existent over the last 5 months and that Mathew was missing the affectionate side of their relationship. Adam agreed however was having problems connecting and promised to make more of an effort.

Adam was slowly making progress and the following weekend the doctors asked Adam what he was doing that weekend and on hearing his reply suggested that he be discharged to a day center to do a rehabilitation course which was a personal assessment course and try to maintain his sanity. The course for Adam was boring as hell however after some time it did help. He was posted to the kitchen for 4 hours a week where he helped out in the kitchen with the chef who prepared the food for the people attending this center.

It was a far cry from the fabulous food he had been cooking in Melbourne. There were people at that center that were attending for years Adam called it the boulevard of broken dreams and could not wait to leave and was constantly saying to the doctors that he wanted to return to work. It was run down and smelled this horrible smell of cleaning equipment.

The doctors advised that he stay with them for the time been and dished up food in the canteen he hated his time there and could not wait to get the fuck out of there.

Mathew kept saying to Adam to stick with it that there was no real pressure on them now. Mathew would call the apartment to check that Adam was attending and making sure he was not hanging around the apartment.

After been home for some months Mathew and Adam were out and about. Adam found it hard to socialise without drugs and alcohol and on no condition was allowed to use or drink.

However some week s later Adam started drinking again. He knew he shouldn't however when you are diagnosed schizophrenic it is a lot to except the alcohol was a crutch for the agony of it all. Both lads caught up with friends and some were surprised that they had returned to Dublin so soon.

Acquaintances in bars would enquire on how was the trip and both lads would say fine that Adam just wanted to come back to Dublin.

They were renting an apartment on Dominique Street in Dublin 1 Mathew was working in a top hotel in Dublin as a conference and banqueting manager while Adam attended a lifestyle management course. Their life was sort of coming together and Mathew seemed a lot happier with the progress Adam was making. Adam had some way to go however under the circumstances he was doing well.

Both lads spent the summer in Dublin it was 1997 it was not an easy ride for them by September Mathew returned to Australia there were complications with his visa and by this stage he was working in Dublin illegally.

Mathew s send off

Adam and Mathew spent there last few days staying at Jury s hotel down on the docks. They caught up with some friends and were out on the town for three final days together. Both guys spoke about their future together and Mathew told Adam to look after himself. That they would be together again in Melbourne by the end of the year. Mathew mentioned that he was going to miss his second home which had become Dublin and the culture he had become accustomed to.

For some reason they spent the night in separate bed s and the next morning Adam woke up to vomit all over the side of the bed where he was sleeping. He had vomited in his sleep and did not remember doing it.

Adam returned to the family home and was still attending the day center that was coming to an end. Adams family were happy to have him home.

Mathew would call Adam up from Australia and ask when was he returning at the time Adam was too scared to return and stayed in Dublin for the immediate future. Adam finished his personal development course and started another course with Schizophrenic Ireland on September 1997 which was for four months. They helped him build his self esteem and prepared him for work the outside world. However Adam started drinking again.

He started a job as a chef in a bar on Dorset Street and started taking drugs again, The job was manageable and for Adam and soon he took over the kitchen as head chef. After work Adam sat at the bar have some fun and usually head out into the night. He would spend Fridays clubbing at Harcourt Street and was partying at house parties somewhere in the city.

Adam s family had a hard time dealing with Adam's behaviour and one day his mum turned around and mentioned to him that she had done all the worrying she could ever do and thought that Adam was purely out to destroy himself.

By this stage Adam was skating on thin ice in work for months on end and was not unusual for him to turn up late and phone in sick on a regular basis. Which meant the bar staff were doing his job. On morning s that he was late he would phone in advance and ask the staff to put the roast in the oven and to prepare the soup and do the brown bread that he was on his way arriving in just before lunch and fly around organising everything before lunch.

One night Adam brought Lola a Chinese girl he was working with out clubbing the owner of the bar commented like Jasus she will be strung out on drugs after Adam was finished with her that night Adam met this gothic guy Paul who brought him home. He was dressed in a full length coat and thick heavy boots with gelled hair he approached Adam and kissed his hand Adam was weary of him but also found him intriguing.

He invited Adam home so they walked Lola to the taxi rank and walked towards Paul s place which was on Pembroke Road it was Friday night. Paul told Adam that he was a vampire and that he lived for the night this suited Adam fine.

They arrived at the flat and sat in the kitchen drinking coffee. Paul started licking Adam boots and both lads ended up in bed. They stripped each other and had sex and afterwards Paul asked Adam could he shave his ass. Adam agreed and Paul got on with his request. It was a kinky moment. Adam liked Paul and thought he was different from the lads that were around town.

The next day they spent a day drinking at Renard's with a friend of Paul s later that night they ended up in a club at the Tivoli on Francis Street on E dancing and kissing.

After clubbing they left in a taxi to Paul s. They had sex and Paul fell asleep. Adam spent some hours in the bedroom dancing in a pair of Versace shorts Paul had passed out.

On Sunday morning they awoke and ended up in a bar on Baggot Street. Adam met some people that he met on a bender some years ago at a party in Step a Side. They chatted for some time and then said their goodbyes.

Paul and Adam hailed a taxi to a bar on Duke Street and finished off the weekend and ended up at Paul s late Sunday night. They fell asleep and later that morning Adam left for work. Mondays were manageable and because it was quiet Adam got through the day fine. Later that day Adam had some beers at the bar and ended up at a night club in Temple bar. After the club was over Adam took another E and before he knew it he was out of his head on a Tuesday morning. Adam caught a taxi to where he was working there were flat s above the bar and luckily the publican s mother was away on holidays.

Adam woke some of the tenants up who lived there looking for somewhere to stay. The Spanish lady who he knew was not able to put him up Adam was completely out of it and left in a taxi to Paul s on Pembroke Road.

Paul s flat mate opened the door to him and Adam walked into Paul s bedroom and was lying on the bed completely out of it. Paul woke up screaming at Adam what the fuck was he doing and how did he get in. Adam tried to calm Paul down however Paul was having none of it. He wanted Adam out Adam was not moving and with that Paul produced a knife and got Adam in headlock with the knife up to his throat Paul threatened to use it if he did not leave.

Adam said go ahead use it and you'll be spending a long time in prison getting over the situation. With that Paul pushed Adam aside and called the police Adam realised that he had to get the fuck out of there, he left the flat and slammed the door and with major anger kicked the door.

On walking down the pathway onto the street the police pulled up and stopped Adam by this stage it was 7 am they asked him who he was. Adam bluffed his way out of the situation by explaining that he was a resident from upstairs and had heard a disturbance from the flat below the guards thanked Adam and with that Adam hailed a taxi and asked the driver to take him to Slatterys on Capel street. Adam spent the morning drinking

Adam phoned work around 10 am to say that he would not be in that day to which everyone roared behind him and thought it was great fun they nearly blew his cover.

Adam s employer had many conversations with Adam and after work explained one day that he was a good chef and he did not want to replace him however his absences from work could not go on. So Mark his employer explained to Adam that he was putting him on a three day week for the foreseeable future, and if Adam wanted he could drink and drug his head off however he was to be in a fit state when he was due into work.

In the mist of all this Adam s old school friend Danny was in touch and was home from Paris he was also an addict and never worked a day in his life. So Adam was out and about with Danny on his days off and sitting in the Globe Bar on Georges Street one day Adam commented to Danny on how good looking this guy was across from them, with that the guy came over he was dark with a white muscle tee shirt on and said hi to Adam, Adam just looked at him the guy explained that they had met before in an early house on Capel Street and did Adam remember him.

Adam laughed and said he had no recollection he would have remembered someone he fancied but must have been really out of it. The guy introduced himself as Mark and asked Adam how he was. He mentioned that Adam joined him and his girlfriend the two of them were having some morning drinks together.

Mark mentioned that a fight broke out with Adam and some other people at the early house they were harassing Adam over been gay. Mark said he stood up for Adam and smashed a stool over this lads head and with that they were all kicked out and ended up in the Boars Head the guys causing trouble who started on Adam followed them all to the Boars Head to continue the arguing. Mark told Adam that he called a taxi for him and put Adam and the person who was with Adam into the taxi. Adam had no recollection of this and was intrigued to know who was with him. They left in a taxi laughing and waving out the window,

Danny and Adam sat in the Globe laughing at this and ended up in Temple Bar for some pizza and wine and later sat in the George for a few drinks. Both guys were chatted up and Danny ended up in the toilet snorting cocaine and left with this guy. He only wanted coke and decided that he d spend the night with this guy just for drugs.

Danny parents died when he was about 18 both in the space of a year. He was left money from their will and blew 150000 pounds living the high life in Paris and returning to Dublin every so often. The last Adam heard of Danny was that he was living in Amsterdam hanging out with an 18 year old guy going to all the latest club s pub s and restaurants.

Both lads met at Marian college and used to skip school and hang out together in the City Centre. Adam brought Danny to the Gay bars not knowing then that Danny was gay too. Danny lived in Paris for some years and when the shit hit the fan in Paris or when he got bored returned to Dublin. Adam was always fascinated about the people he attracted into his life when he was younger because they all in some way had similar lifestyles. Danny never managed to hold a fulltime job and his siblings threw him out and the last time Adam heard of Danny he was sponging in a flat in Stoneybatter off a transsexual drug addict and was borrowing money off everyone around him promising them all that he was waiting for money to come through from an Aunt who died and that part of her farm was going to him. As soon as the will came through he up t and left everyone around him high and dry.

Friend s were saying to Adam that he should stay away from Danny because all Danny was interested in was going out and getting off his head. And that Adam had enough of his own problems to be dealing with.

Adam knew that he needed to do something about his lifestyle because he d see the alcoholics coming into the bar he was catering in on Dorset Street and knew that if he did not sort himself out that he could end up like one of them. Mathew was always on Adam s case about loosing the game of life for good and ending up a sad and lonely man this had always played on Adam s mind so he attended alcoholics anonymous and lasted the first attempt for six weeks and ended up back out there drinking and drugging.

Adam was also in touch with Mathew and wanted to travel again.

Mathew wrote to Adam and

Well hello Adam

I hope you are well. I'm writing to you after your phone call the other day saying you want to come to Australia. I think it's a great idea life is fantastic here even better that I remember it. I have just started my fulltime employment. Food and beverage manager at a hotel in the city, the job is fantastic I love it. My plan is to live at mum and dad s until November this year to save money. At least 8 000 Australian Dollars because I never want to have no money behind me again, like the last couple of years. Its great living with them, there is no hassle and no rent I can drive the car whenever I want (fantastic) so if you decide to come over I d love it. But there have to be some rules it would have to be a partnership we would both have to work and save money. There would be no running off to Virgin Mary s with the last 40 dollars like before what I mean Adam a good quality life, nice things around us, the ability to go on nice holidays, and enjoy life together.

I think about you all the time and reminisce the old days we had a fantastic time together when things were good. And that is the way I want it again, and I believe it would work.

First thing you would have to do is make sure you keep all our visa information together and bring it all over. Last time I saw it, it was all in your room in a purple envelope, all that stuff is really important and needs to be kept, next either apply for a 12 month working holiday visa or a tourist visa either will do and when you get out here we will pay the money and reapply for an independent visa. I think the best time for you to come over is just before Christmas. That way it gives me enough time to save money and get a flat together and it gives you time to save your airfare and some extra cash to get started.

You would make it in time for our famous Melbourne summer and our hot Christmas day.

I look forward to hearing from you soon. I miss you very much and think about you all every day. Keep safe and well hope you are behaving yourself.

All my love Mathew.

This was March 1998.

By this stage Adam was home since May 1997

Adam was managing to keep his job at the pub and see his friend s who were all concerned about his welfare tHose who knew Adam well started mentioning that he was slowly killing himself and that one day something bad was going to happen. Adam was hearing stories about other people he knew who were either missing or had died. In a way Adam was hoping to start afresh with Mathew in Australia. However his lifestyle in Dublin however bad it was going would be a hell of a lot worse in Australia.

Adam used to spend his night at the George on a regular basis and walk out the door pissed at the end of the night. He was missing Mathew and wanted him around. On standing outside the George Adam blacked out and later awoke in a police cell banging on the door shouting let me out. The police arrived and made some comment on the state Adam was in earlier before when they picked him up. No matter how many blackouts Adam had he always managed to find his way home. However his condition was getting so serious and Adam was blind to the fact of it all. On different occasions summonses were arriving at the house one was for Valentines night Adam had no recollection of the night in question.

The summons read

You hailed a taxi from town and arriving along the Oscar Trainer Road you announced that you had no money to pay for the taxi. Due to this the driver brought you to the local police station at Coolock where you refused to pay for the taxi. Due to this the driver pressed charges and a statement was signed.

Adam had no recollection of this until the summons arrived. What the fuck was he doing out in Coolock when he lived on out in Dalkey. He phoned the police station and asked for the officer in question and asked to speak to the officer who dealt with the situation. She told Adam that he was out of it that night and had no money to pay the taxi and the driver was taking the matter further because of Adam s attitude, she explained that it was unfortunate for the matter to be taken to the district court.

Adam asked how he left the station and the officer mentioned that Adam asked her to call him a taxi and the destination was Dalkey. Adam was trying to remember what he was doing out there and who was he with it was all a blur. The guard mentioned to Adam that she was sorry that it was been brought forward so off Adam and Mother went to court. While sitting waiting for the case to be brought up there was a lady standing at the box up for not paying for a fare on the same night on the Oscar Trainer Road. Adam turned to his mum and whispered to her was she in the taxi with Adam that night. They both started to laugh and later the woman was ordered to pay the fare and put some money in the poor box.

After everyone was dealt with Adam expected his name to be called out the Judge looked down at the two of them and asked Adam s Mum, did she have summons with her. Both explained why they were there and the judge mentioned that the case had not been presented and that they would hear no more. Both Adam and mum left the courthouse laughing hysterically about the situation and Adam s mum mentioned the fact that after that she could do with a stiff whiskey.

Mathew was never there when Adam phoned or else he was out clubbing. Adam suspected Mathew was seeing someone else after all a year had passed and both lads were living separate lives. Then Mathew announced one evening to Adam not to come to Australia at Christmas that he was coming to Dublin Adam was thrilled and was looking forward to seeing Mathew. However the news Mathew had for Adam was not what he expected.

Mathew and Adam hooked up two days after Christmas out in Dalkey. They had drinks at the Club and Mathew commented to Adam that he was like Patsy out of Absoulutely Fabulous Adam laughed. They walked Vico road and upto Dalkey hill. Mathew commented to Adam on how beautiful Dalkey is and was aking Adam what type of birds were flying overhead. Adam commented that they were magpies and Mathew thought they were lovely.

Then Mathew came out with the blow that Adam was not expecting however deep down he knew that his life was in Dublin. Mathew explained that he had met someone else and that they were in Dublin together and that they were living in Melbourne,

This was not what Adam wanted to hear and became quite upset. They ended up again in the club bar all Adam wanted to do was get pissed. Mathew explained that if they were from both the same side s of the world that things could have been different. However Adam s life was in Dublin and his life was in Melbourne. Mathew mentioned that his mum missed Adam and was sorry to hear that they were splitting up.

Adam thought that they were going to spend more time together and ring in the New Year together however on hearing the bad news suggested to Mathew that they were going to keep their holiday over Xmas separate and make the most of their last days together. After some time that passed Adam walked Mathew to the dart station and left Mathew onto the train that was going to Howth. That was the last time Adam saw Mathew.

It was not a good Christmas for Adam after his life changing news he spent most of it with his family and friend s who advised him that he was better off in Dublin where if he ran into any trouble he d have his family and friends close by.

Adam returned to work after the holiday season was over and spent a lot of time drinking alone and having one night stands this went on for some time and he lived a life of self destruction once again. Drugs came into the equation and he swapped drink for drugs and drugs for drink six months on drink and six months on drugs, eventually his employer in the bar let Adam go due to his absences. So Adam found himself out of work and doing a rehabilitation course. Which sort of helped and his family were all there to help to.

Meeting Jean
And Flying To Budapest

Adam met Jean in a sauna in Dublin and decided to keep in touch with him when he returned to Budapest. They had hung out in Dublin and had gone out for dinner later clubbing on a summers Saturday night. Jean was staying at the Berkely court hotel in Ballsbridge where they later spent the early hours of Sunday morning where they slept in each others arms. Adam left the Berkely Court Hotel Sunday morning and both lads kissed each other goodbye and promised to keep in touch. Jean flew home to Budapest and Adam jumped into a taxi home to Dalkey.

Both lads kept in touch by E mail and on the summer of 2001 Adam and a friend of his flew to Budapest for 16 night s on a trip. At this stage Adam was sober 6 months and while up in the sky while the air stewardess was passing with the drinks trolley Adam decided that he d order a bottle of wine. Adam s friend George asked Adam was he sure and Adam responded that it was grand that they were both on holidays and were only responsible for themselves. Adam chatted to the lady beside him she was in her late sixties and was wearing her best suit. She commented to Adam that she had been thinking the night before who she was going to be sitting beside on the plane and told Adam that she was delighted that it was him.

Adam was drunk and high when the plane touched down in Vienna which was where the changeover was for Budapest Adam and George said goodbye to the lady and wished her a nice trip she also wished the lads a good trip and that it was nice to meet them, later the lad s boarded the plane to Budapest from Vienna.

When the plane landed in Budapest Adam was pissed and high from the excitement of meeting Jean. They passed through customs and walked through the arrival s to meet Jean and his friend Maria, Jean was smiling and waving at Adam when he came through and they greeted each other with a hug and kiss.

Adam introduced George to Jean and Maria and the four walked to the car park and drove onto the motorway to bring them to their hotel.

Adam and Jean sat beside each other in the rear of the car while George sat in the passenger seat with Maria driving. George and Maria chatted about the lives and what they did for a living. While Adam and Jean were holding hand s and chatting about what they were going to do for the time that they both had together in Budapest. Phats and small was playing on the radio this time around while we were driving into the center of Budapest. Jean suggested to Adam that he have a key to his apartment in Budapest and Adam agreed that that was a good idea.

Jean was thrilled when Adam arrived through the arrivals gate he was jumping up and down.

They dropped their bags at the hotel and george stayed in the hotel room that night while Adam and Jean decided to go out that night. They arrived at a bar that was an arty type of place and paid the entrance fee to go downstairs to this trendy large bar with a dance floor.

Jean introduced Adam to the staff and they ordered beers and sat at the table with their arms around each other gazing into each others eyes like love puppys. Jean warned Adam to be careful in Budapest of the Indian Gypsies that they'd chance there arm on a tourist and take advantage of a tourist. After downing a couple of beers they proceeded to the dance floor and the Indian gypsies were all over Adam.

Adam was reluctant to entertain them and was looking over at Jean laughing at the attention he was receiving from these strange looking characters. One was in drag and was wearing a leopard skin dress, with a matching handbag and with long black hair she was off her head and was having a good time. How she stayed in her high heels was a mystery she was hilarious the club was quiet except for the gypsies they were adding some atmosphere to the establishment.

Adam and Jean left around 4 am and walked to Jeans flat it was a lovely summers morning and Adam produced a bottle of Bailey s to Jean as a warming present they opened it and poured themselves a lavish measure and almost polished off half the bottle they were late dancing to Jennifer Lopez waiting for the night and later slept in each others arms.

It was a great start to the trip and the following day they picked George up from the hotel and drove around the city looking at the sights and landmarks. They walked up to the palace and from passing along the river Danube Jean pointed out the Budapest bithches, which Jean explained were rent boys. Some were looking at Adam and Adam thought they were cute and he was loving the attention.

On walking up to Buda in the hills they overlooked the city and the houses of parliament it was a gorgeous day and Jean and Maria gave the lads a run down of the history around the castle.

Later they drove past a waterfall coming down the side of the cliff it was really beautiful and Adam commented that it was all very cultural.

Jean laughed and mentioned to Adam that he needed it Adam laughed and said thanks. They later returned to the hotel to freshen up it was Saturday night and the three lads ended up in a club.

Adam was downstairs while George and Jean sat upstairs. Jean was tired and decided to call it a night so Adam decided to stay on and party. He later ran into an m and m lookalike who he later brought back to the hotel they were staying in and arriving on the 7th floor entered the hotel room to George. Who was lying awake concerned about Adam.

George was giving out to Adam about Adam s behaviour and that the m and m lookalike should leave. Adam was having none of it and decided that he was going to hire another hotel room until the morning.

At this stage of the night it was bright and on arriving down to reception paid for another and later that morning both lads fucked, said their goodbyes to each other. The m and m look a like kept saying to Adam sexy boy they were the only bit s of English he could speak they both said goodbye about 9 am.

Adam fell into bed about 9.30 AM, to a George, he was trying to talk some sense into Adam about his drinking and behaviour. They both were in a strange city and with Adam drinking something bad might happen and then they d be in trouble.

Adam had met George in a psychiatric hospital in Dublin in the mid 1990's and they became good friends both with mental health problems and also gay they were good for each other always looking out for each other and helping each other along. George was pointing out to Adam that if he got into trouble that he was not in the best state of mental health to help him out.

Adam told gerorge not to worry that he was able to take care of himself and that they were covered with health insurance. George pointed out to Adam that he was drinking too much and that he was not supposed to be drinking at all.

They later slept and caught the local tram to the center of the city to meet Jean at 2pm. George got off at the wrong stop while Adam was busy chatting to a couple for directions about the underground transport system.

While the tram doors closed, Adam noticed George out in the middle of nowhere and carried along in the direction of the center of Budapest. Unaware where he was going himself they had no cell phones to contact each other so Adam got off in the city center and caught the underground to the other side of the city to meet Jean on the directions he had been given over the phone by Jean.

Adam arrived to a station beside the river Danube to meet Jean and the two lads kissed and caught an over ground train to a remote gay hillside to sun bath.

Jean inquired about George and Adam burst out laughing explaining what had happened to George and Jean asked was he alright Adam commented that he was fine and Jean told Adam that he was crazy.

They got off the train at there destination and walked up to the swimming pool paid the entrance fee and climbed the steps to the hill that was awaiting them it was fabulous with a view overlooking the city it was a hot sunny day lovely.

Both lads settled into the grass with their towels and rubbed suntan lotion over each other and held hands together while they soaked up the sunshine. There were a lot of good looking Budapest guys sunbathing on the hill with guy s in groups and guys by themselves.

Jean asked Adam how he coping off drugs and Adam said that everything was fine. Jean was happy for Adam and was happy that Adam was spending time with him in Budapest both guys were thinking about George and hoped he was alright.

Adam spent the night with Jean they had some drinks in Jeans and later slept naked together. The following morning Jean had work so both lads arranged to meet later that evening for dinner near Jeans.

Meanwhile Adam phoned George in the hotel and arranged for them to meet in the Centre of Budapest in a square called Octagon to catch up. Adam asked George was he ok and arranged for George to bring his passport to use at the bank to cash some travellers cheques. George arrived at the square to meet Adam.

Adam was sitting there over a cappuccino and was happy to see George arriving. Adam told George about the hillside and the swimming pool and asked George what he got up to after they lost each other the day before George mentioned that he famillarized himself with Budapest.

George ordered brunch and both lads sat in the square absorbing the atmosphere of this unique city. That afternoon the lads cashed travellers cheques and Adam later returned to Jeans to leave the money in a safe place in Jeans flat he put it on top of the kitchen cabinets and thought that there was probably no one else using Jean s place as far as he knew.

Later that day the lads spent the day exploring Margaret Island enjoying the sunshine and stumbled across a small zoo that had some gorgeous peacocks, hens and other birds that they had never seen before.

Later that day they spent the day at the local swimming pool chatting and checking out the talent.

That night Adam hooked up with Jean and he bought him to a Chinese restaurant where they had a slap up meal they later walked the park across from the restaurant enjoying the summers evening.

An hour or two later they hooked up with George and spent the end of the evening watching a drag show in a cool gay bar in Budapest.

That night Adam spent the night with George back at the hotel while Jean spent the night at his place. The following day both lads awoke and spent the day at the pool. Later on they met Jean and some of his friend s and had dinner at a traditional Hungarian restaurant Adam liked Jean s friends and they chatted about why had they picked Budapest to visit.

Adam explained that some years earlier he had been to Prague and enjoyed the Eastern European feel and since meeting Jean in Dublin and keeping in touch thought that it be a good idea knowing someone in a different city to come visit.

Later that evening they spent the night at a trendy gay bar overlooking the Danube and looking into the distance there was a view of the palace of Budapest. After some drinks Jean left to go home and told the lads that they should check out the leather bar that was around the corner.

George and Adam entered the leather bar about 12.30 am and were given a drinks card which was later to be returned to the bar and paid for.

Adam lost track of the drinks he drank and was chatting to a lad he met at the pool who joined in the session they were having. George decided to call it a night while Adam stayed with Bolauge. Bolauge was all 6ft 2ins handsome Hungarian hunk who with Adam was having a ball with. At about 2 am Boulage left and Adam was there by himself. The bar was full of mazes and dark rooms with a stripper dancing alone in a cage Adam was dancing too beside the stripper with a bottle of poppers and having a ball.

Meanwhile Adam picked up this sexy cute young Hungarian guy who he decided to invite back to the hotel room. On leaving the bar. Adam realised that he did not have enough money to pay all the drinks. At this stage he was very drunk and with the bar staff and door staff around him he screamed to them look, that he did not have enough money to pay for the drinks, explaining that Boulage that had left earlier he should have fixed up his share of the bill.

To this day Adam still does not know how he wrangled his way out of it and left in a taxi to return to the hotel with this sexy Hungarian guy.

On arriving to the 7th floor hotel room, with his new pick up. George commented on how good looking he was and asked where did he meet him.

Adam mentioned that after everyone had left that he meet him just as he was leaving himself some hours later.

Adam suggested to the guy that they have a shower together and on asking this request realised that the guy was a male prostitute and started asking Adam for money saying to Adam sex business sex business. Adam thought that there was no way he was paying for sex he had never paid before and was not about to start. He told the guy to take his clothes off the guy was having none of it and so was Adam. Adam ordered him again to go into the bathroom at this stage it was 3.30 am and they were causing a scene. With no one able to agree Adam dragged the guy out from the seventh floor into the lift down to reception and dragged him through the reception area with the rent boy screaming where is my fucking money.

171

Adam thought fuck this and the staff at the reception area said listen just give him what he is looking for and get rid of him. Adam agreed and went back to the room for the safety deposit key and took out the equivalent of 40 euro and gave it to the guy and told him to fuck off.

Later in Dublin Adam was telling some friends about the situation and they told him about someone they knew who had his throat slashed with a knife by an Eastern European rent boy and survived Adam was lucky.

Adam was sensible and with his street wise credibility knew how to cope in Budapest. The following day both Adam and George had lunch and spent the day sunbathing and bathing at the terminal baths under the hotel which is a 5 star bath house with fabulous Turkish statues embedded into the walls with water running down them to the pool lovely.

That evening they hooked up with Jean and some friends to have dinner the Hungarian lads took them to a fashionable part of the city with cafes and bars they had some dinner and chatted about hotel Gellert where the bath house is and all commented on how good it is. After dinner the lads jumped on a tram and caught a bus up to the top of a hill where lies a fort and at night time you can see all over the city with an amazing view of the city with all the bridges lit up and a fabulous view of the palace.

That night Jean told Adam he wanted to sleep alone and Adam was gutted about the situation. Jean held Adam s hand and told him that he was a nice guy and to enjoy the rest of his stay in Budapest Adam agreed.

The following day Jean flew out to Cyprus for a week and Adam was alone in Budapest apart from George. So Adam hooked up with Boulage who had given Adam his phone number.

Adam called around to Boulage s apartment and greeted each other with a kiss. Later they stripped off and had sex on the lounge floor Adam left inviting Boulage to come stay at the hotel the following night. They smiled at each other when leaving. Adam returned to George at the hotel and they had an early night.

The next day was spent having lunch, which was usually their first meal of the day and later at Margaret Island by the pool. Adam was looking forward to Boulage coming around and met him at Mc Donalds in the city.

They stopped off on their way to buy some beers and returned to the hotel room Goerge was out hanging out in some bars by himself. Both lads turned the key in the hotel room and poured themselves a beer and sat on each of the single beds in the hotel room.

Boulage told Adam about himself that he was an addictions counsellor for people that had problems with drugs and alcohol Adam laughed and thought how ironic. He did not mention to Boulage about his situation and Boulage proceeded to tell him about his brother who died of a heroin overdose on the street s of Budapest and that he still missed him.

After a couple of beers Boulage asked Adam could he open a bottle of sparkling wine Adam said sure and both lads drank the bottle of wine in between having sex. The hotel room was trashed and sheets were everywhere and empty bottles of wine and beer scattered on the floor they had a great time and later about 12 am Adam said he was going to bed. Boulage asked Adam was it ok to have another bottle of wine Adam agreed and said when he was finished to come to bed. George was still out. Adam slept for two hours and awoke to find Boulage sitting beside the hotel window drinking a bottle of brandy.

Adam asked him where did he buy the brandy knowing that he had ordered it on room service. Boulage mentioned that he popped out to the off license which Adam knew was untrue.

Adam thought of joining him and remembered that he had to check out the following morning so decided to go back to sleep. At about 5 am Adam awoke to see that George had returned and that Boulage was unconscious on the floor lying sprawled out on the hotel room floor in his briefs Adam thought nice and that he was relieved that Boulage had stopped drinking. Adam fell asleep till 7 am and later saw Boulage sitting by the window drinking the rest of the bottle of brandy. Adam said nothing and later awoke to Boulage unconscious on the floor the reception were calling asking Adam when were they going to check out Adam looked at George and both lads agreed in 30 mins.

Boulage was lying on the floor and Adam was pouring water over him. Trying to wake him up he was slightly coming round and Adam was pulling his jeans onto him with some difficulty. He was still only slightly coherent. Adam counted what he had drank and calculated that he had drank a bottle of brandy 1 and a half of sparkling wine and three large bottles of beer. Adam thanked god that he did not join him at the window, because he knew that he d be also in the same state too.

The hotel reception were on the phone again asking when were they leaving and Adam told them they d be out in 20 minutes. Adam put Boulages shoes on and could not find his tee shirt so he lifted him up and dragged him to the lift on the seventh floor and pushed the button for reception. He dragged Boulage through reception and put him into a taxi and told the driver to drop him into the centre of

Budapest the driver was reluctant however on Adam pointing to Boulages wallet the driver drove off.

Adam returned to the reception area with the receptionist saying they had to pay their bill and that the room was only for two people, asking who was the third person Adam replied that Boulage was a friend who popped round after this night shift finished and that he drank too much and was there only for a few hours.

George was on the 7 th floor and checking the room for anything that they might have forgotton. Both lads fixed up the bill and had lost the address of the hotel they were staying in that night.

Adam s hangover was awful and George was having a spell of some schizophrenic symptoms Adam was standing there with a map guessing the name of the hotel that they were staying in and loosing patients with the whole situation. Eventually the right hotel name came out and the hotel receptionist repeated the name and Adam agreed.

George was relieved and so was Adam so off they drove in a taxi to the hotel hoping and praying that it was the right one. On driving down some unknowing streets they finally arrived at the hotel they had spent the first two nights at. Both lads were relieved and decided to have a nap. It was their last night in Budapest and Adam was intending to make the most of it. They hung out in the hotel and had something to eat and later that night Adam put on his best shirt and PVC pants and headed into the center of Budapest to meet some Polish guys that he had met at the swimming pool earlier on that week.

The last night in Budapest was a blast with the polish guys and some American s that all ended up in Budapest best gay club it was Saturday night and everyone was revved up.

Adam and George were telling the lads about their hotel exit, and how they had trouble finding the other hotel also too about Boulage. The lads were laughing and after some beers they were all dancing lee the polish guy was asking Adam was he intending to go to Warsaw and that he was welcome to stay if he ever did.

Adam and George spent the night dancing and George left early to return to the hotel to rest for the journey home to Dublin. Adam stayed with the polish lad lee and drank some more and both lads had a fabulous night dancing and chatting.

Adam mentioned to lee that he had to leave because it was 6 am and that he had to be up at 9am for the journey to the airport they both hugged and lee told Adam he was welcome anytime in Warsaw.

When Adam left the club outside it was sunny and bright. He walked to the underground and remembers standing at the top of the escalator and then remembers standing on the platform with a train approaching he had blacked out at the top of the escalator and came round on the platform with the a train approaching it was about 6.30 am.

Adam boarded the train and tried not to think about the flight, which was in 4 hours time. He arrived at the hotel and said good morning to George who woke up as he arrived. Adam mentioned to George to wake him when he needed to and fell asleep. Two hours later George woke Adam up with a cup of coffee and told him he had half an hour to be ready. Adam had most of his packing done and tied up a few loose ends that he had to take care of.

The lads packed their bags and booked a taxi to take them to the airport the journey took 30 minutes and they checked in and did a spot of shopping in duty free and boarded the plane. Both lads had a good time in Budapest and mentioned at some stage to return.

Three hours later they landed in Dublin hailed a taxi and were dropped off in South Dublin.

There has been no contact with Jean since he left and to this day there has been none. Adam kept in touch with a friend of Jean by E Mail after for some time and then lost touch.

The rest of the summer in Dublin Adam studied the ECDL course he was doing and spent some time looking after an older gent in a wheelchair who had the misfortune of having a stroke. Adam met Tony who he looked after through a friend of his,

Tony was delighted to have Adam around and look after him once a week and take him to the shops and off licence to do some weekly shopping. Adam would drop around to the nursing home where Tony was and help him from bed into his wheelchair and take him to the local shops to buy what he needed for the week.

After that they'd sat in Tony s room in the nursing home and chat about Tony s experiences and Adam s too. Tony was a lecturer at Mountjoy College for marketing. Tony was constantly advising Adam on what he should do and knew about his drug problem and alcoholism.

Adam would arrive to Tony and on occasions help him shave and cut his nails dress him and help him with some walking too. Tony was always saying to Adam to think about his future and that he should stop drinking. He was concerned about Adam and was always free to advice him. He mentioned to Adam that he could not make someone like him up and that he never met anyone like him. Adam was always casual about it all he was only 26 and was out to have a good time. However there comes a time when you've got to face yourself

177

and that tomorrow will always come even if you don't want it to. Tony was delighted to have Adam around to visit him and Adam kept visiting him until he died three years later.

Unfortunately though both men fell out one day in the supermarket while Tony was ordering some roast beef Adam advised him to order some more. Tony said to Adam, don t tell me what to do you fool, and Adam snapped back to Tony how dare you speak to me like that. That if he did not apologize he'd leave him in the shop and that he could make his own way back to the nursing home.

Tony never apologized to Adam so Adam marched him up the road to the nursing home dropped him to his room and told him that he could prepare his own tea and organize himself out of the wheelchair and back into bed.

On leaving his room Adam turned to Tony and said do I get an apology and Tony refused stubbornly. Adam left and that was the last he saw of Tony 3 months later he died and Adam and Brian attended his funeral, which was quiet service in Mount Jerome.

Tony was better off dead because he lived life to the full and had an excellent career and was living a gentleman s lifestyle, He used to fly to Hidelberg and was always chatting about the German men he meet there.

There was one German he'd see and off to the park they would go for a picnic and drink wine and champagne. Then there was his aristocrat friends in London where he'd attend dinner parties and socialize. It was sad that he died alone and had hardly anyone at his funeral life can be like that though.

Strange for someone who had a good job and never bought his own house and really set himself up with security. He had many contacts in Ireland which were all of good stock and often told Adam stories about certain people he knew here in Ireland. They had an interesting friendship which lasted for about four years.

For the rest of the summer Adam passed his exams after returning from Hungary.

South side Partnership

So now it was time for him to look for a job. He searched the fas web site and found an office administrator job in Dun Laoghaire. He phoned the company and set up an interview. The two women who interviewed him for the job commented on his c v and said it was fascinating Adam took it all in his stride and cracked a few jokes and left the interview feeling confident and happy. The company he applied to is a company that help s disadvantage people return to work and improve their skills.

A couple of days later they offered him the job. Adam started the job in South Side Partnership. On his first day his employer mentioned to Adam that the person comes first and the job second Adam was delighted to hear this and was full of enthusiasm.

The company catered for people who are from ethnic minorities, single parents, people with disabilities, people who also have poor education and from disadvantage backgrounds also people who have had problems with drugs and alcohol too,

They help people get back on their feet again and encourage you to better yourself. They also run workshops on confidence building, stress management, writing skills, computer packages, job searching, conducting your c v, team building, health and safety, communicating skills and offer support in Adult learning.

Adam was lucky to find this job on the internet and only realized what they did when he phoned one day. He stayed for two years and did quite well and also started a second job in an Adult Shop Dublin 2.

There was a nice bunch of people in the office in South Side Partnership and some of the staff also had problems with drugs too it was a great support network and one women who really helped Adam was a lady called Siobhan they had an instant connection Adam was still drinking and taking drugs however he was also dong recovery in AA and was sliping and sliding all over with drink and drugs, Siobhan was a good support to Adam and in a way Adam was a good support to her. Adam saw in Siobhan how well she was doing and Siobhan saw in Adam that if she was using she'd be having the problems that Adam was experiencing.

There were days when Adam was up and there were days when he was down. He received a lot of support and helped out his colleague s with his computer knowledge and spellings

Outside in the garden there was a nice bench and on a sunny day Adam and the woman next door would sit outside smoking and drinking cup s of tea chatting while the boss was out. Also other people dropped around from the office around the corner and there was always good fun. The company worked well.

In the building there were professionals who ran the company and also people who had problems in their background it ran well and there was a good social scene.

On occasions everyone would gather together and have gatherings together for birthdays and if someone was leaving. It was the time of the world cup and Ireland was doing well and the company would have lunches in the local pub beside them.

Adam was doing well and with taking on the job in an Adult shop had a lot of disposable income to socialize.

He was dancing in the POD one night when Adam met a guy called Neil. Neil was dancing with his top off on E, Neil turned to Adam and asked him did he used to work in Trinity College Adam replied yes and Neil asked Adam did he remember a guy approaching him on a Friday night after work to ask him out for a drink, Adam replied yes and Neil told Adam if was him.

Neil mentioned to Adam that he had spent the day picking up the courage to ask Adam out Adam turned him down and kept going he was on his way out to meet friends, however looking at Neil Adam realized how handsome he was, suddenly the D J changed tracks and on came Ilo rapture the lyrics started with tonight I laid my eyes on you felt everything around me move got nervous when you looked my way but you knew all the words to say, and your love slowly moves right in all this time I don t know where you've been please I'm worried don t you know my love I want you so sugar you make myself complete rapture tastes so sweet mesmerized in every way you keep me in a state of daze your kisses make my skin feel week Adam was also on e too. Adam took his top of too and both lads were checking each other out both lad s were fit and tanned.

The following track that played was volcano let your body be free and Adam lead Neil by the hand into the middle of the dance floor. They kissed and danced together and by the end of the night Neil asked Adam home Adam said cool so they left the club happy and high.

They hailed a taxi and jumped right in the driver commented and replied two fucking faggots. Adam was ready to lay into him when he realized that he was his sisters ex boyfriend. They both inquired about how each other was and Gerry asked where too, Neil responed to the four courts and off they drove.

Both lads arrived at the four courts and said goodbye to Gerry. They took a lift to a fifth floor apartment and came out into a fabulous apartment overlooking the city. Adam commented very nice and both lads sat down and had a drink. Neil was in finance and both lads laughed about the brief encounter they had some years back. Neil was interested in what Adam had been doing since he left Trinity College and Adam told him that he was out in Australia for a year and had spent two years with and Australian guy. Neil also was out in Australia and was doing very well for himself since his return.

After about an hour of chatting they moved to the bedroom and stripped and were happy with what they saw. Adam kissed Neil on the bed and Neil asked Adam was it ok if they just held each other. Adam was interested in sex however realized Neil just wanted to be held so agreed.

The next morning both lads had coffee and walked into town Neil was off to see some friends who had been to an after party and told Adam that it was nice to see him after all this time. They did not exchange numbers and on other occasions would stop and chat and kiss. Adam has not seen Neil in some time and reckons he is dealing with his e problem and thinks that he suffers from mild depression. Extacy is a strange drug when you first take it makes you feel so good and then before you know it your taking it most weekends and dancing your head off. There is some bond on the dance floor between people that are on E and then when a club is over most people congregate outside organizing an after party in some underground warehouse or in someone's apartment. However E is a false emotional bonding and most people who do it are involved with it for a period of time and then move on. You can go for days and loose track of normality. Just what you need if you want to escape from reality.

The Adult Shop

An adult store is definitely one of the most interesting jobs that one can have. You learn about peoples fetishes and what makes people tick. Friends of Adam were saying to him how could Adam work in somewhere like that dealing with the kind of people that shop there.

Adam s reply was that you deal with the same kind of people in all sorts of jobs that it was no different to working in a supermarket that all walks of life have to shop for food and looked at the adult store in the same way.

It is fun and you get to meet all sorts of people transgender, the gay community, straight people, bisexuals, prostitutes, macho builders coming in looking for ladies boots, guy s who are killing time waiting for the girlfriends to meet from work, army guys, strippers, dancers, office people, loners and older teenage and college dudes.

Other people would come in and start chatting about their lives and talking about their families and what they did for a living you ended up sitting there like some sort of counsellor and they be chatting about their fantasies.

Other guys would come in and if the shop was quiet would ask to try on the leather and rubber gear and call you into the changing room and ask for your opinion. One bi guy was trying on a leather pouch and stepped on the bum strap and broke it he came out of the changing room all embarrassed and apologized earlier on he was on for sex. Adam was laughing and mentioned not to worry.

Other guys would try on different sized shorts and briefs and pouches and stand in front of you erect one guy in particular mentioned to Adam that he was a very good looking young man and would he like to have sex. Adam dismissed him with a reply saying that he'd have no problem pulling on a Saturday night in a club in his tong the lad was left alone standing to attention disappointed. Other guys would browse the dvd isles for over an hour if you left them alone and others would cruise each other and play with their dicks and then leave usually followed by the other person. There was also the darker people who came in and Adam avoided these by reading and usually not letting them stay too long saying that he had to pop out for a few minutes and to come back later. There was plenty of offers for sex and Adam usually had the pick of the bunch it was pure fantasy for Adam and he was at work so he had to try and keep some sort of reality.

One lady came in with her partner and you could see that they had had a few drinks they were looking for a vibrator so Adam asked them what size would she like. The lady replied darling what is the standard size that she did not want one that was too big. Adam replied was she sure and they had a good laugh. Adam suggested to her the rabbit one that that was the most popular and that it was on sex and the city she said darling that would be fine she left with a smile on her face.

There were also drug dealers and addicts shopping for toys and guys who would come in on a Sunday morning looking for rubber vaginas so they could go home and get their rocks off. Adam knew a lot of the customers and was always chatty but kept the darker ones at bay and knew who to talk to and who to avoid.

There was one freak who would come in he was a drugged up tranny who was always dressed in black wearing makeup and a dog collar with doc martin boots with fish net stockings. He arrived from England by ferry and always spoke as if he was about to collapse basically if he thought you'd listen to him he'd be there all day. He was always giving Adam flyers for dance parties over in England and mentioned that he should go and try one he mentioned was the gathering of the souls Adam always subtly manoeuvred him out the door after about 15 minutes he was too much.

Adam loved this job and got to know a lot of the customers from out and about there were also the famous Irish gay guys too that would come in for Amyl or Viagra or a dvd to pass the time on a boring Sunday afternoon.

The phone would ring and people were always asking were there any extra services the lads knew about in the city also there were prank calls and people calling from the country looking for someone to stimulate their sexual fantasies. There were also orders from Australia and the Uk for different films.

The police were watching the shop at certain time s too and one customer who came in one day was browsing for about half an hour when Adam approached him he asked him was he looking for anything in particular the guy said he had just done a line of coke and offered some to Adam the guy was fat and looked rich. Adam said right and that if he needed any help to give him a shout refused the cocaine and sat behind the counter. The fat guy turned to Adam and said he thought Adam looked stoned when he came in and Adam told him that he was clean over three years thanks.

Adam amused himself by reading the guy was on for sex however Adam was having none of it. After some time the fat lad bought some porn and left after been in the shop for over an hour. Some customers were in trances in the isles of that shop and would be there for over an hour they'd leave with nothing and say thanks.

What was going through Adam s head with the fat guy was that he could do a line of coke finish work however if coke was taken the fat lad would have wanted sex Adam was only thinking about where the line would take him to if he did it however he wanted the fat guy out of the shop and Adam thought to himself that he was not a piece of meat. The fat lad left after buying some porn. Adam was definitely tempted to do drugs it was the end of a Sunday day however decided against it. It was all to like old familiars and Adam was happy when the fat lad left he closed the shop and caught the Dart to Dalkey and that night stayed in and watched some television.

Then there were lads that would come in on a Sunday morning horny from the night before looking for some rubber vagina to play with because they had not had a shag the night before so Adam would help them choose one which was suited to them. On one Sunday afternoon this sexy German guy arrived in and Adam and this guy instantly clicked.

The German guy asked Adam where he was from and Adam replied Dublin. The German guy introduced himself as Strauss and asked Adam where he hung out Adam replied the usual places and Strauss asked Adam out on a date. Adam agreed and when he was leaving asked Adam did he mind if he kissed him Adam looked at Strauss and then both guys ended up kissing each other and exchanged numbers.

Later on in the week they hooked up in a café near St Stephen s green had coffee together and later ended up in the Market bar for some drinks. Strauss was tall good looking and muscular Adam was happy with the way he looked they chatted about the gay scene in Dublin and London.

Strauss wanted to move to London and set himself up over there. Adam talked about some of his London experiences in clubs and how different London was compared to the clubs in Dublin.

Both lads got on well and later Strauss drove Adam to Pearse street Dart Station said goodbye and promised to keep in touch,

However that was all that happened between the two and later when they met just nodded at each other,

Strauss later met a lad from Killiney and started going out with him. A friend of Adams who knew Strauss told Adam to stay away from him that he was bad news that he was into sleazy sex and that he be no good for Adam with his past history of drugs and raves.

Some time later they ran into each other and just smiled and acknowledged each other and that was it.

There was always something to keep Adam amused in the store and he soon knew who to chat to and who to keep his distance from.

One day Adam and his workmate Mark were playing with a black 12 inch rubber penis. Mark mentioned to Adam that it was his baby so Adam told Mark to put it in a pram and take it out for a walk that the baby needed some fresh air. That it was unfair to have the baby cooked up all day in the shop and that if the Authorities found mark working with a baby in an Adult store they'd prosecute. Euro cycles euro baby retail shop was over the store and Mark mentioned that he should take the 12 inch dildo out for a walk in the pram, Adam replied that once the baby was giving the love and attention of its mother that it be alright.

They were always slagging each other off and about how many abortions they had been through.

They were others who came into the shop and started telling you about their fantasises. One lad who looked wrecked would try to talk to Adam about his dressing up in ladies cloths with his mate he was not much to look at and came across as quite boring Adam never gave him much time he also looked depressed and quite repressed and when he arrived at the door Adam refused to let him in. Adam thought that it was a business not a fucking counselling service.

Adam advised certain customers one guy was chatting to Adam about his boyfriend. Adam asked him how long were they together and Martin explained that they were with each other three years and that when they were out and about they usually ran out of things to say each other.

Martin explained to Adam that he was loosing out on the opportunity of meeting other guys,

Adam pointed out the advantages to Martin of staying in the relationship. They were having a good time and sex was good too also the relationship was varied and that both lads had something stable together,

Also that they were in love and that when your single on the gay scene you soon become tired of the one night stands and hanging out in bar s can become isolated and lonely.

Adam told Martin that it s no picnic having lots of causual sex and that did he really want to undo what they had going with each other. Martin agreed and left the shop thanking Adam for the advice Adam replied anytime and to enjoy what he had,

A lot of guys think that the grass is greener on the other side whichever way the coin is. Adam stayed in the shop for 5 years however the novelty left after about three years and for about 2 years was thinking of how to move on and change into a healthier environment.

Adam saw the bright side to porn and the dark side too and thought to himself that there was no way he was going to end up on the dark side especially as you get older and certain practices can end up making you darker than you might have realised. Adam spent the next two years knocking guys back and really thought about himself and where he was going in life with this job.

However the money was easy and the job was socialable however there is no future been a sales assistant in a porno store unless you own it.

Barcelona

Flying to Barcelona Adam was off the booze for about 2 years he had just been let go from a job working as a chef and with the effort he put in and was thinking fuck it after putting in so much effort in his recovery too and doing his best to leave the adult shop behind. So he travelled with Bob to Barcelona and checked into a fashion guest house just off Plaza De Gracia and with a stroke of luck just happened to stay nearby from one of Barcelona s top gay clubs.

While landing in Barcelona myself and Bob caught a bus to where we were staying and arrived into a double bed room the two of us looked at each other as if to say I m not sharing a bed with you and while the house guy realised oh your not a couple immediately changed us to a twin room. It was very stylish and had marble floors with high ceilings with a bathroom off it and double doors leading out to a small kitchen with windows that opened out onto a view of other buildings.

The style of the apartment was fashion and pop art in the centre of Barcelona. Myself and Bob sat down both at this stage with mental health problems and looked at each other and said wow it s amazing how in just a short space of time you could be in another part of the world and together left and bought food for our weeks stay.

The shops were just 2 minutes nearby and while I browsed the food isles decided on parma ham with mascaponi cheese with baquettes for lunch something that was quick to prepare so we had lunch in Barcelona thinking wow we had a week to explore this place.

So out we were on the street s of Barcelona near the old town exploring and gathering our bearings. We ended up walking locally around just to see where we were exactly and decided to rest for an hour. After an hour of rest we showered and got dressed and made our way to the underground and got off at the harbour it was a beautiful summers evening and we decided to browse the restaurant s to see what was on offer.

After walking about the harbour we ended up in the Ramblas and decided to have dinner in the main square off it where we ordered salads with bread and desserts. On our way to the restaurant I was approached by guy s selling drugs my friend do you want some cocaine I had no interest and brushed them off I was more interested in the street artists work out on the Ramblas.

After dinner we looked through our Gay map and decided to make our way towards the gay district and see what was happening. It was a Wednesday night and after catching our underground arrived out at the Gay district where we noticed different boutiques and cafes.

The gay area in Barcelona is big and off different streets. It was the celebrations of San Juan and Friday was Bank Holiday in the city. There was a street party going on we found out on Thursday and there was a small stage set up in the middle of the area.

The first bar we ended up in was a bar done out in Green and White with two flat screens with porn films on I thought the bar was cool and sat with Bob and decided I wanted a beer. Bob looked at me and said are you sure and I mentioned to Bob fuck it I was on holidays and thought about having a week of no responsibilities Bob was reminding me of my recovery and that I was taking a risk and I mentioned to Bob that I'd keep it in control.

After chatting to a cute guy at the bar we chatted about Dublin to and he mentioned that he had visited some years ago. He used to date an Irish man and he asked us how long we were staying and we replied that we had just arrived.

The cute Spanish guy mentioned to us that we had arrived at a good time because Gay Pride was on this week and that there was a lot on. I laughed and said thats why we were here and Bob just looked at me again and asked was I sure about drinking.

I reminded Bob that if I made it through Budapest I'd make it through Barcelona and not to worry and ordered another drink. By this stage I was creating a high in my mind about the next 6 days and decided to take it easy on my first night in a strange city. So after three drinks with Bob left and walked back to the Fashion guest house and had an early night.

The following day we ended up down in the sports stadium on the beach sunbathing together and watching the people pass by. We were enjoying the sunshine and the cute slim guy sunbathing in front of us I always picked the beach with the cutest guys and settled in well that day on the beach. mmm

After sunning ourselves and swimming till the sun dropped into the ocean we left and walked to the apartment and sat in the kitchen drinking coffee, each of us were listening to our music players and thinking this was great. We ended up chilling for about two hours and then we got ourselves ready and left and explored Plaza De Gracia and found the Gaudi building and stood outside admiring his architecture and thinking that it looked like a complete fantasy and thought what a brilliant mind he had.

I was looking forward to visiting his Cathedral and always associated Barcelona with the Gaudi Cathedral. After dinner on Placa De Gracia we ended up walking to the gay zone and decided to have drinks in some bars.

We ended up in Dietrics and as you walked in you walked through heavy curtains and into a bar that had orange lighting along the side of the bar. From there was a D J to the right high up in a box with a fluorescent lighting and mirrors around the dance floor.

I ordered drinks and Bob said to me was I sure about this and I replied yes that I was and reassured Bob that if he thought I was overdoing it that I'd knock it on the head. Bob mentioned to me that if he wanted to leave at any time and just hang out in a café that he was fine with that. All the guy s in the bar were hot and looked well there style was jeans and trainers with muscle top s and myself and Bob sat under the D j box on a sofa checking everyone out there was a good crowd there for a Thursday night and after some drinks we ended up at the street party for a beer there was about 500 people there with outdoor drink areas and drag queens and singers on stage it was all in Spanish and so we had not got a clue what they were saying so we left and ended up in a dark bar beside the first one we were in on the night we arrived.

Bob was into the younger guys who I was not really interested in and preferred the first bar which we were in on our night of arriving. After a drink and finding out that gay pride night was on Friday and Saturday beside where we were staying we decided to have and early night and left and returned to our new apartment for which we had for the rest of the week.

By this stage I had stocked the fridge with bottles of Peach Schnapps and beers which by now I was drinking during the day and early in the evening I thought so what it was only a week before in Dublin I was on a three week binge which I had completely thought after been let go from my job now I was free in Barcelona and was here for Gay Pride and it was all an adventure which could lead us anywhere.

So I sat in the kitchen with a peach schnapps and pineapple juice thinking about what the next night had in store. By two am I fell asleep and so did Bob.

The next afternoon we had breakfast together and thought about the next two nights and decided to spend the day on the beach sunbathing and chilling before the night advents took off later.

We had dinner late Friday evening in Barcelona s gay area and decided that it was one of the best meals we had the restaurant was done out in white with a huge lampshade hanging from the ceiling very trendy with a good crowd. After dinner we ended up in a bar across the street which was busy and arty.

From there we jumped into a taxi and arrived at Salvation beside where we were staying and paid into and found it had two areas with a dark room off one it was not very busy and so we ordered drinks and stood together watching the talent arrive the two areas had bars beside the dance floors and a hallway between them.

We had psyched ourselves well up for the night ahead it was about 12 and the club was starting to fill. Bob was cruising around and enjoying himself by this stage he was not to concerned about my drinking and either was I because we were only 5 minutes away from where we were staying. So we were dancing and checking out the lighting above us there were blue and purple lights flashing and dry ice released every few minutes.

We stayed there till about 4 and then left because we were told that the best night was on Saturday so we decided that we'd have an all night on Saturday and make it to the beach for some sun.

After returning to the apartment we sat in the kitchen Bob with a beer and Adam with a beer too. We had landed in Barcelona on Wednesday and had three great days, and tomorrow was another good night ahead.

So we slept late and arrived at the beach around 2.30 and spent 5 hours in the sun sunbathing and drinking coffee and smoking cigarettes. Bob decided to go for a jog and I was swimming and toasting myself by the beach. There's such a good feeling about lying in the sunshine and feeling good about yourself. I was not too concerned about my drinking after all I was away from home and when your away your not to concerned about your life in the city in which you are living in.

The two of us had not met anyone however The German doctor and his friends we were chatting to on the first night said that he'd see us around and when we left them we both said that maybe we should have stayed because they were cute.

So Bob and myself were hoping to meet some cute guys for Gay pride in Barcelona in Salvation's night club. After jumping on the underground to the apartment we sat there in the kitchen both having beers and thinking about where we were going to have dinner that evening.

We decided to eat in and have a few drinks chill and shower and take it easy. Bob tried on jeans and tee shirt and Adam advised him to wear the one that had more colour in it.

I dressed myself with a new tee shirt I bought in H and M the other day with a dark pair of jeans the tee shirt was light blue with black stripes and asked Bob what did he think Bob replied gorgeous darling and we both laughed. So at about 12.30 we left and walked into Salvation and ordered drinks at the bar. It was much busier and was almost packed to the gills.

I was creating a high in my head and thought that I'd love and ecstasy but decided to drink. Bob was smiling at me and we both toasted to each other. Bob was moving about and so was I checking everything out inside Salvation.

At about 2 am I was well on my way and ended running into a guy I knew from Dublin and by this stage decided to ask him did he know anyone with ecstasy and just as it happened he did.

He bought me over to two drug dealers who were in their early 40 s and mentioned that I was from Dublin and looking for E they checked me out and I stood there in a state of anxiety and thought that these two could be dangerous and that I was about to do was a big risk. Any way the guy s asked me how many did I want and Adam replied one please.

They looked at me cautiously and decided that I was cool with it and sold me one for 15 euro I dropped it and walked about the club in panic and while thinking what was going to happen realized that I had to get out and have some breathing space back in the apartment. So I left the club with a stamp on my arm and realized that I was been followed by the two guys.

What was going through my head at the time was first the panic about E and the problems I had encountered so many times in the past and the second was the two drug dealers following me in their car.

There were other guy s in cars cruising around outside Salvation anyway and in some way this relaxed me on arriving at the door to the apartment I turned the key and closed the door behind me. I took the lift to the fourth floor and entered the apartment and ended up looking at myself in the mirror and thinking that I looked all right so I poured myself a large peach snap s and sat in the bedroom listening to some music.

After two drinks I was in a much better relaxed stage and was looking forward to the effect of E after about 2 years of not having any and doing a very good job in recovery to get off it all.

So while I came up on E I was dancing casually around the bedroom smoking cigarettes. Now I was high and didn't give a shit and sprayed aftershave on myself and checked my look in the mirror. I looked great and decided that I was ready to return to the Club.

On arriving outside I was now in a carefree attitude and walked by the drug dealers who were parked outside and walked into Salvation and stood at the bar and ordered a diet coke.

Then I moved towards the most happening area of the nightclub and was dancing with a guy looking at me. It was all so done before as far as I was concerned and I thought about my past wild experiences in London and that it was not the same because I was over drugs however that night I decided to myself that I'd never to E again. It was over as far I was concerned it all felt so mundane to me now or else I was just getting older and more mature a bit of both really.

So for two hours I danced and thought that Ecstasy was not good to take in your 30 s. The ones I was on in London were much better however I was giving a lot of attention by a lot of cute guys who were looking in my direction and smiling and I was smiling too. It was enjoyable and good to visit that place again in my mind however in my heart I knew that this was not the path I wanted to be on again.

I had come so far and was not willing to jeopardize what I had going for myself. And with dealing with drug dealers you can trust no one. Even the guy from Dublin the conversation was hi how r u how long you hear for ok and then I asked have you got any E that was it nothing else later on in the early hours of the morning there was a smile and that was it was I expecting too much or was it just a place I needed to visit and check where I really was in life.

There were highs and lows from it and self questioning too and I thought that it was all so false and then about 4 30 I was coming down and decided that I wanted a drink and stood at the bar feeling unhappy about myself. There were drag queens looking at me who seemed so happy and I was feeling alone and full of self questioning.

Bob arrived beside me and asked me was I alright and Adam replied yes I was happy to see Bob and mentioned nothing about taking E to Bob. Any way it was getting late so we drank till about 5 am and chatted about the crowd and what we were going to do for the rest of our stay.

We both wanted to go to Sitges and spend some time there it s only 45 minutes by fast train out of Barcelona and is one of the nicest Gay Beaches in Europe. With a good mix of bars café s and clubs also all located in one small pretty town.

Bob looked at me and asked me was I sure I was alright and I replied yes. To be honest I was feeling insecure and lonely and on a low. So after a drink with Bob I ended up dancing till 6 am in Salvation and was looking around at different guy s ending up on highs and lows from the E and music by the time the last track was playing one guy looked at me and put his hand s to his cheeks and created a smile towards me as if to say cheer up.

Outside it was bright and the sun was coming up and I was chatting to some guy s who were from America living in London and talking about London s gay scene. They were off to an after party called space and invited me along to it I was not that interested however did not want to go back to the apartment because Bob was with a guy he met and out side earlier on Bob mentioned to me did I mind if he bought him back I replied not at all and mentioned to bob that I was staying out for a few hours any way and to relax and enjoy himself.

So with Adam in limbo about going to space and getting further off his head the only alternative was to go to the sauna which I thought was the best option and said goodbye to the guys who invited me along.

So walking through the old town with a map and a pair of sunglasses I was feeling better about myself and ended up meeting an American guy who was also looking for the same sauna. So after chatting together and walking about the street s of the old town both of us found the sauna. Smiled at each other to be honest I could have had sex with him after chatting to him for 20 minutes he was cute and he felt the same about me.

We paid into the sauna were given key s and climbed the staircase to the locker room s and arrived into a changing area which was half full of guys coming and going. We stripped off and both of us were happy with what we saw of each other naked. So with towels wrapped around us we walked around the cubicles together and commented that there were a lot of cute guys.

We found a cubicle and ended up on a leather bed and started kissing each other and playing around. The

American guy was two or three years younger than me and he commented to me that I was very sexy and I replied that he was hot too. We spent about three quarters of an hour together and then decided to go our separate ways it was a pity because we both like each other and the American guy was leaving Barcelona later that evening if he was staying on it would have been great to spend time with him.

So I cruised around the sauna downstairs and thought that I was in another sauna in another city. After browsing the cubicles I found a guy who I knew was on he gave me a lot of attention so I walked into the cubicle and the two of us started kissing and snorting poppers after playing around we fucked and after wards just spent about 15 minutes lying beside each other looking at each other in a way that we had been out all night and the two of us just wanted some company together to fill a need.

We started taking more poppers and getting even higher and with the Spanish Guy and myself playing around for another 20 minutes we stopped and relaxed and afterwards we said goodbye to each other in the darkly lit maze of cubicles.

So I showered in the open showers with other guys naked and relaxed in the café down stairs and was cruised by a guy who was good looking. By this stage the sun was shining in and it was about 8 in the morning and I thought to myself that I might as well come with this guy and so we ended up in a cubicle together he was nice and in a way the two of us looked lost together in a haze of an orgy in an early morning sauna.

So after about 30 minutes of kissing and playing around with each other we both came. and chatted for some time the guy from Barcelona was happy to be with me it was mutual understanding between the two of us because half way through been with each other we stopped and just held each other the sun was shining through a dark lit room and it was about 9 pm a classic gay encounter between two men who had been out all night looking for their ideal partner again.

I left and thought about him and myself and how as you become older as a gay man it becomes more real you develop and change in different aspects of your life. I walked into to the apartment with Bob in bed with his Spanish guy.

Bob mentioned to me that if I wanted to go to bed just give them 5 more minutes. I replied that there was no rush because I was going to stay in bed for most of the day anyway and walked through the bedroom and into the kitchen where I sat by the open window looking out onto the buildings and decided that I wanted a drink.

I poured myself a large peach snaps and sat there in a haze thinking about my life and what was going to happen when I returned to Dublin. So after one drink I poured another and bob mentioned that his friend was leaving.

I waited for him to leave and got into bed with a double peach snaps and mentioned to Bob what a night. Then I told Bob that I thought about suicide a lot and that if I died that it would not really make a difference to anyone and that if you are not happy in this world what is the point in staying.

Bob mentioned to me that I should never give up and that a lot of people loved me and were happy to have me in their lives. I sat there with my drink smoking a cigarette and with that the glass smashed on the floor and shattered everywhere. I said fuck it I'll clean up later that it was now 10 30 on a Sunday morning and that I needed to sleep. Before I fell asleep Bob mentioned to me that I had been through so much more so than other people and that to rest and that we'd have an easy day when I awoke so I turned over to Bob

201

and kissed him on the cheek and said good morning and to wake me before 4.

So I dozed off after 15 minutes before I fell asleep I thought that I'd love something like this apartment in Dublin and watched the sun shine in through the curtains.

After a deep sleep I came back to life at 2.30 to an awful feeling of guilt and it reminded me so much of my past day s in Dublin, London and Melbourne where after a night on the tiles was in a state of panic about how to organize myself.

Bob asked me how I was and I replied that I needed cigarettes and a drink. So I got dressed and walked to the off license and bought some juices and bottle of peach snaps and arrived back to the apartment and made coffee and smoked some cigarettes it was 4 in the afternoon and Bob suggested that WE D take it easy and just spend time out in Place De Gracia for a few hours that it was Sunday and not much would be happening anyway. We were looking forward to Sitges and spending some time on a nice calm beach.

So after coming to life the two of us had dinner on Place De Gracia and sat outside a restaurant Sunday evening. There was a family beside us who smiled over they saw something in me that was of something special and sensitive so that made me feel better in myself. So after dinner we returned to the apartment and sat in the kitchen listening to music and I had some beers.

It was an early night on Sunday and the following day we were going to Sitges we travelled there by train and had lunch across from the Train Station and we walked through the town and out onto the promenade.

It was a nice sunny day and my spirits were lifted and I walked the beach in my sexy red shorts and with Bob heavier than me and not as well dressed we settled on our towels and looked at each other and said nice. There were about

200 other guys on the beach and there was a children s playground behind us.

Adam thought that it was a healthy environment in comparison to Dublin I had never seen much to do with a gay area associated with children. So we settled into the afternoon sun and swam in the sea.

There were a lot of sexy men around who looked great and toned. So much healthier than Dublin I suppose when your away everything look s better especially when the sun is shining. After an hour of soaking up the sun I ended up in Parrots Bar in the square of Sitges alone drinking a beer and looking at the other guys together drinking they looked as if they were there for a few hours and did not look as healthy as me no one spoke to me and I was thinking that I was getting older and the attention I received in my early days of life was coming to an end. Or else it was just the afternoon and no one was bothered maybe later mmm.

So after two beers I left and bought myself a fake Gucci Watch and returned to Bob with two coffees and together we sat there thinking that we were having a good trip and that we were returning to Dublin on Wednesday. So for the last days we decided to go shopping and visit the Gaudi Cathedral.

After taking the fast train from Sitges into Barcelona we had dinner in a restaurant somewhere in Barcelona it was Monday night and we ended up in the gay area walking in and out of bars unable to decide which bar to go to some were too quiet and we stood out on the street trying to decide which ones would be cool to check out and after twenty minutes of indecisions we agreed on the first one we had been in on the first night.

Bob replied thank god darling that you decided on one finally after walking in and out of about 5 and we sat down at the bar and we were chatting about Dublin and that how it was a small city that s compact within the center of town. I replied that I knew so many people there Bob replied Darling your famous in Dublin and with that I sat there in my bright G star tee shirt and Jack and Jones Jeans subtlety smiling and almost did not believe it.

So after talking about Dublin and thinking that it was a good city to live in we thought Barcelona has more to offer as a gay man. That the people were not as friendly maybe because we were not from here we thought that everyone knew each other in Dublin or had slept with someone that we knew through someone else and because I was on the scene almost 20 years that a lot of people knew me and Bob told me that I was a good friend to have and that the two of us were good for each other. I agreed and we left after our second drink and walked back to the apartment together.

We sat in the kitchen drinking beers and listening to our CD s touch me in the morning and last thing at night was one and sharing tracks together then I was listening to Charlene never been to me and Bob was listening to some of David Bowie and every so often we looked across at each other in some knowingly way and give each other an understanding look I had met Bob in a psychiatric hospital when I was going through my depression and Psychosis and Bob was in for well I never found out why Bob was in for he never said why. But I had my suspicions

So after sitting there together for about an hour drinking coffee and beers I got into the shower and washed myself from head to toe and shaved put on some sexy shorts and poured myself another large peach snaps and got into bed listening to some dance music and thinking that I was going to return to recovery when I flew into Dublin that the last three week s were great and also crazy I thought about the last two weeks in Dublin and the slippery slope I was on and also about the other night on E and how unhappy I was from taking it.

So after a peach snaps I fell asleep in a nice safe relaxed state and thought about my last day and night in Barcelona and thought that I was going to make the most of it.

Tuesday we asked the gentleman who had given us information on where to go and directions for the Gaudi Cathedral and he mentioned oh this one was in the square to the right of the old town and that it was just a 10 minute walk we replied great and thought that we d walk we arrived into a beautiful square and walked into the a church it was very peaceful and we lit candles and said some prayers. To the right of the church was an area which had a garden in the room which was open air that had a glass cage surrounding it to keep people out in the middle of the garden was a man made large pond with rocks built up around it which had terrapins sunbathing and the others were walking around the garden. There were immaculate Geese which were so white with there lovely yellow feet with plants and flowers in which they looked so peaceful.

In the pond were different coloured gold fish black and orange, orange and white and ones that were completely orange.

I turned to Bob and mentioned it was like the garden of Eden and we thought it was so beautiful and full of peace and tranquility.

We spent about twenty minutes walking around the garden admiring it looking at the animals that were so well looked after. We realized that this was not the Gaudi cathedral we left and took the Barcelona underground to Gaudi's and running out the door of the train I screamed at Bob look your handbag and for a split second Bob was about to run onto the train with the doors closing and collect his handbag I laughed and Bob said to me that there was never a dull moment when I was around.

So standing on the escalator we arrived outside to a fabulous view to the right was the Gaudi Cathedral where we looked in Awe at each other and said wow it was something else. We had seen it in films and just stood in the park drinking coffee and smoking cigarettes thinking that it really was something else. We paid in an walked around I was thinking of a guy I was seeing about a year ago in Dublin who was here he was wearing a medal that he bought when he was here.

I had been talking to Bob about him and mentioned that it was unfortunate that he was an alcoholic because we would have been good together. The guy I was seeing was a guard in Dublin and one night he mentioned to me that people were like the Gaudi cathedral yet to be completed and always working on themselves and that's what life is about. I remember him saying to me that like I was just a boy as far as he was concerned because I was only 32. There was an age difference of about 14 years.

We climbed the steps to the top of the cathedral and Bob was afraid of so he left early I stayed on and took in the amazing view overlooking Barcelona and thinking that this was special after about two hour s of spending time there we jumped on the underground back to Place de Gracia and spent the rest of the afternoon shopping I bought some sexy boxers in H and M and a false diamond cross and some tee shirts.

Late in the afternoon we sat outside on a bench thinking that this was our last day and that tomorrow evening we would be home to Dublin. So with our bags of shopping and presents for family we walked through Barcelona to our apartment and sat in the kitchen thinking that we should pack and organize ourselves for the last night out. We ended up having tea in and some drinks I prepared some mascaponi cheese and parma ham baquettes and did a light mixed salad with some honey dressing which we had with some mozzarella cheese.

After showering and dressing we ended up in a taxi just off the gay area and sat down in a bar beside this cute guy we ordered coffee and beers and I fancied this handsome stranger beside me. He asked us where we were from and he too had been to Dublin and worked there for a year as an engineer. He introduced himself as Paulo and asked us how long were we in Barcelona for and I replied that we had been here for a week and that this was our last night.

He said oh and asked us where we had been and Bob laughed and said everywhere he was from the Bask country and offered us a drink. I was thinking that I'd like to bring Paulo home to the apartment however was not rushing into anything too soon.

So after our drink Paulo invited us to a bar across the road he mentioned that it was a late bar which was open late on Tuesday s and recommended it as the place to be on Tuesday s so we took him up on his invitation and the three of us left and Bob decided that he'd go on somewhere else I asked him are you sure and Bob said yes.

Outside I put Bob into a taxi and asked him was he alright and Bob said yes that he was tired and that he was going to the apartment to finish packing I had already packed and was organized to wake up the following morning and just walk out the door with my suitcase.

I had other ideas about Paulo and was hoping to bring him back later on and asked Bob did he mind Bob said sure but to make sure he was gone before 8 am because we had to check out and organize our bill and return the keys.

So off I skipped into the night with Paulo and arrived at the bar which was designed in dark brown wood with mirrors and a lounge area with steps which brought you out into a beer garden.

Myself and Paulo ordered drinks and stood along one of the wall s. Paulo replied to me that I was a nice guy and it was a pity that I was leaving the following day and I agreed too and told Paulo that he was a nice guy too.

So after another beer Paulo started talking about pain in life and that his Grandmother had been in a concentration camp in the second world war and that some of his family were killed and how it had an effect on him and that life was full of twist and turns. I agreed and told him nothing about myself just that I used to live in London and Melbourne and that I was a chef and thought that life was always good when you were somewhere else.

Apart from talking about travelling and working that s as far as I was willing to go with Paulo and let Paulo do the talking apart from commenting about different guy s that were around and the music that was playing and talking about the décor of the bar.

We had three drinks together and I decided to leave and jumped into a taxi and said goodnight to Paulo with him saying to me that it was nice to meet me and I replied to Paulo that it was nice meeting him too.

The taxi driver asked where to and asked me where I was from. I told him I was from Dublin and that I had been staying in Barcelona for the past week. Bob Sinclair was on the stereo world hold on and I was asked by the driver did I want to go to a club that was around the corner Adam told the driver that he needed to organize himself for the following day and that he should have an early night it was about 1 in the morning.

The driver suggested to me was I sure and said come on it's your last night here I should stay out and so with that we were driving to Barcelona s best gay club on a Wednesday morning about 1.30 in the morning we pulled up outside and I paid the driver and without a care in the world arrived down into the basement of this club.

There was a bar to the left with a beefy bar man serving beers I ordered one and was on the dance floor dancing with a group of guys and girls who seemed to be on E the floor had cool red laser lights moving around everywhere and the walls were painted black with some strobe light s flashing on and off every so often.

There was a dark room off it and after I finished my beer I ended up in there checking out some guys I stopped off with some on and off and then left after 15 minutes and ordered another beer feeling alone I was thinking who could I talk to and with that Paulo appeared in front of me with a smile and asked me what I was doing here.

I explained about the taxi driver to Paulo and he mentioned that he was happy that the taxi driver persuaded me to go clubbing. So the two of us spent the early hours of Wednesday dancing together in Barcelona. At about 4 A M we left and walked through the streets of Barcelona chatting and looking at different buildings and about 5 am arrived at Paulo s hotel he wanted to invite me in however because it was the first night and he replied that he usually did not do something like this so we agreed that it was better this way and Paulo replied to me that he wanted to make sure I returned back to my apartment safely.

So walking through the streets of Barcelona we walked past Place De Gracia and down to the fashion house apartment on the way we passed some police standing beside their motorcycles and 15 minutes later we were across the street from my apartment.

Standing across the street myself and Paulo were in each others arms kissing each other I said to Paulo was he sure he did not want to come up for coffee and take it from there but Paulo was thinking that our time together should just be remembered like this. So for about 30 minutes we embraced each other with kisses and hugs. I was so high and happy and thought it was a lovely way to end this trip and on leaving Paulo on the other side of the street with the bin men going by and dawn appearing we waived goodbye to each other and that was it.

I walked into the apartment and told Bob all about my night and poured myself a drink.

We were leaving at 10 for the airport and I thought that I better have some sleep. So Bob woke me 3 hours later and we ended up checking out after breakfast.

We took the underground with our luggage and ended up at the bus station for the bus to take us to the airport. After hanging around the bus station there were a lot of scruffy people there with not much to do I didn't care because I had no money left and was expecting some money when I returned to Dublin.

The bus arrived and the two of us got on and sat there looking at each other and thinking what an amazing week we had had together. We arrived at the airport and checked in and boarded Ryan air for Dublin and were airborne in the sky I slept for most of the journey and so did Bob and we were awake for about an hour of the flight home.

On arriving in Dublin we ended up taxiing it to Connelly Dart Station and jumped on a dart to Bob s in Black rock and I continued onto Dalkey. Later that weekend Adam was out with friend s in the front lounge and on Saturday night back in Dublin I was feeling good about myself.

I was off the booze again and got myself back into recovery it was a rocky two week s in Dublin in a bit of a panic about how I could have ended up on booze. My sponsor at the time was helping me and advising me about what I should do and all he kept on saying to me was meeting s meeting s meeting s.

My friends were aware of my slip and so was my employer in the Adult Store. His reaction was not good he had mentioned to the others who also worked with me that if I was back on the booze that I was out the door and gone.

So I had another wake up call when I settled into Dublin after been back for two weeks and ended up meeting in brown Thomas s two of the guys I worked with advising me to stay off the booze.

People were talking in the bars about me been out of control. So straight away I got myself back into the rooms and kept myself out of trouble. A mate of mine was saying to me how did I manage to do it and just about get away with it all. On that sunny afternoon in Brown Thomas I left with the advice I was given and kept myself drug free and sober.

After been lectured in Brown Tomas I took everything on board and decided to get back on track and keep myself out of trouble and do all the right things I phoned my sponsor in AA from home and he commented to me that I sounded edgy and I agreed the last three weeks I had battered myself with drink again however enjoyed the splurge and was aware that I could loose my job and have hassle with my family my sponsor recommended meeting meetings meeting s that they were the key to unlocking all the uncertainty in this life we spent about an hour and a half on the phone to each other and I was taking it all on board.

My sponsor recommended me to listen that that was a good way to recovering and also a way of learning a new skill. I picked up on this pretty soon and realized that for my years of abuse through drink and drugs that I thought I knew it all however listening to older people s experiences and taking the advice that was been given to me was now on a new path.

The Adult store was manageable because I usually worked alone apart from my boss been there to delegate work for me on changeovers this suited me fine because I did not want to be around people in work. So the job was secure the crazy thing about addictions is that you just get drawn in and without realizing it you are in complete isolation again.

Anyway it paid the bills as someone famous once said to me and gave me a lifestyle I was used to and the other guys I worked with knew the situation I was in.

However Archie knew there was something up with me because I was so unhappy. Archie mentioned to me one day that he knew this girl in Italy and told me about her that she was continuously unhappy until she found a good therapist and once she had found a good therapist she was much better in herself and that she was not so unhappy any more.

With that I tried to cry and however I was unable to manage it. My employer asked me did I want to go home and I mentioned that I prefer to be working and not on my own in the house with my parents. So after a few months Adam found himself a therapist in one and four who I spent a year with until she left.

Most of what I talked about was my drug lifestyle and how I was now getting older and wanted out of it all and from looking around at older guys on the scene who were still on drugs I thought about my future and decided that I did not want this life for myself.

After my slip in Barcelona I learnt a huge lesson about unhappy I felt in Salvation by 6 in the morning and walking the streets at 7 with the sun shining and ending up in a sauna it was just all too familiar to me and was now becoming boring.

I needed another outlet and decided to do a course in Web Design however four months into the course I dropped out I was still not connecting with the real world and was quite concerned about why. For 17 years it was sex drugs, bars and nightclubs.

I found reality boring however realized that I was missing something within. The other guys on the course spent lunches together while I spent my time in the park alone and dreading going back after lunch some days I was skipping classes and in the end just dropped out and thought that I'd just return to the Adult store.

I knew most of the customers and a lot of the guys that were gay that shopped there. It was social to me and I felt comfortable there. It suited me and because I was close to Archie and Jack thought that it was where I belonged for the moment.

Another escapism for Adam. There were guys coming onto me a lot and Adam enjoyed the rush of it all and with some I teased and with others I had sex when the shop was quiet you could be on your own for over an hour with a customer cruising you and when it was quiet I thought it was a rush and something to pass the time.

Other guy s came in and tried on leather and rubber and asking for my opinion for what I thought. Most of the guys would stand there with pouches on and thongs semi erect waiting for me to make a move.

And then while in the back room some would ask me for another thong or pouch so I'd return with pouches on

213

hangers and arrive back to the changing room with different styles. By this stage a lot of the guys were naked standing there semi erect I was on for it with the good looking ones and it took care of my void in life, it also made me feel wanted and I enjoyed the attention to with the mystery of what was going to happen next when the doorbell rang.

Not everyone I took up the offer with, however sex and cruising passes the time. I had a free hand there however was not really realizing that in my subconscious mind it was doing me serious damage.

There were married men coming in and guys who were waiting for their girlfriends to finish work and they'd have an hour to kill. It was certainly a buzz and other time s guys I knew from the scene would pop by for coffee and a chat.

On my break I was meeting friends and after work I was out and about sometimes in the Boiler house having sex actually that was becoming a regular occurrence taking Viagra and helping myself to a bottle of poppers and off I'd go.

There were also married men coming in and asking me for Advice about how they could spice up their sex lives and they'd also complain that they were unhappy in their marriage s and were experimenting with there gay side everyone has it to some extent.

One night shortly after returning from Barcelona I was out and met a guy who I bought back to the store and we spent the early hours of the morning on the floor having sex and trying on different fetish gear. There was a bottle of poppers shared between us and while I was having sex with him felt like such a whore. It was all starting to catch up with me now and I wanted out however wasn't unable to find a way.

I was enjoying it and it was like in the Verve the drugs don't work this is what was happening to me. At about 7 in the morning we sat outside under south William Street in the basement and had coffee sitting there in our shorts together.

I thought it was all exciting and also becoming boring I had dropped out from the Web Design course too and was thinking seriously about my life now.

I started to take stock now of my future and wanted a way out into something that was going to keep me mentally stimulated.

So before South William got busy on this cool autumn morning I locked up and tidied the store and was dropped by this stranger to the Dart Station. I slept till the afternoon and started work again at five hoping that I had left the shop in a fit state. I phoned earlier that day to check with Archie to ask was the owner happy with the way the shop was left the night before and Archie said there was no nothing out of the ordinary.

Except that there was a bottle of poppers left on the counter outside the door. That was it we were always covering up for each other it was such an edgy job anything could happen and especially with tourists it was easy to have fun with one because it was anonymous you'd never see them again anyway.

With all this going on Adam was cruising too and having affairs and just got caught up in sex addiction. He was not in the real world and was completely cocooned in a dangerous environment.

There were dangerous people that came in I knew the type and kept them at bay and after ten minutes it they did not move I told them that I had to pop out and would be gone for half an hour.

If the shop was too hectic I cleared the floor and told everyone to come back in 15 minutes. Because everyone would start cruising each other and don t get me wrong it was completely entertaining and fun just at times it was just too much and depending on the state of mind I was in I entertained it and other time s got rid of certain ones who had let themselves go in life.

There was a scum element to it that I hated and never entertained it other time s guy s would follow single girls out and some were dangerous people. Other customers were groups of guys over for a stag and hen parties too it was a huge buzz and very psychological.

You found out people tastes and what made them tick. I loved guys my own age coming in alone and chatting to me especially the ones I was attracted too. There was always flirting going on and on and off there were encounter s in the famous back room.

By this stage Adam I had been there 3 years and knew it was going to end some day however was uncertain when.

A group of male strippers came in one day and were all straight and needed underwear for their show and they stripped off to their underwear two were in the army and did it as a side line and the others were builders. They spent about an hour trying on all the designer boxers and thongs and coming out to me and asking me for my opinion.

I was in my element because they were posing for me in what kind of moves they were to do later their bodies were muscled and they were hot straight open minded guys. However after an hour they were becoming out of control trying everything on.

I thought that I'd have to control the situation because after all it was a business and that I was supposed to be working instead of entertaining the troops. So after an hour I asked them were they buying anything and in the end they bought some shorts and left and thanked me for my help in hysterics of laughter because of the last hour and a half.

THose toned bodies and butch two army guys a gay man s complete fantasy.

It was complete fantasy and I was in the middle of doing the twelve step programme which was gradually bringing me into reality so I took my lunches and toddled off to Molesworth Street meeting s and sat then in the afternoon working through the 12 step programme.

Commuting home on the dart I thought of the others on the dart who were in nine to five jobs and thought that I had a unique life and one day it was going to be changing however I did not want it to change.

After three years in Adult Store I moved to Temple Bar and we all set up home there and got the business off the ground. However this time it was different for me I was thinking now that I was getting older and thought what type of future did an adult store hold for me. The owner wanted a cruise club in the basement where I was to be part of. Taking customers coats and charging them to use the fuck club.

I knew I had issues with sex and did not want to be part of it so for a year and half I was constantly talking to people about leaving this Adult world behind and hopefully sailing off into the sunset or some other fantasy to keep me amused. By now I was knocking back customers and not taking them up on their advances I wanted more for myself and while still in therapy was flying off every two month s on holiday s having affairs and out partying in some far away land.

I was learning a lot about life in recovery and was delighted that I had come so far by this stage I had a new sponsor with a man who was also sexually abused and we had a close relationship together on a sponsorship basis.

I knew that from the moment we met that there was something between us there was a sense there. I knew it however did not know how much influence this man was going to have on my life.

In the beginning we'd chat outside meeting s and Trevor asked me was I looking after myself by this stage was turning a blind eye to my sex life and although working in the Adult store and doing recovery was facilitating a lifestyle which Trevor told me was keeping me sane.

I was still running from myself and one summers night while walking through Christchurch Trevor asked me what had happened and why could I not stay still for a long time and was always on edge by this stage I started to panic and tried to hail a taxi. Trevor kept probing me what had happened and I was in a state of wanting to run.

Trevor suggested to me that we drive around town and chill that he'd drop me to the dart station and if I wanted to talk I could and if I didn't that was fine too.

We ended up a Lincon place with me opening up about my past this was the first time I spoke to him about Australia and what had happened in Melbourne all the drugs, drinking and sex escapades.

Been sedated on my last day and bought through the airport not remembering a thing and boarding a flight and waking up on it not knowing where I was. Part of the abuse came up too and Trevor told me that it was all mental.

Adam was chain smoking in Trevor's car and was on edge. Trevor told me that we were special because we had both survived sexual abuse and that he'd help me with the rest of the steps. So we arranged to meet every week for coffee in town and in David Norrise's house on South Great Georges Street where we worked through the 12 steps.

Trevor was training to be a counsellor and had a lot of experience in counselling and bought me through the 12 steps. The third step by the end of it I wrote a letter to God thanking him for the light I had in my life. The two of us sat there on the patio in the middle of summer with birds flying around the garden and drinking coffee.

Trevor commented on my letter that he said god that was great. I noticed everything in the garden and how peaceful it was and how the two of us had bonded together. Trevor mentioned to me that the letter was a delight and asked me to read this letter to god Again thinking of the gratitude which was in it and I read it again and thought how much light was coming into my life.

This was step three and I still remember the special afternoon we spent together in David Norrises garden. Watching the fish in the lily pond and birds flying around sitting there having coffee and been so relaxed together.

However much the Adult store was killing my spirit and although I worked there for about three years until I started watching gay DVD s I was getting lost in sex. I was never short of action and however was getting drawn into the Adult world.

One day while chatting to a customer I was recommending DVD s to watch and while browsing through the isles I noticed that with the other guy I was getting more absorbed into the whole trance state of been addicted to sex. With that I stepped back and left the customer to what I had recommended.

I sat beside my 12twelve step programme working and I was reading one of the steps. I knew my time in the adult world was coming to an end I had seen too much sleazy characters come in especially the older men who smelled and had let themselves go with health appearance and were completely filthy. I was taking serious stock of my sex life now and looking at these older men who were horrible and thinking I could end up like this I was far to handsome and genuine to go down this road for the rest of my life however by this stage I was addicted. There was one older man who came in and bought poppers and Gay porn and would pick his arse in the shop he was disgusting and always s angry and commented to me one day that the younger generation thought they knew it all his problem was that he had abused sex for such along time that the only way he got release from sex was though a bottle of poppers and young gay porn magazine, the guys in the magazine were 18 and I reckon this horrible person would step over the mark as with a minor. I hated him coming in and just wanted to get rid of him as soon as he arrived. I thought how tragic this was and knew something one day was going to give either me or the owner firing me.

I knocked back so many come on s for the next two years and while on my breaks outside the shop in Temple bar noticed mainstream society passing by and commenting on a sex shop. I was also going through emotional shocks because of it never knowing who was going to come through the door with another guy in cruising mode.

Also there was a cruise club opening up and I certainly did not want anything to do with it. The agreement with staff was that we'd have to clean up at the end of the day and I thought cleaning up other people s come you must be joking.

There was also the cruise side to it that I wanted out of and knew that I was in a serious dilemma and while still in therapy my therapist had mentioned to me that I had found a good way to survive after my history with drugs and was doing exceptionally well considering the circumstances.

However my therapist was leaving and I was going to be in Limbo with the last therapy session I had with her I burst into tears because she was leaving me and I had found this occurrence all too familiar in my life just as I was beginning to get close to her. She told me to take care and look after myself.

By this stage in recovery the clouds were beginning to lift and I knew that something good was going to come from the Adult Shop where I had now spent nearly 5 years there and for Two years I had been doing a lot of work on myself and working through the 12 steps programme.

However on step six I was in a state of running and wanted to revisit London all for the wrong reasons I wanted a drug and drinks binge and was becoming bored with reality. So preparing in my mind the rave scene and what adventures I could have for 48 hour s was just a familiar occurrence which I didn't need so I phoned an old sponsor and met him in Dunne and Crescinis and sat there chatting for over an hour.

My old sponsor was with a Dublin Bus Driver who I noticed had so much peace of mind. The three of us sat there talking about what I was going to do and the bus driver was saying to me that I must be on such a high in my mind to contemplate this trip to London and that there must be so much flying around.

I agreed and after over an hour the two guys told me to take care and not to do anything to rational because I could end up dead. The London rave scene had been far too easy for me because I was staying in the best of London suburbs and I knew most of where to go.

This was because I was out of therapy and left for 6 months with nothing to keep me grounded except my meeting s which by this stage I was becoming bored with although I had made so much progress.

Sex was less and I was seeing a guy from South Africa who was telling me not to let life pass me by. I knew that I was playing with my life however I had a self destructive streak inside me that I did not want to end.

Realizing my drug induced psychosis and sense of adventure and also my sensitive side and vulnerability I left South Fredrick Street and decided to sleep on it and the following morning awoke and thanked God for the two men from recovery meeting me the day before and decided to stay at home.

Even writing now London had a huge impact on my life because it's just so fast and exciting and some of the drug s I did there were the best in my life also too the clubs a massive gathering of gay men.

I was running, running and running and still wanting to run 6 months out of therapy I thought now what.

Another time on Step six I phoned my sponsor and I mentioned to him that I wanted to go on another spree and with that Trevor was in Dun Laoghaire in a café within 90 minutes.

When Trevor walked in he dropped step six into my hand and told me he d return in half an hour and I was to read it. I took Trevor s advice and ended up at a recovery meeting sharing about what I was about to do.

The gentleman that was doing the chair had something in his life that I wanted. He was happy and content and was also dying. He had gone through a nightmare with his drinking and had created so many problems over his drinking period and after I shared what was going on and that I had just left my sponsor after an emergency meeting the gentleman saw in me something because he quoted Barbara Streisand's song people that need people are the luckiest people in the world he knew I was gay and at the end of the meeting he came over to me and said son you did the right thing you phoned your sponsor got to a meeting and did not drink.

On his parting he told me that you could be sitting at home and make any decision you want and if the door bell rings you can either answer it or not depending on what mood you are in. This gentleman had been through life and was still married and had raised a family and now had 6 months to live he was leaving this world peaceful and happy and not angry or sad I thought but happy.

He had time and in his later years time had been good to him and I left that meeting in a state of peace which in emergency's I got grounding and stability from. So for the next couple of months I spoke continuously about leaving the Adult Store the time had come and I had completely lost interest in it anyway.

But I was left with a decision about my future and was unsure how I was going to break back into something of a normal life. Always running and trying to connect and out of therapy was left in an unsafe position and thinking about my connection with myself and the world because most guys I was with thought that there was something missing with me.

I knew this too deep down however did not know what it was. Even working in Black rock hospice I was connecting on a one to one and thought of the connection I had with my mum and the outside world, and how I was living in the world now.

In Black rock hospice I was cooking for the dying and served too. I was always happy alone, Thinking about my life and how I ended up in a religious organization and thinking about my future. One day on my way to work while also working part time in the Adult store filling in for lads on their day s off and for appointments they had I in a way just did not want to work.

I stood on Black rock main street one day in a hoodie and faded jeans smoking a cigarette looking out in a state of God this woman who had let herself go came up to me and so in my face said another Irish looser smoking himself to death.

I turned on her and told her actually I was on my way to work and that she should mind her own fucking business and to look at the state of herself first I told her to go get a makeover and to fuck off and leave me alone. She looked at me in disbelief. I was taking no shit from her. At least I was not as far gone as she was thank god.

The following week she spotted me in the bank in a designer shirt cashing my pay check I ignored her and thought how well I was looking. She looked at me and thought to herself mmmnnnnnnnn what s his story.

So a year passed at Blackrock hospice with a lot of insecurity and I left. And returned to the Adult shop again thinking that it was easy money and in a gay environment where I could do whatever I wanted. Always stepping back to my old way s and trying at the same time to find something that was going to keep me In the real world.

One of the sisters there was asking me to return to college to finish my exams I just thought it was too much hassle and decided on the amount of hours I'd have to put in for what I thought reality no thanks so I thanked her for her offer. I was also thinking how I'd fit into it even though it was one day a week it just was too much to deal with.

I was set up with another therapist and I liked her she seemed to be with it more she was the same age as myself and has a nice personality. Through working with her she d ask me how much of me was in the room today and where I was in touch with my body by this stage I hated to Admit it that I was living in my head and conscious of my penis.

I filled her with nightclub stories and drugs and sex and my life s experiences this was the norm for about 6 months always avoiding sexual abuse and carrying on meeting different guys and cruising the internet. After six months my therapist mentioned to me that if I took that away what was left I thought what else is there to do.

Time was moving on and we were talking about my future and after a lot of Wednesday afternoon sessions I left one in four in bit s on different Wednesdays. The amount of stuff which was coming up was unreal and because I was used as a sex object from a young age I lived like one too.

I remember my therapist saying to me to be careful on my way home because I was in a state of acting out due to my low mood which usually took care of me when I had sex with a stranger for some days after. It lifted my spirits however I knew how vulnerable I was becoming thorough my sex addiction now and because I was meeting the 14 year old boy who was abused for three years I was now reverting back to him in my head which was scaring the shit out of me.

So after therapy on Wednesdays I d phone a friend and explain how I was feeling without going into too much detail on what I d been talking about. I remember tHose Wednesday s now thinking back to how on one hand I was very isolated in my mind now that I was dealing with my sex addiction and how as well as the fact that I was feeling a great loss in my life too.

The adult store was the last place I wanted to be now however I needed the money to keep my lifestyle going in seeing my friends and having some sort of social life. Because it was part time I was able to handle it however if it had been fulltime I'd have walked out along time ago.

So after my therapy on Wednesdays I'd go home to my parents and cook dinner I remember one striking memory that stood out to me was that I told my therapist about a neighbour who would follow me when he spotted me and I told her that I went with him.

She immediately commented on how striking that was because I came across as young boy who had to go with an older man. We delved into it further and she commented that it was a high price to pay for intimacy and I was more scared on how appearance wise I looked 36 however in my mind I was now reverting back to young boy who had been hurt and abused and was now trying to fix myself and have some control over my sex life.

Don t get me wrong I enjoyed a lot of my sexual experiences however there were a lot I sold myself short for and just ended up with any type after cruising for hours and in the state of desperation I just had sex to get the addiction out of my head.

Dublin is a small town and soon while working with my therapist I was thinking that sex was not doing it for me anymore however in my mind I wanted to continue but my body was saying something completely different to me now.

I had destroyed myself through sex however on the other hand I was crying out for love. Most people who come into therapy regardless if they have been sexually abused or not are looking for love. In some ways I loved Wednesday s because of the freedom I had however when I was not acting out my freedom in therapy was confined because I was in two minds one in working through my problems and the other feeling free when I was having casual sex although now I was realizing the damaging consequences it was having on my life. When I was feeling good I'd spend the afternoon after in the city center sitting in a café or browsing the cloths shops and popping into some friends.

I've got to admit though when the sessions were bad I just returned home and isolated myself in my room and would not go anywhere.

Hence the fact I was becoming more cagy in the adult store. I'd always had a guard up and the way I dealt with sex with someone was to have casual sex because this way I was not letting anybody in however doing this was having drastic consequences on my sex life and having a relationship with anybody. I suppose I was still having relationship with myself and my therapist was bringing up so much for me and it was scaring me to death.

So any trips I took I always flew out on a Wednesday and returned the following Wednesday for which I could avoid what else there might be to handle.

Berlin Gran Canaria

In the middle of all this 5 of us flew to Berlin. I booked five of us on a flight with Aer Lingus to Berlin from Dublin. The hotel we were staying in was 20 minutes from the center of Berlin. The owner of the adult store suggested to go to the Kit Kat Club which I was looking forward to seeing.

We all meet at Dublin airport and were delighted to see each other. I made sure to share a hotel room with someone who I was comfortable with James who I met in psychiatric hospital I definitely did not feel comfortable sharing a bedroom with. There was something always edgy about him and although I had my suspicions about him I did not want to be in a room with him for four days.

Although we shared a room in the south of France however it was separate beds we had in a twin room. So I shared with one of my closest friends, while were sitting in departures lounge in Dublin having breakfast the 5 of us were in great form. There was a business guy who asked us where were we travelling to and we commented Berlin he mentioned that we were going to have a mad weekend and we all laughed.

We all had seats together at the rear of the plane and we settled in well while airborne. After arriving in Berlin we collected our baggage and arrived out at arrivals and caught the over ground to the closest station to where we were staying and hailed a taxi to our hotel.

The hotel was fabulous very posh and contemporary it was designed with large front windows from floor to ceilings from the outside and corridor s to the hotel rooms were grey and white with beautiful grey carpets on the floor.

Inside the rooms were done in white and a large double bed in a light blue color through the hotel room. There was a glass cordoned off sliding door into a walk in bathroom which was decked out with black tiles and glass mirrors everywhere nice.

Martin and Joe were staying the room beside myself and Carlos, James was on the floor below us we unpacked our bags and sat in our room having drinks and decided on what to do for the rest of the afternoon. We decided to have lunch locally and we picked a restaurant near by which Martin commented on that it was cheap and cheerful I just thought that it was middle of the range and the atmosphere was great and the food was fine. That was the situation about the Celtic tiger everyone got themselves caught up in money and which address you lived in and what each and everyone had material wise its amazing now how people have come down to earth.

After lunch we walked through the Tier garden and it was a beautiful sunny day we passed the memorial park where there was a monument s there explaining the dates of the first world war and second were so many people lost their lives and it was shocking to see how many Jew s were killed and how much torture people have to go through on this earth. The memorial park was filled with tourists looking at stones made of date s and people who have died.

We arrived out at the Brandenburg gate and we were amazed at how big it was and we decided to walk through the area were the Jewish holocaust memorial maze was located there were droves of people walking through this area and so many tourists about.

We stopped off for coffee and decided to watch the world go by and walked through the Tier garden on a beautiful sunny day. Later that afternoon we decided to relax in the hotel room and decided to check out some bars there was one I noticed which looked cool. Later on after drinks and chatting we called a taxi and arrived at this bar in part of Berlins gay scene.

We arrived into this pink bar which had white fluffy pink wall paper on the walls and there were mirrors in the room at the end of the bar it was a cool disco atmosphere and with a large disco ball spinning around from the ceiling.

People were smiling at us and there were a few nods and winks from people. All of a sudden there was black drug dealer waving a bag of grass over at me and I thought fuck off that I'm not interested and brushed him off in a fast but friendly look he was disappointed and by this stage I thought was just go away. The five us laughed and we ordered our drinks. Abba was playing dancing queen and we thought how Pricilla Queen of the Dessert mmm.

We decided to sit at the main bar and these people moved a stool towards us and I decided to sit down. With that this guy manoeuvred over to me and put his two legs in between mine and was becoming very relaxed I was delighted with the attention and he asked me where were we from. We started chatting immediately and the rest were looking at me laughing at how I attracted someone so fast.

He was a nice guy and he asked me what did I do for a living at this stage I told him I was working in an adult store in Dublin part time and doing industrial cleaning also. Pasko mentioned that he was a psychotherapist I just started to laugh. I remember the psychiatrist who came onto me in Lisbon and I thought here we go again. The others thought it was hilarious and later after our drinks we left with Pasko and caught a taxi to Toms bar in the other part of Berlin which is gay. Of course James was left with the girls who joined us as well and Pasko while the four of us flew off in a taxi and Martin commented to me how he could not believe that I just left James with 3 strangers on the corner of Berlin.

I suppose looking back it was not a nice thing to do but at the time I thought it was hilarious and I remembered my aunt one night forgetting her son at a wedding in Clontarf Castle after drinking all day and I just cracked up laughing.

After arriving at Tom s bar we entered and I bought a round of drinks for the four of us and we stood at the bar looking around it was rough gay porn bar in Berlin and there were DVD projections on the walls of hardcore porn. The crowd was fine and at the end of the bar there were barrels and a pool table where you could sit and everyone was cruising each other and checking each other out. It was dark and bright with neon lights everywhere and I recognized a guy I was with from Dublin some time back we just nodded at each other and that was it.

After looking around and sitting together at the end of the bar we cruised the dark room in the basement it was dark and dingy and damp with a lot of guy s cruising around and the aroma of poppers was everywhere there were guys in darkrooms having sex and myself and Joe commented on different guys and grouped some on our way mmm lol.

The situation in a dark room or if your cruising is that the time just fly s by and after about 30 minutes of messing around without having sex you leave and prepare yourself

231

for someone later on when your more relaxed and I suppose cruising rooms are like testing the water after another round of drinks upstairs I decided to see what was on offer in the basement and picked up on this guy who looked cute and was very well endowed.

Looking back now and talking about this experience with my therapist in Dublin about three years later and also about the couple in Lisbon I was with for three days there blockages which were coming up in sex and although I was having sex with this guy in the basement of a dark dingy dark room somewhere in Berlin and not even feeling the feeling of sex and intoxicated with poppers I was thinking how was this happening to me and was I really over it all by now.

My body was not connecting and I was thinking how was this happening to me and was I really over it all by now. I had not connected in with any guy in a relationship since 1995 and it was now 2005. Where was this going to end and how was I going to change my lifestyle I remembered Joe mentioned to me about Berlin that it was all not about sex clubs and of course Pasko was with James somewhere else in the middle of Berlin and we had no idea where he was. It got me thinking and how even with a guy who was nice I did not connect with him and when I ejaculated I did not enjoy my orgasm.

After leaving Tom s bar we decided to have a drink next door at the bar and James was sitting there with Pasko and the girls we met earlier on and we were all happy to see each other. By this stage Pasko was sitting beside me and although I liked his personality he asked could I come back I decided to wait and see.

After one drink Martin and Joe decided to leave and I decided to leave too with that myself and Pasko kissed there was nothing there and decided there and then that he was going his way and I was going mine.

So he walked us to the taxi rank and we jumped in and he said goodnight and said he was sorry that he could not come back because I was a nice guy. I waved out the window and Joe commented on how it was amazing the way I could just pick someone up and drop them at the same time I replied that he was not my type and that there was no chemistry between us definitely from my side and what was the point.

We arrived back at the hotel and kissed goodnight to each other and left Carlos and James in the gay district of Berlin. Back then and even now I was always sleeping and just fell asleep straight away. Carlos arrived in about 4 am he was talking over me in a higher state of consciousness and with jewellery hanging over his chest was giving out to me for smoking in the hotel room I told him to go to bed and that he was out of it on booze and that his breath was stinking and to shut fucking up. Dictating to me how to behave on holiday and he was out of his head.

I rolled over to the other side of the bed and fell asleep to a renaissance chill out c d and awoke the next day to Joe and Carlos preparing for the gay pride march that was happening in Berlin. I arranged to meet them later on and stayed in bed till about lunchtime.

Sometime in the afternoon they arrived back with bags of shopping and we sat in the hotel room having drinks and chatting about the Pride party in the Tier garden and how the March in the center of Berlin was good with guys walking their dogs in PCV hot pants and guys on floats in harnesses and how it was all so chilled with the response from people in Berlin.

That night we left the hotel and walked through the Tier garden and the statue in the middle of the park was jammed with people standing around the stage where there was a d j playing house music and the sky was starting to turn dark we ordered drinks and the five of us absorbed the atmosphere and we were taking photographs and we all seemed to be amused by each other.

After about an hour one of the D J s announced that there was a D J coming on from Detroit and this black guy appeared on stage we thought it was Frankie Knuckles and laughed when he announced his name as someone else.

There were guys everywhere and it was all very well run a fight broke out and one guy started kicking the shit out of this other guy with the crowd of people scattering everywhere. It was kind of scary however the police intervened and broke it up all the same the guy in combats looked violent and scary while he was kicking the shit out of some poor guy.

After this the d j played his set for another hour while I walked through the crowd for coffees and drinks for us. It was excellent and we all decided to go to another club after the pride party in the park.

There was a firework display and the war of the worlds was playing for the last track looking into the sky in Berlin with all this happening we commented that there'd be nothing like this organized in Dublin for Gay pride and we walked through the tier garden with two hot guys who directed us to a taxi rank and myself with Joe and Martin decided to relax back at the hotel where we had an early night.

Carlos and James ended up in some club in Berlin when I returned to the hotel I was thinking I should have gone however I decided on intuition to stay in with a feeling of sensitivity and regret for not going too. So I slept early and Carlos arrived in at 5 am with James and commented on how the club was brilliant and that it was something else with house music I was thinking of my clubbing days in London and trying to imagine how it was and thought there was the Kit Kat Club tomorrow night where we could have another night of clubbing.

James was thinking on how there was no comparison to Dublin and Berlin with clubs and we started talking about that it be a cool city to move to with the diversity which was on the scene in Berlin and that you could have whatever you wanted. I thought yes I could live in Berlin and however I thought about how I knew so many people in Dublin and even when I was living in Melbourne for almost a year and the problem I encountered there were so many and how I was safer on home ground in Dublin if ever anything was to happen my mental health again. James also had mental health problems too and agreed that its a lot safer to be in your own country if ever anything unstable was to happen.

We fell asleep at 7 am and later that afternoon did a tour guide of Berlin. The one thing that stood out about the tour was there were very few churches in Berlin and that people were not very religious the guide was mentioning. Apart from that rents were cheap and it was a well built up city with small green areas scattered here and there. We passed a naturist park with people sunbathing naked and the most colourful part of the tour was the Berlin wall were Checkpoint Charlie was located after looking at part of the wall that was left, divided by east and west check point Charlie had the best atmosphere were the original check point still stands for tourists to see and bullet holes in the walls around were the café s still are and how colourful and free it all looks now with a feeling of hope that still lies within humans which gives us a statement of how free everything in life is capable of been without the destruction of wars between different countries and races religions and cultures which is the way it should be.

There's no such thing now in this world as someone commented to me once everyone has an opinion on something and especially when your working you really come into your reality within this world.

Later that evening we ended up having dinner in a restaurant by the river in Berlin. Watching boats pass by and all of us were in a very relaxed state of mind. We ended up in the Kit Kat Club and we entered into this run down looking stately almost haunted looking house with no life from the outside at all after all its famous in Berlin and there was no one around. We thought we were in the right place and you could hear nothing from the outside. We knocked on the door and three guys opened and asked us where were we from I told them we were from Dublin and heard about this place and that we were here for the Kit Kat Club the bouncer told us it was a sex club and that if we wanted to come in that we'd have to take our tops off I thought with the rest of us that this was cool and it was no problem to us that we were open minded about what we were going to experience.

With that we entered this old run down house mansion and left our coats in the cloakroom and walked down the barley lit stairs with candles and entered into the darkest gay club I've ever been in, in my life.

There were lights on the ceiling with old cables hanging from the lights the staff were wearing G strings who looked so thin and malnourished and almost a feeling of death about the club. It was crazy there were guys in chaps and guys in rubber just standing around the dance floor in groups or just by themselves and the music we were expecting to be house or hard house was hard core techno so many of the guys looked unhealthy and pervy. There was also alot that looked good.

The five of us stood together and we all thought the same thing oh my God what are we letting ourselves in for and laughed. We ordered a drink at the bar which looked like it was about to fall down with the wiring or electrical s and it was damp and dark dark dark!

Myself and James were together and for about half an hour we were indecisive about staying and for about 30 minutes we asked each other shall we stay or just go somewhere else. At one stage I flicked my ash on the dance floor and expected a rat to go running across the floor and after about 30 minutes I commented to James fuck it we might as well stay that we d probably never be here again or else if we were it be in quite a while.

One big guy cruised James who was in his 50 s in leathers and I commented to James that you are what you attract and burst of laughing James stood close to me and the 5 of us had a drink together and decided to have a look around the rest of the club.

There was an area with guys in it sitting around on benches cruising and waiting to score and also there were guys sitting around having sex. From the stairway into the basement there were groups of guys together and to be honest it looked like a meat market with tissues thrown everywhere and it looked like something that you'd keep cattle in.

The five of us stood looking and from there it was a maze of corridors with guys having sex to be honest with you 10 years ago I would have been in the middle of it however now by this stage of my life I was over it all and looking for someone special in my life which I was now searching for years.

From there we left and walked the candle lit stairs up to the top floor with white and red walls there was a guy in the corner getting fisted and with a group of guys around watching and playing with their dicks. In the toilets there was a young guy on a pissed wet floor in a rubber mask wanking it was fucking mad and off the wall we were all just saying to each other this is mad.

After having a look around I decided to return to the dance floor hoping that I'd get fucked just joking I wanted to get into the music after ordering another drink I saw this guy with his head been fucked through a square kind of frame which was looking onto the dance floor in full view of everyone the guy looked scared with banging techno playing. Nobody was dancing and the majority was just standing around.

The guy looked drugged off his head and after that I decided to have a look upstairs which was more relaxed the theme night was called Berlin Bonking Bastards upstairs was completely different in the main dance area which had neon purple light s with a snow effect on the floor there was a guy on a swing swinging back and forth and there was a German guy dancing in a kilt he was one of the best looking guys there so I just ordered a drink from the girl behind the bar who I had to ask three times for a drink and thought she is drugged out of her head we laughed and with that this guy approached me and started talking to me.

He seemed mad and he told me about the guy in the kilt was a doctor and that if I wanted to have sex with him that I should just ask him, however I knew he wasn't interested in me however I was happy to just dance beside him. I snogged the mad guy and thought I was not that interested it was just a quick group and kiss which could have led somewhere however I just held back.

The music upstairs was more trance and the club was brighter with girls around and guys playing with themselves it was more tastefully done so I spent about an hour there with some of the others.

There was another cute man there in a harness and leather hot pants almost white with black hair he seemed like he had a good temperament and personality he was looking over at me and I was just intrigued by him and thought of my experience in the dark room in Toms bar and thought that I was not really interested.

After dancing for about an hour I decided to look for the others I walked around the club looking for them and for the first time I felt lost in a club in my mind and also feeling vulnerable and a bouncer picked up on my insecure vibe and winked at me and smiled and I smiled back I just did not feel safe in my own skin and thought were are my friends after about 40 minutes I found them and was thrilled to see them.

We stood on the dance floor and the d j played this amazing techno track I want to be rich and I want to famous the others looked at me and started pointing to me and I just laughed. I recognized some porn stars from the D V Ds that were on sale in Dublin and I was thinking how someone could wind up dead in here.

So when down in the basement was clearing out myself and Carlos spent the rest of the morning dancing up stairs the others left and by 7 am myself and Carlos left on a high that was so hard to explain awed thinking how crazy this world really is and how mad some places can be where you can end up and experience. Carlos was talking to the driver who he was talking to about the Kit Kat Club I was just exhausted from dancing and thinking about the cute guy in the harness and hot pants who I could have had sex with however when we came across each other in the toilet and looking around the dingy dark cold room I thought to myself I' m better than this and just buttoned up my fly and left the gents and thinking I d rather take him to the hotel however it was tricky with Carlos staying in the same room.

That's as far as I got to have sex with anyone in the Kit Kat Club. So driving through the street s of Berlin about 7 30 am we ended up in the hotel room dancing to the Bee Gees more than a woman and Barry White Can't Get Enough of your Love. We fell asleep about 9 and slept till about three and we woke up feeling wired and almost in a comatose state of being for about an hour after this.

It was our last night in Berlin and we just had a quiet night in Berlin sitting around the hotel room and out for dinner admiring the sights for our last time in Berlin. We ended up in a café the four of us looking around a food hall and admiring the food we sat at the table with our breads and salads and the four of us decided to find something to do for the rest of the evening Carlos Joe and Martin decided to look at me and with that I started to burst out laughing Carlos commented that I'd probably return to bed and I thought well we are on holidays and responded why not mmm. The others cracked up laughing and later on that evening we just hung out in the hotel and packed our bags and watched television.

The next day we checked out and caught a taxi to the station and boarded a train to Berlin Airport. We ended up arriving two hours early due to a misread in our flight time and the five of us just looked at each other and said oh god.

So we sat around departures on two leather black sofas and just had a good laugh and while boarding our flight we decided to leave each other in Dublin because we were all sick of each other by now joking on how we could get rid of each other and change our friends as soon as we got home.

And burst out laughing we flew into Dublin shared a taxi to where we were all staying.

Sitting in the taxi driving through Dublin the taxi driver commented on us that we all looked like good friends and that we looked close I replied that yes we know each other a long time and that its good to have people around you that you know.

So on our Monday afternoon we ended up going our separate ways and I arrived home and my parents asked how was your trip. The first thought that entered my head was the gay clubs we were in and I thought what am I going to say they would have died if I had of told them about the Kit Kat Club.

So I replied that we all had a great time together and that Berlin is a city worth visiting. With all its history and that the people are laid back and chilled I commented that it is an easy city to live in if you are gay and they just looked at me.

I slept that Monday night like a baby and thought that I had to work in the adult shop I ended up in town the next day and decided to come down after my 4 days in Berlin. I hooked up with a friend of mine and gave him a present of some Marlin Monroe Coasters and he was thrilled with them and I stopped off to buy a pair of jeans in Jack and Jones too. There was an older man in the store where we worked and he commented to me that he'd love to sleep with me I thought to myself dream on Gran dad and I left and stopped off for a coffee and jumped on a train and arrived home.

I slept like a baby that night and was working for most of the week after that. I was in Dragon clubbing the following weekend and was in the sauna after until the early hours of Sunday morning.

Summer in Dublin was cloudy and it was also one of the best summers I had in my life. I was seeing a healer who was helping me with my head and after sessions with her I always felt so relaxed and calm. I was over with friends on a Sunday and having dinners in their place and life was ticking along nicely.

However life was good and I certainly was not complaining about anything I was doing well for myself and was calm in my mind too.

So for another few weeks I stayed in the Adult store and one day I just had enough and walked out the door I was so absorbed with sex that I just could not take anymore and while stamping a customer's loyalty card I thought fuck this what a waste of time in my life. I was also rattled on what was coming up in therapy and was having moments where I was feeling vulnerable in my mind.

The owner asked me was I alright and was I taking drugs the night before he was always watching me to see how well I was performing I used to pop tranquilizers at times when I had to work afternoons with him because I felt on edge. I remember him saying to me at times I came across as so relaxed and other times my hands were shaking, On this day when I left he was chatting to a customer about a sex club and to be honest I just panicked because I did not feel comfortable with myself now that I was dealing with myself who had been sexually abused.

Time was moving on and Adam knew however in a way did not want to get off this merry go round and take the plunge into mainstream society.

He thought he was wasting his life here and doing a pissy little job and in the end walked out the door. His employer on leaving mentioned to Adam that he owed him money and Adam just put his hands in the air expressing his body language to him whatever. It was something like 15 euro and the guy is a millionaire.

After that incident Adam sat down at Central Bank and watched life go by for an hour and thought that what now and thanked God he was still living with his parents. No job no property of his own some money in the bank and 5 years in the Adult Industry. Now it was all over and Adam thought about what was next.

He could not have gone any darker with sex because he was aware of that from the customers that he saw who came into the shop and the mess they were in. There were DVD s of Bondage and people tied up and Dominitrixces and people pissing on each other and the customers that were in there not all but I say about 25 % were into it and all the crap which filled Adam s head for now the best part of 5 years.

Something about Adam is if he concentrates on something he usually gives it his all and feeling like a homeless person now after it all though where to next.

While all this was happening I was meeting my sponsor who was helping me through this and we meet up and talk and try and help one another.

So I walked out and since then I've never worked in an adult store it was one of the best move s I made in my life leaving that store.

Now that I was completely out of addictions there was more to deal with and because I was not working I was starting to get scared because how was I going to deal with all this mess.

Leaving the Adult Store And Flying To Marbella

While I was helping a guy in recovery who was also sexually abused we decided to fly to Marbella.

Unfortunately the guy I was helping was abused by his parents and I was lucky that it was an outsider who abused me if you can call it that. The guy I was helping just made me feel grateful about myself because there was no sexual abuse in my family.

However I resented the fact that I was a middle class boy who lost a lot of his heart between the age of 14 up until his early thirty s. and I still did not feel the loss until I ended up in the YMCA however it was now the middle of summer so myself and my sponsee flew to the south of Spain to escape from reality.

Adam looked after Paul through Dublin Airport and checked everything in and Paul was in an anxiety state by the time we were up in the air Adam was advising Paul to just relax Paul kept saying to Adam that his head was wrecked so Adam suggested to Paul that he have a large whiskey thinking it would calm him down.

Paul ordered his drink and after half an hour felt worse he had been popping tranquillizers and using them as a way to relax. So Adam was calm and Paul commented to Adam that he flew very well Adam got clarity up in the air and knowing that he had a week in the sun made everything feel alright.

He could handle Paul because he knew where he was coming from Paul and Adam had conversations about been abused and the effects it had on their lives. Adam was still the 14 to 17 year old boy in a mans body of 35 and because Paul was abused much younger resorted back to the very little boy who still had nightmares from the age of 3 his sexual abuse was more serious Adam thought because it was his Dad that abused him Adam felt more in a better head state because it was not from his family that he was abused and Adam really thought that because he resorted back to his 14 to 17 year age had a lot of adventure inside him and also had a lot of worldly experience too.

So Paul fell asleep and Adam read and three and a half hours later they were in the south of Spain feeling a sense of adventure. We were picked up at the airport and driven to the hotel Adam had been on the freeway before and recognised signs for different towns. He felt well travelled and with Paul beside him he thought that they were going to have a ball.

Adam had been visiting Paul in Dublin and meeting him in the Irish Film Centre for chats and in a way they were counselling each other and Paul saw how well Adam was doing. Adam wanted to help Paul because he was a nice guy who needed to be guided around sexual abuse and away from booze.

The horrible thing about sexual abuse is that you cocoon yourself in your world and act out self destructively you want to numb the pain and what ever way you can do it you will do it Paul s was through booze you already know what Adam s was through.

Anyway we checked into reception Adam looked after everything and Paul ended up in a bar having a drink. So with Adam organizing passports and booking forms and thinking to himself that Mathew did all this for Adam when he left Australia.

And bought him home to Dublin now Adam was doing it for Paul and this made Adam feel how much progress he had had over 10 years.

Adam arrived into the bar and asked Paul was he alright and that we should drop our baggage into our room. We arrived into the room and felt great to have made it together to Marbella.

After unpacking we had another drink at the bar it was late and Adam thought the bar was dingy and Paul thought it was great that this was where it was all going to happen Adam sensed different and could not wait to find where the rest of the night life of Marbella was.

So he asked some ladies over at another table where was good to go and they mentioned that they should check out the arena after about an hour in the dingy hotel bar Adam left with Paul and we ventured down to Puerto Banus and found an array of restaurants and bars all lined up beside a fabulous boating harbour it was a nice night and warm Paul and Adam were delighted to be out of Dublin because the summer was wet which had come to an end now over in Dublin it was almost October.

We walked around the harbour and watched some fish swimming by the boated area that were anchored into the side of the pier and generally liked what we saw. We walked into a bar and ordered some drinks the music was house music and Adam and Paul absorbed themselves into the Marbella club scene there was a street parallel with the arena which consisted of other bars and small night clubs there were ladies of the night from Brazil checking us out and asking us did we want to get a room Adam was completely disinterested in them and with Paul by his side he felt special because he was away with a guy who was not gay and they were sharing a room together and having fun.

So after checking everything out we ended up outside a bar along the street looking at everyone pass by. We ended up chatting to a Swedish girl who was working behind the bar and Adam asked her how long had she been here. She replied two years and loved it and Adam started inquiring about how much was an average apartment to rent.

She told us that we were a good looking couple and asked us how long were we together. Paul replied he was straight and Adam was the one who was gay. She replied oh and thought we should get it together. Paul is good looking Adams type and Adam came across to Paul in a sexual way and Paul told Adam that he was coming onto him and that he was not gay and the three of us laughed.

We had three drinks and Adam ended up in the club next door where the crowd was good and Paul sat chatting to the Swedish girl. There were no Gay Clubs in Puerto Banus and Adam was hoping that there'd be something.

At about 3.30 Adam joined Paul and by this stage Paul was pissed there were a crowd of criminals behind Paul and Paul was totally oblivious to them sitting there talking to the Swedish girl Adam knew the type and with Adam in full view of them they were looking at the two of us.

Adam was becoming restless and decided it was time to leave. The criminals were doing business together and were aware of Adam and Paul. And every so often they looked over at us thinking to themselves who were we and with that Adam said to Paul if he wanted to stay that he was leaving because they looked dangerous.

With that Paul was up in flash and mentioned to Adam that he had a good sense of character and that he was so naïve. We walked through the back streets of Puerto Banus with South African guys selling carved statues and into our hotel and sat on the balcony listening to Sissor Sisters Filthy and Gorgeous and sat there for an hour listening to other tracks another one was Alone Tonight where the lyrics go I wrestled with Angles all of my life looking out on the Marbella night sky with the moon at the side in the distance from our balcony.

Paul and Adam fell asleep around 5 am and awoke about 12 and ended up having coffee beside the swimming pool Paul started to drink and Adam found two sun lounges that were beside him and settled into one and was looking forward to a day in the sun. There was a clear blue sky and hot by 12 in the afternoon and about 30 degrees.

Paul mentioned that he did not like to sunbath for two long and Adam noticed his negative state he was in he started to get boring and Adam explained to Paul that he was staying here for the day.

So after swimming and about two hours later in the sunshine Paul left and ended up alone on the balcony. Adam spent the day by the pool lapping up as much sun as possible he could take and in the evening decided to go shopping for food.

We ended up in the shopping center and Paul got freaked out he said he could not handle it and that he was going back to the hotel where we were staying. So Adam got a trolley and filled it with Salmon, Shrimps, Steak, vegetables and salads with different pastas olives and dressings organized coffee and juices and breakfast cereals he was weighed down carrying the bags returning to the hotel and thought Paul was in a mess.

So later that evening Adam cooked for Paul who was sitting on the balcony and bought him out steak with garlic butter with a mixed leaf salad and sat there watching the sun go down. Paul just sat there in a slumber state and Adam thought about the rest of the holiday,

We ventured out and sat in a bar we ordered Soda and lime and Paul was drinking chocolate liquors. All he was interested in was drinking and Adam thought the he was in for a challenging time over the next week how was he going to be entertained. So we had an early night.

On days out on the balcony Adam was reading articles to Paul to keep conversation going. There was an article about a guy in New York who was sexually abused and it explained his lifestyle he lived in a complete fantasy around his lifestyle and how he lived he was a model and worked in the fashion industry and was a complete fantasist and wild child running around New York City and drinking and taking drugs. What stood out in the article about him and stuck with me was it questioned who he really was and it made me question who I really was too. The guy had a good life and seemed to have his fingers in a lot of pies which I had myself at different times in my life too however because it was never stable I either had it all or on other occasions had nothing. Never having a consistency and it also got me questioning my own running about.

Never really settling for what I had. There was also another article about a guy in London who was gay found hung in his apartment in central London and it described his suicide letter which he left behind. It was found by the Metro Politan Police and he described how he was unable to keep up with gay life and that he ended it all because he was getting older and was finding it hard to keep up in modern society. The police commented on how he was a good looking man who probably could have had a relationship if he wanted. The police officer who was involved in the suicide discovery mentioned it was one of the hardest cases to deal with because he himself was gay and had more insight into something like this in comparison as to someone who is married with children.

I looked at my own life and thought how good looking I was and that in the gay world expectations are high on looks and fashion. I was also thinking about my own sensitivity and found it hard sometimes too.

Adam thought about his own sexual abuse and how he lived his life up to this point he was delighted to be out of the adult store and sitting on the balcony in the sun overlooking the apartment block and swimming pool.

Paul was totally withdrawn and unhappy and saw in Adam something that he could aspire to.

The rest of the week was based around booze for Paul while Adam was just interested in sun and eating well and thinking what was next for him in Dublin. The week passed well with Adam and Paul bonding well together and hanging out by the beach bar and having a relaxed time. Puerto Banus was cool and laid back there was no gay scene there and on some night s we ventured into the center of Marbella and walked through the Salvador Dali Sculptures and found a gay bar off the square which was empty when we arrived.

Adam was thinking of the weekend ahead and what we were going to do for it.

The nearest gay club was in the Costa Del Sol which Adam calculated would cost 75 euro to go to by taxi and suggested to Paul to bus it to the Costa Del Sol and in the morning return in a taxi this gave the two of us a boost because we were looking forward to the adventure.

However when Saturday arrived money was coming to an end and both lads thought that they have some time recovering after been out all night and returning to Puerto Banus from the Costa Del Sol was just too much effort so they decided to give it a miss. Adam was thinking that he was getting on in life and all his club days were coming to an end in the way that he lived his life before and that it did not interest him as much now.

So both lads spent their weekend in Marbella and just chilled out in the bars and ended up in Seven drinking and talking to some girls. Paul told them Adam was gay and they seemed more relaxed around Adam and Paul. Paul was interested in sleeping with one of them however after two drinks they left and Adam was happy to be on his own.

It was so cliché oh your gay this is amusing and do you have a boyfriend and when did you first realize you were gay and all the usual questions that go with it. The girls were talking about clubs they were going to in Ibiza and were leaving the following morning they were pretentious as far as Adam was concerned and Adam was thinking about his life and that most of it was based around night clubs and that he was now reaching a stage in his life where he knew it was becoming boring to him now and that he wanted something else to stimulate his mind and was looking at Paul high from booze and getting nowhere with the girls. It was all becoming so boring to Adam now and also costing him a fortune. He also realized he was getting older and the crowd was getting younger.

So after the girls left Adam and Paul ordered drink and sat there looking around at the crowd. There was a gangster sitting in the middle of the bar with some Asian girls around him there was champagne around the table and he was well built and looked like he was hung like a horse. He was wearing sunglasses and tight jeans and looked completely unstable and exciting.

The girls looked like they were into an all nighter with him and Adam cruised the crowd while Paul sat in the other area of Seven. Adam fantasized about the gangster and about his days when he was off his head on drugs and the wild days he had when he was younger.

The girls were in their twenties and were swarming around him. Adam stood there with his 8 euro soda and lime and thought about drugs and the unstable life that goes with it and thinking to himself now how he had changed and about having some sort of regular relationship with someone and some sort of stability in his life.

He was in a different head space now and although he was attracted to the drug lifestyle he was also scared of it too.

So after about an hour of analyzing and thinking Adam left with Paul and they ended up sitting on the balcony chatting and thinking that they made the right decision about staying in Puerto Banus. They both agreed that an all nighter was too much and thought that it was so much of an effort too.

So we fell asleep about 5 am and awoke Sunday afternoon and just sat on the balcony with little conversation. Paul mentioned that Puerto Banus was just a tourist trap and over expensive and that there were better places in the world to visit and spend time in.

So for the next three days we had meals together with Paul popping tranquilizers and antidepressants and uppers with sleeping pills and with him drinking and sweating on the balcony. His health was a mess and he reminded me of what I used to be like.

Adam looked after him with his mood swings and at one stage Paul phoned a counsellor in Dublin who told him to come in off the balcony and lie down for a while. It was a reminder of Adam s mess in Australia and how Mathew had looked after Adam.

And now he was in the reverse situation looking after Paul he thought it was amazing how relaxed Adam was now about his life and how Paul needed his guidance.

So after two more days in the sun, Adam and Paul flew home to Dublin and Paul told Adam that he was going to work the recovery programme and quit drinking.

It had been a week of pills and booze for Paul and Adam stayed clean. So Adam bought Paul to meeting s in Dublin and dropped out to his apartment and cooked food for him. Paul wanted Adam to move in and Adam was thinking of it however did not want to be around Paul s negative state although the offer of his own place was inviting and to be living his own life was also appealing.

Adam got Paul sober and Paul was feeling a new lease of life he commented to Adam that he was lucky to have him in his life and Adam felt a sense of achievement with Paul.

What you learn in recovery you pass it on and help others with. However because we had been sexually abused we resorted back to the hurt boys from the age that it happened.

Unless you have counselling for it you can never explore the insecurity and damage that you have experienced and develop in a confident way with in yourself. Adam saw Paul s three year old and inner damaged child and Paul saw Adam s inner damaged teenage boy it fuck s up your self esteem and perception of yourself and although Adam and Paul are both good looking men they are damaged by sex abuse and for someone who has never been abused see themselves in a more sexual and attractive way.

That s why you need professional help dealing with what s going on inside your mind and body. Withdrawing into yourself protects the inner person who has been sexually abused and from others seeing your vulnerable hurt self especially in social situations where you can feel completely vulnerable and exposed that is why drugs and alcohol can be such a crutch however in the end they will just destroy you.

I also felt my inner loneliness which was niggling away at me inside in the way I connected with the world in some way s having a feeling of solitude and that I should connect more however my habitual nature was second nature to me now and I thought that it would be hard to break now.

And when you sober up you are left with all this to deal with or else you die or end up on the same pattern for the rest of your life. It's a vicious circle because you are never letting the person who has been raped grow from this and end up going through life like a victim and the raped person will always surface it can happen at any given time. I ve got to admit during my therapy when it was horrible reliving my abuse I felt like a victim in society especially meeting the hurt 15 year old boy inside me. Where now I have grown a lot within and feel stronger inside now after 2 years out of therapy love has a lot to do with healing within now and knowing my boundaries.

People who have never been abused are more confident about themselves and carefree. However Adam had cocooned himself in a world that was completely dangerous by the end of his seventeen years of drinking and drugging and one night while he was on the dance floor in a night club looked around at the crowd of older guys and thought that the men in their 50 s were sad and lonely and Adam thought this is not the life he wanted to have when he was 50.

Out side in the beer garden later that night there were asking each other for cigarettes and Adam picked up on their insecurities and how he had no intentions of ending up like them 50 and still taking drugs and trying to get a younger gay guy into bed for a one night stand.

He was now becoming more cautious and responsible and was doing well in therapy and realizing the bigger picture about himself and was gradually meeting himself however he was still running and not really connecting with life and was finding this quite a challenge to enter back into the real world however Adam knew this was vital for his development to do this.

So the next weekend Adam met up with a mate of his in Dublin and ended up in Dragon and for some reason with his magnetic vibe he had a lot of people around him. I was asked by a friend of mine would I be interested in going to Gran Canaries in three week s time and I was thinking since I walked out of the Adult store thought why not and flew off to Gran Canaries on a major high. Thinking how do I do it. Later that night I was dancing in Dragon having the time of my life and had all my friends around.

I was wearing a sleeveless red top and just living it up really someone commented that I was sex on legs.

For the rest of the three weeks wait I decided to look for a job. There was nothing which interested me and flying out to Gran Canaries was the only thing on my mind.

Myself and James flew out to Gran Canaries and arrived in our apartment complex it was 4 am and looked around and thought what a dump we were staying in and burst out laughing together. The whiff of the fridge was dreadful and we thought we could not live here for a week with the state of the fridge and got it removed and replaced with another one.

The surrounding walls were cordoned off with corrugated iron and to be honest it made what was supposed to be paradise cheap and tacky. What we paid for this apartment was a disgrace for what we were expecting at least the weather was hot and all we were looking forward to was a week in the sunshine and relaxing by the beach and having fun. We sat there in this dingy apartment which was designed out of something like which was in the 1970 s of cheap furniture and a small lounge come kitchen listening to tracks on an I pod.

We decided to fall asleep about 6 am and awoke at midday and shopped in the local supermarket and filled our new fridge after having some coffee sitting outside on the balcony looking out at the swimming pool. It was a hot sunny day and we spent the afternoon sunbathing and swimming. After having a shower later on we ended up in the Umbro Centre having dinner and relaxing in a gay friendly restaurant having steak and enjoying our first night out. It was hot and bustling full of people coming and going through the shopping center. I started to notice how my head was feeling and how anger had surfaced in my head now that I was in therapy and thinking that I felt harsh it was only the beginning of what was surfacing for me.

After dinner we sat on the ground level looking out at people coming and going there were so many gay guys passing by and we were sitting there in our designer cloths checking out the guy s who were hot mmm.

After two drinks we ended up in construction listening to some house music sitting on stools which had barrels as tables. I ended up in the cruising area and thought back to my last trip here where I met a 6ft 8inc guy 5 minutes after I walked in which was about three years ago. For some reason the dark room did not have the same appeal to me as it had before and to be honest I was looking for something more in my life now. So I cruised around and left without doing anything. We sat outside and ended up in another bar on the first floor where we got talking to some lads from England. One asked how long were we here for and he asked me did I have a boyfriend. I replied no and he commented on how come because I was a good looking guy.

I was thinking true and however thought of the low opinion of myself which I had as if I did not deserve love with a guy.

We sat there checking out the crowd and thought that it had changed to a lower level since we were there before. There were guys in jeans leather chaps and tight tee shirts cruising around. The dark room was damp and smelly from heat and amyl nitrate floating in the air.

We ended up in the club later on which was empty and danced for about an hour also checking out the dark rooms there too. I did nothing and was in a totally different head space since I was here before. The time before I was having sex casually and enjoying most of it especially with the tall Dutch guy who I spent most of the night with he was cute thin with blond hair and dressed well. He was an artist and back in his apartment he had framed boxer shorts of guys who he was with and was framing them. Which I found amusing.

Around 4 am we jumped into a taxi and ended up sleeping 5 30 am and awoke at midday lounging around by the pool sunbathing reading and swimming, drinking coffees and smoking. The weather was hot and in the low 30 s which was great for unwinding and just baking ourselves in the hot sun.

I was thinking back to three weeks ago in Marbella and now here I was again in Gran Canaries. I was thinking about my mate Brian who killed himself and was thinking where he was now, and our friendship together.

Later on we had a late lunch and did some shopping in the local supermarket the usual water, juices and snacks too I bought 600 hundred cigarettes and for the afternoon sat outside on the balcony smoking to my heart s content.

Swimming every hour to cool off, applying lotions and listening to my spirit of summer C D from beach style c d s collection.

Later on we phoned for a cab and arrived in Meloneras and had dinner at a strip of restaurant s together chatting away I was thinking that my life consisted of dinners and night s out in bars and clubs where everything was great. After sitting there in 28 degrees we thought about checking out the boutiques to see what was on offer.

I bought myself a cool pair of G star combats and thought I'd sit in for the rest of the night lighting candles and absorbing myself in the late night sky.

James ended up out by himself after trying to convince me to go out however I was happy to just relax listening to the music from the apartment bar.

Sitting there drinking orange juices and with my feet up enjoying the warm night breeze. The sky was littered with stars which were high in the sky and everything was relaxed and calm.

I ended up sleeping around 1 and sat by the pool it was hot and I was reading a Jackie Collins novel about a show girl in Las Vegas who was seeing a handsome entrepreneur.

I was totally absorbed into it with all the different characters and thinking about how life is sometimes hard sometimes easy depends on your mood.

James ended up out again that night and I sat in with my box of special k crash dieting and thinking that I was on my own again and how I withdrew into my own world. Feeling alone and thinking at the end of the day here was another day over and how I was sleeping on my medication which I was now taking for almost 20 years.

I was sleeping a lot the last time I was here too and Brian who I was with on holidays the last time commented on how I managed to sleep so much.

James was taken back on how much I slept also.

However James was surprised on how I did not even bother to go to the beach and how I just sat around the balcony reading and swimming.

I was thinking the same too and how in Dublin I was more motivated in what I was doing. Meeting with friends working out in the gym in Dublin, and also working part time.

The following night we were out again in the Umbro center and had dinner with an acquaintance from Dublin who was also there too. We were sitting in the restaurant having dinner and listening to a drag queen singing hey big spender and some Shirly Bassey songs and Kylie also do the loco motion.

Later David ended up in a trashy Gay come prison theme club which was just for sex. He looked kind of tragic leaving us and saying goodbye on his birthday entering this club by himself. He asked us did we want to join him I'd no interest and we wished him well.

Myself and James ended up on the third floor in a bar having drinks and enjoying everyone coming and going. By the end of the night we were dancing around poles and most of the guy s were only interested in cruising with the best looking guys I was thinking of my life of relationships which I had not had one in such a long time and after all these years I was still alone. With nobody to share anything with James commented to me that I wanted him to ride the arse off me for years and I replied that that would never happen and thought how James wanted it to happen badly for years.

From listening to his cruise escapades in the Umbro Centre each morning after been out all night I was thinking of my own sex life and how I had changed over the years from been the same to now withdrawing into my own world and not really having anyone with me.

So after 5 days of doing the same thing almost every day I decided to go out and celebrate our last night out. We ended up in cruise and construction and later on in a club I was messing around with some guys where my boundaries were completely different now.

While dancing outside James commented about a hot guy who was dancing in a pair of leather studded jeans with a pouch that was studded too he was checking me out and I was doing likewise.

After dancing for about two hours I sat down about 5 am and was thinking was this the life I really wanted. Some people who were there were in bits and the others just seemed to be doing the same party circuit.

The leather studded guy picked up on my vibe and joined me and asked me where was I from and I replied Dublin. James was taken back from the two of us feeling so relaxed together and when everything finished up we were outside on the balcony with the sun coming up together in each other's arms kissing.

Later in the morning we ended up in his apartment together until 7 am and he walked me to the gates of his apartment in his red tight shorts. He was fit and tanned and asked me how long was I here for and could we meet up later on tonight. I mentioned how I'd love to but unfortunately I was flying home later on that afternoon. He commented on how it was a pity he was very gentle and good looking and sex between us was good.

So I walked through the garden with him waving to me and saying goodbye. It would have been nice to see each other again so I hailed a taxi and ended up arriving to my apartment about 7 30 in the morning.

James asked so where were you and commented I suppose you were with the cute guy I replied yes actually I was and he put his hand to his mouth and yawned which I thought was selfish and inconsiderate since I spent the last 4 days listening to his cruising stories having sex in alley ways after out clubbing.

So I mentioned I was off to bed and left him too it. Later in the afternoon we packed and checked out of the apartment complex and decided to sit with our luggage outside the apartment waiting for our bus catching the last of the sun.

There was a track on my mp3 player playing it was the spirit of summer and James walked over to me and handed me a flower which he picked from a tree. I thought that the two of us knew each other so well however I could never really imagine the two of us as a couple together. We had a close friendship and as far as I was concerned that was it for me.

We flew back to Dublin sometime in the middle of July and arrived back to summer in Dublin. George Michael was playing and I had organized tickets with friend s to go and see him.

It was a beautiful summer s evening in Dublin out in Balls bridge and myself and George arranged to meet in a bar for drinks before with some other friends. There was a good atmosphere and after our drinks we were waiting at the entrance to see George Michael.

We bought some coffees and stood inside the arena and waited for him to come on stage. It was a bright summer's afternoon in Dublin and when George came on the crowd erupted into cheering and applause.

The stage was done in flat screens and a lot of silver metal displayed about also. He arrived out onto the stage in a dark suit and was looking good. One song he dedicated to his uncle who killed himself and he was explaining to the audience that how his uncle was gay and sensitive and growing up gay in his time was not easy with been excepted by society.

The lyric s of the song were about that he never really got to know him and myself and George looked at each other thinking that we both had health difficulties and also that we were gay also.

He played for two hours with a crowd that was enjoying the atmosphere and after the concert we left each other and I jumped on a bus home while George ended up in town.

I was now unemployed and thought what was I going to do for work and contacted an employment agency in Dublin and spoke to an ex colleague who graduated to a work placement officer and arranged for an appointment to see her.

I was still in therapy for sexual abuse and while I set up a meeting I mentioned to her that I could only work part time because I was dealing with something in my life which happened 20 years ago.

So after our meeting I left and to be honest I felt that life was passing me by I was still living with my parents at the age of 36 and I had never set myself up with my own place which I could call a home. The pattern of changing jobs and drifting in and out of meaning less employment was starting to catch up with me now.

However I knew I still had to do work in therapy and was looking for an answer which I spent avoiding in my mind hence the fact I never really connected with life however standing at the bus stop I felt a big loss in my life now because I had not managed to set up a life of my own.

So after some searching from my ex colleague a part time job was available in a gym in Dublin 2 which I ended up going for the interview.

So Adam applied for a job in the YMCA on Angier Street and while he sat in front of three women they asked him what experience did I have on reception and Adam thought of his five years working in an Adult store and backtracked to his office Adminstration job with South Side Partnership.

One of the ladies told Adam to relax and Adam spelled off his Administration responsibilities that he had had in South Side Partnership. The interview went well and a week later I was offered the position on reception

They explained to Adam that the job involved working Saturdays and Adam was not happy with this because he wanted to have his Saturdays free to go clubbing so after been offered the job he agreed that he was willing to give the job ago.

Returning to London
Sober 2008

Before I started I flew to London and two weeks after I started on reception in the YMCA.

While flying to London I was a nervous wreck however I needed to go over some old ground to see where I was at this stage of my life. Also my uncles ashes were scattered on Hampstead Heath and I was living in Melbourne when he died and I was unable to attend his funeral.

So with a suitcase in one hand and a return ticket to London I flew out of Dublin with Ryan air to Gatwick and boarded a train to London Bridge and caught a taxi to my uncles flat and arrived to a gorgeous sunny day and ended up in Tesco buying some sun tan lotion. All my items were taken from my hand luggage in departures because the security staff were giving out to me for packing so much in hand luggage and I was giving out to them because it was over 100 euro s worth.

The security staff suggested to me that I should check it in and I replied that there was no point because I'd miss my flight.

I was scared because of my return to London after all the drugs I did there and little did I realize that I was in for some surprise.

After shopping in Tesco on Kennington Road I sat overlooking central London with my uncle thinking that some day I could end up here. Although I thought it was selfish I was subtly thinking about my isolation in Dublin and that did I really want to be isolated in London with the gay scene just ten minutes walk from where I was sitting well maybe maybe not I was thinking. I was also thinking of people I was hanging out with before in London and thinking maybe I might run into some of them.

Myself and my uncle were bonding and from completely different worlds in lifestyles the good thing we had in common was that we were gay. There was a friend of Albert s popping around for dinner and I was anxious thinking that in my psycho state that I did not want anyone around.

So after chatting about all the family and what was happening in Dublin we relaxed into the evening and met one of Albert s friends.

The three of us had a wonderful evening and sat about chatting about different aspects of life and also about my state of my mind. My uncles friend commented to me that I was very low spoken and also distant and my uncle commented that I was analyzing everything that I was taken in.

I agreed and thought this was the way I was and my uncle's friend thought that was just the way I was. He asked me about friend s in Dublin and was there any women in my life. I mentioned that there were some and that I had a lot of friends and they both agreed that I was popular in Dublin.

Sex abuse surfaced on this evening to and my problem with alcohol and drugs and I explained that I was in London to say goodbye to my uncle's partner and the next day I was off to Hampstead Heath. With that my uncle explained that I had had problems since I was 14 and that was the start of me going off the rails when my abuse started.

The two of them asked me did I have much love in my life and that all the family loved me and that I needed to love myself more and relax which I was finding it hard to do.

They thought I was angst and I explained why I was nervous because London was where my problems with drugs had started. My uncles friend advised me to see London as a tourist now and to see some tourist attractions and that the war museum was just near by and to spend the week taking it easy.

The night ended with goodbyes and good wishes and we cleared away the dishes on the table and started to wash up. After everything was cleaned I felt like a stranger in London now and thought about the people that I knew from 15 years past.

We sat on the balcony having drinks and I was asked what was I doing with my life because I was now in London again after such a long time and that I had travelled through London and had drifted through London in the 1990 s and had lived in Australia and what did I really want to do with my life.

I explained that I was starting work now and that I was concentrating on this area of my life. I also explained that I was here for a spiritual journey to say goodbye to Gordon. So we spent the rest of the night talking about family members and what was happening over the next couple of days.

I was told that I was welcome anytime and that it was getting late so it was best to turn in. I slept till 10 am in the morning and left after breakfast sitting out overlooking central London on a warm sunny August morning.

After walking to the tube in Elephant and Castle I jumped on the tube to Hampstead Heath and was quite fragile walking through London again. While in Hampstead Heath I noticed how peaceful it all was and thought about the time I had spent with Gordon in London and was proud to be saying goodbye to him now in the famous Gay cruising area of Hampstead Heath.

After about an hour and a half I left the woods which were scattered with men and other's having sex in some of the bushes. I wasn't interested and was conscious of my heart and how I was not that interested in having casual sex anymore. I had spent so many years having casual sex that now all that I was interested in was having someone to love and end up in a relationship with for us.

I wanted to see the men s ponds and go swimming so I left the cruising area and started walking towards the ponds with no idea really knowing where I was going. After about half an hour of walking through Hampstead Heath I met a guy who was standing by a tree. He was good looking and the two of us smiled we were both lost in the middle of Hampstead Heath on this nice summers afternoon. So the two of us navigated our way together chatting about how he hated the underground tube. Ben introduced himself to me and for some reason I already knew his name but did not want to freak him out.

I knew this day was special and so was Ben. He was wearing shorts and had black hair and was very handsome I explained to him the purpose of my day and Ben was amused. I left out the part that I knew I was going to meet him. Which I had planned in my mind.

After walking for about 30 minute s we found the pathway to the ponds and walked into a courtyard where the changing area was. It was relaxed and on this cloudy overcast day we stripped off and walked the pathway to the ponds. Ben was naked and I was wearing a pair of blue shorts. Ben jumped in first and I jumped in after Ben we were swimming about together and the two of us were enjoying ourselves. The water was murky and still with green grass by the banks and rushes in the water with some ducks and birds gliding through the water. There was a feeling of calmness there which felt good surrounded by the outside busyness of London which seemed so far away.

After about 15 minutes we got out and showered together and the two of us were relaxed together. There were cameras everywhere because of people who were been mugged and attacked. Ben was in good shape nicely proportioned and well hung mmm.

I found Ben cute however he had a partner who he was living with in West London and I was just enjoying been with a nice guy.

We sat together in the overcast sun shine in the changing areas both relaxed in each other's company.

There was an American playwright from High Gate sitting to our left in a pair of white Calvin Klein's who was checking me out I thought that we could spend the afternoon together however I just memorized my previous experiences which I spent a lot of time running around and all the time I had wasted on casual sex. He was good looking with dark hair and he was doing preparations for his play.

There were others there too and one older man was sitting there semi erect with a younger man about 5 feet away the two of them were cruising each other.

I was more aware of how easily unsettled I was with casual sex and sat with Ben just relaxing. After sitting in the sun we ended up swimming together. If Ben was single I was going to ask him out however I mentioned nothing because he was in a relationship with someone else so I just enjoyed the time we were spending together.

After showering together and smiling with the two of us checking each other out we sat together for about 20 minutes and Ben got dressed and mentioned to me that it was lovely to meet me and to enjoy the rest of my stay in London. His last words to me was party hard we had been talking about different London Gay Clubs which id been in and there were some Ben had never been to. I thought about my wild days when I was younger and thought about Ben living in London and he had concentrated on his career and I had concentrated on my social life.

We kissed each other goodbye and I had sat there looking at the other guy s that were coming and going. There were some queens that looked battered from the E scene in London who I gathered were off it now and had found a better way of life off drugs they were looking at me and I was looking at them and thinking how we had battered ourselves through drugs without anything been mentioned.

It was just a knowing by the way we looked at each other. I was still tempted by the American play writer however decided that I did not want to get lost in London with someone I did not know and thought that it was too much of an effort to spend the afternoon with him and thought that if it did not work out that it be just a wasted journey spending two hours trying to navigate my way on the London underground to Kennington I was also feeling some fear inside me too.

So after leaving the ponds I spent about an hour and a half walking through the Heath and left by the park into Hampstead.

By this time people were returning from work with their families who were the same age as me. I was thinking about my life in Dublin and that I was still living with my parents and how did I not have my own home. The architecture of the houses in Hampstead were well designed and in a peaceful part of London and most expensive. After looking in the windows of art galleries in Hampstead and admiring the art in windows there was one of a beautiful shoe which was decorated with butterflies which caught my attention I thought that it was very creative and would be good to hang on the wall of a home if only I had one.

So I arrived in Hampstead tube station and jumped on a tube to Kennington and walked out of the station in a red rugby top and light brown combat shorts.

There was a Rasta guy sitting on his mountain bike smoking a joint and was smiling at me he was hot and behind him there were two young guy s together who seemed to be a couple.

The three of them looked at me and I was interested in the Rasta guy however I d a lot of nervous energy and walked by them and mentioned to them how gay Kennington is and laughed. While entering the newsagents I bought some juices and biscuits and left with the two guys smiling at me. What I was thinking was I could end up with the Rasta guy in his place having sex however what was going through my mind at the time was that I was looking for something more in my life now other than casual sex.

The Rasta guy was tempting however I walked to where I was staying and arrived in after my day on Hampstead Heath. My uncle commented on how I looked reformed and asked me how was my day. He mentioned that I seemed to have had an adventurous day and asked me what was I going to do tonight. It was Wednesday and I decided to stay in. Albert was going out and I was quite happy to stay in by myself and relax I was still feeling sensitive.

So I relaxed in the apartment by myself reading and drinking tea and coffee. The book I read was about a guy who worked in a telesales company and decided to take other peoples credit card identities and flew half way around the world on credit cards living it up and shopping till he dropped. I felt at peace and in the back of my mind I was thinking about the London gay scene. I thought about the guys I knew about 15 years ago and thought to myself where were they now and who was I going to run into when I decided to venture out.

Wednesday night passed and on Thursday I was sitting around thinking that I should do something however I just stayed in chatting with Albert. Later on I was on the tube to central London and got off a Piccadilly square and ended up in a bar in Soho. It was all lit up in blue and red neon lights and the crowd was aged between 20 s to mid 40 s and was packed for a Thursday night.

One guy cruised me and stood beside me and asked me where I was from he was from Sri Lanka and was in London for two weeks on holidays. After having a drink together we left together and walked through Compton Street and ended up in a bar on Charring Cross road.

When I walked in there was a guy who came over and introduced himself to me he was hot and asked me to spend the night with him if I wanted to. He had a shaved head and worked out in the gym.

After settling in after an hour I realized how uneasy I was feeling and my attitude towards what I would have felt comfortable with 10 years ago had now all changed there were other guys raising their glasses to me and I was standing there in my blue adidas top with faded jeans thinking a lot of people found me attractive while listening to some house

271

music it reminded me of my past and how alone in my life which for now had gone on so long. Robin S show me love was playing and also Sybil the love I lost was also playing too. I was now feeling my emotions which for years drink and drugs took care of for me. I was also thinking about Mathew in relation to Sybil's the love I lost and wished for the D J to change the fucking track.

The Sri Lankan guy asked me to spend the night with him however I was not in a right state to do anything because of the uneasiness I felt inside me. I wanted to be with someone however I felt like I was now standing in London with a completely different attitude and thinking that I' m still living with my parents in Dublin.

And how the turmoil inside had not been dealt with. Feeling a loss of connection in my life for such a long time and wanting to connect however feeling that I'd been like this for such a long time. Although some of the guys told me how sexy I was inside I did not feel it at all with the confidence I had had and now was somewhere lost inside me yearning to be free.

The Sri Lankan guy asked me home and I thought that I had no intentions in throwing myself away with sex any further and after I told him no he asked me did I want to have sex in the toilet I felt worse and just walked out of 79 Charring Cross Road and into Trafalgar Square and jumped on a night bus to where I was staying in Kennington and I arrived in feeling better and slept till lunchtime on Friday.

On Friday I was talking to an aunt of mine on the telephone and she asked me how I was and that how I was now off drugs I told her that I was fine I was sitting out on the Balcony looking into the skylight of London she mentioned that I had learnt my lesson and invited me over for dinner on Sunday.

The following day in Tesco I bought her a beautiful bunch of flowers and bought some fresh fruit for dessert. We drove to the other side of London and arrived into Harrow.

It had been a long time since I was last there and felt relaxed sitting there talking to her.

She mentioned to me that we carry a lot around with us as people and we talked about my grandparents who had now passed away. We prepared for dinner and sat there having a really good conversation. Later that evening another aunt arrived who I used to stay with some 17 years ago on and off while I was setting myself up in London. We were having fun which I was missing from my life and I was amazed on how happy I felt. A cousin arrived too and with her daughter and a friend also. When we sat down for dinner I felt uneasy with the girls there and thought of my sex life and how bad it had been and how these young girls had their future in the big bad world.

I started thinking about my sexual abuse and how that at the girls age I was abused I felt so uncomfortable and one of my aunts commented on how fragile life really is and my other aunt just looked at me thinking that I was a bit of a mess. It scared me because I thought of the two young girls as they could be abused by people in the world that abused me. To be honest I just wanted the meal to be over and my cousin picked up on my uneasy vibe.

After dinner myself and my cousin sat in the garden having a cigarette and I commented to her that I know what your thinking and she commented that she was not thinking anything bad of me. I looked into her eyes and saw in her and early childhood that we had had on family gatherings and with that I broke into tears thinking of the loss I had had in my life. I was feeling love to my family however the guards I had carried around in my life to protect from these feelings were now starting to catch up with me.

She hugged me and assured me that she was not thinking anything bad of me and she thought I was lovely. My eccentric aunt arrived into the garden and asked what was the matter and why was I upset to be honest I sat on the grass that night feeling like I was at a party with so many mixed emotions explaining what had happened to me from the age of 14 to 17 I ran from myself for so many years. My aunt commented how I did not lose my sense of humour and how we were together now after such a long time.

Later that evening the two young girls did a sketch of a play they learnt in school and I thought how calm I felt now because I was amongst members of my family having fun and not feeling like I was standing on the outside looking in for which I had spent so much of my life doing.

The next door neighbours bathroom was beside my aunt s kitchen where through the frosty glass you could see him sitting down on the toilet it was so funny because all you could make out was a body frame sitting down through frosted glass from the kitchen window we all cracked up laughing because it was so unexpected to see someone using the bathroom from a kitchen window. It could only happen in London where so many people are crammed into a large space.

After drinks and coffee we left about 1 am and drove through London and I got out at Vauxhall and walked into the arches feeling scared and excited about venturing out on the London gay scene. To be honest I was expecting to find the bars packed and there was not so much going on by this stage it was about 3 30 on a Saturday morning and I had not been on the gay scene in London for about 15 years now. Still I was expecting clubs to be kicking until 12 in the afternoon.

I checked out another bar in the area and walked in about 3 am there were about 60 people there who turned around as I walked in I must have been right on time. I was thinking where was the night club expecting to find what I used to before when I was in London.

I asked the door staff was there anything happening about and they commented that they were closing about 5 am and if I wanted to pop out and check out somewhere else that it was fine to return for a late drink. So I walked through the bars of Vauxhall very sensitive and thinking that I was nervous and noticed that everything was closing up. So I turned into a side street to see if there were any saunas and reluctantly passed one and decided that it was better if I just returned to the first bar I was in on Kennington Road to see if there was anyone to talk with.

I returned about 4 am and ordered a soda and lime and decided to stand in the beer garden and look at what was happening. I started talking to a local guy who was not that good looking and another two had just hooked up the four of us were chatting about Dublin and two of the guy s had visited Dublin and thought it was a good city to live in I agreed.

The History teacher spent time in Kilmainham and was talking about its history where they originally had hanging s of prisoners I added that it was now a museum.

After one drink together the council lad mentioned to me that this bar was having their 5th birthday. Which was on a Sunday and that I should get myself down here because it was going to be an amazing night. I was happy to be having a good night out in London again. The two lads who hooked up moved to another area and I walked about the bar on a quiet night after all it was 4 15 am Saturday night Sunday morning. At the beginning of the bar there was a dark room off it which was done in neon dark red light s and in the back there were about 25 guys cruising each other.

There were a nice bunch of guys and seemed relaxed cruising each other and others were having oral sex I thought how guy s who were so macho and at ease with their sexuality and calm in comparison to some of the guys in Dublin.

One guy who was well built moved in on me and I started playing around with him however I was feeling sensitive and after touching each other up through our jeans I decided to just back off and he respected my boundaries.

I wanted something to happen and deep inside me there was another part of me that wanted to back off. He just touched me in a patted manner on my chest and smiled I stood there in the dark room for another 10 minutes and lit up a cigarette thinking that it was now nearly 5 am and I thought it be great to relax in bed with a lover if only I had one and cuddle up in a more relaxed manner.

I was also thinking about the therapy I was in for sex addiction and sex abuse which I was going through for my addictive personality and how I was in a dark room in Berlin where the sex I had with a guy who meant nothing to me analyzing and apprehensive and thinking of how in my mind I wanted to control my emotions which were always mixed with excitement fear happiness sadness and loss of something deep inside me.

So I walked out of that bar and walked Kennington Road and into the apartment before I opened the door there was a cute guy walking in front of me where he was looking back I was horny and thinking we could have some fun together so he stopped and we played around in the hallway. He had nowhere to go and I was thinking of bringing him in however I was not willing to take the risk.

So we left each other and I slept alone on Sunday morning in London. I felt great that I was out the night before and was looking forward to the night ahead because it was on until 5 am.

Albert was going out to a party in Green Park and I was in for the night until 11 pm. I left the apartment after a shower and walked to the bar I was feeling scared and excited at the same time and recognized someone in the queue from Dublin. I was standing alone and the other guy was with some friends.

It bought me back to the days I was in London in the 1990 s sometimes by myself and other times with friends. It took 45 minutes to enter inside and once inside the place was kicking and there were a lot of colourful characters inside it was like a scene from the 1970 s and people were all dressed up in outfits it blew me away because I was now back in a scene which made me feel good.

I ordered a drink and was standing on the dance floor there were fishnet camouflage on the ceiling with multicoloured fish and stars and a huge disco ball spinning around the crowd was all in a fantastic mood and so was I it's amazing how when you are in a good mood everything seems clear and calm.

There was a cute Indian guy in a red bandana dancing near me and other guys were dancing with their top s off I knew that it was going to be fun the music was excellent Kandi Station you got the love was playing and other tracks mixed into house music 70 s style updated to 2009.

Although I was not drinking I felt great inside myself and the Rasta guy from the tube station was dancing in the middle of the dance floor. People were aware of me and I was aware of them. There were other guys dancing in leather harnesses and women dressed in feathers with younger guys dressed in jeans and tee shirts.

The good thing about London is that when you are in a club no matter what size it is there is always a lot of colour and creativity. Outside on the street it is a completely different story everything grey with large designed buildings and rundown council estates with private houses across from council estates it just all blends in.

Standing in the que earlier on the traffic was flying by with London busses passing a major crossroads in Vauxhall.

I was dancing for about 1 ½ hours when suddenly Grand Master Flash started playing love can turn around with that something of an amazing energy rushed through my body from head to toe and the lyrics started with this is how it started my dreams are broken hearted and I want you baby were coming from the speakers when all of a sudden there was a guy in the d j box announcing on the microphone please everybody raise the roof for such and such in the house tonight and everyone raised their hands in the air and cheered by this stage I was looking around and thinking who could this be for and with that a mate of mine who I had not seen in 15 years appeared in front of me and wow it was even a bigger rush with that he commented that I never thought I'd see you again and with that I lifted him up and swung him around.

The feelings that were inside me exploded into an emotion that I'll never forget Chad asked me was I living in London and where was I staying I commented that I was staying about 20 minutes from here and he introduced me to his friends. He asked me how long was I in London for I told him I was here on a spiritual trip to do with a relative that had died some years ago.

We were just so happy to see each other again after 16 years. We exchanged numbers and we were both amazed to see each other again. The last I heard of Chad was that he had died of a drug overdose by some fucker who was his ex in Dublin making it up.

We had drinks together and were so taking back from our meeting we arranged to meet on Monday.

I spent the night dancing and at 4 am I was dancing to Diana Rosse s trance track baby love in the middle of the dance floor. It was such a good night and I was happy with myself for stepping back onto the London Gay Scene after so many years off been away from it without doing any drugs.

After all it had been a big part of my life which I had some amazing experiences from the past and now that I was drug free I felt more in control of my life now. So after chatting to two of the best looking guys where I was tempted to spend time with one of them however I realized by the tension in the back of my neck that I'd be unable to relax which one noticed in me and was rubbing the upper part of my back.

At 5 am I collected my jacket and walked out of the bar feeling happy with myself for not doing any drugs and having such an amazing night. It was a big step to take and I was proud of myself now that now that I felt that there was nothing in life which was going to hold me back now. I walked through Kennington to the apartment I was staying in and slept until midday. I met chad that afternoon in a bar in Vauxhall and I was feeling insecure that he would not show. Earlier on chatting he told me that he loved me and was looking forward to seeing me again and catching up.

So I walked through Kennington again to meet Chad who arrived with his partner and sister in law. We had drinks outside in Vauxhall and I was feeling happy to be with Chad after such a long time.

I was explaining to him about an ex of his telling me in Dublin how he had died of a drug overdose and Chad responded what a cunt that he was alive and very well living in London with his partner thank you.

So after having drinks together and catching up we ended up in a restaurant in Vauxhall laughing and just so happy to see each other it was a nice reunion.

I left the restaurant for a cigarette and stood outside alone thinking that my life had been such a rollercoaster ride and thinking back to when I first met Chad and now I was standing in the middle of London alone and also thinking back to when we first met.

Chad had met my abuser and there were not many people in my life who had met this person.

With that I burst into tears because although I'd spoken before to friends in Dublin and my family about it there was nobody who was in my life who had met him and for three years while I was abused just at the end of it Chad had come into my life and the abuser was calling around to me where I was living in Dublin asking me to move to England with him that he'd offer me a good life there.

So I was standing alone in Vauxhall outside this restaurant thinking that I'd spent so much of my life alone, and not really having anybody in my life to love me.

I was feeling the rest of my life had been very adventurous with no one who had been a permanent fixture love wise except Mathew.

So I dried my tears and arrived back to the table and had a starter. I could not contain my emotions after that and just suddenly fell apart at the table and broke down into tears.

Chad asked what was wrong so I explained to him what was going on in my life and thinking that Chad was one of the only few that had met my abuser from my past.

I told him about who he met all tHose years ago and what had happened to me before.

It was all coming back in flashes and Chad opened a door in my mind that I had suppressed for so long.

He was holding me in his arms at the table while I was lying against his stomach in floods of tears he commented to the rest that I was very fragile and that after dinner we should just walk along the embankment of the river Thames. We had planned to go to a bar and have drinks and to be honest I was scared now to enter any gay bar because a lot is based on sex and checking out different guys and now that I was finally meeting this hurt abused boy inside me I needed something more gentle in my life.

After I calmed down Chad had a cigarette with his partner and I sat at the table with his sister in law. We started talking and she told me that her job in Northern Ireland was dealing with people who were sexually abused.

She mentioned to me that my abuser was responsible for the way that I was in the world now and that would I consider confronting him and forgiving him for what he had done to me. I'd considered it alright in a different light and had spoken about it to one of my therapists in Dublin about tracking him down and making him pay for what he had done to me.

Because although I had so much sex I was repeating the pattern in my mind of been abused again. In a lot of situations I admit a lot was painful however there was also a lot of experiences which I enjoyed. I knew I'd been groomed and because I had been treated as a sex object from such a young age I was now 36 and needed the professional help of getting over this trait. I had inside me also this and also meeting the hurt abused boy inside me at the age of 36 now it was all starting to surface.

I'd ran around half the world never settling for anyone or even myself and because I was living at home now I'd the advantage of doing so but now it was all starting to come out in the open and to be honest Chad opened a door which I could not escape now that I was off drugs, booze and left the adult store which in a way cocooned me in my own addictive cycle which I admit took very good care of me and also did a lot of damage too.

It's amazing sitting here now typing this and realizing now that I'm 38 I know I still revert back to the small boy who was brutally raped and I do a very good job at protecting him even though I know I'm not fully connected with life. Which in some ways bothers me because I miss out, but in another way it protects me from been hurt it has not been long since I'm out of therapy and the rawness of it all and my subconscious mind helps me to live life this way.

So after our night in London we ended up walking along the River Thames taking some photographs on the river outside the houses of Parliament. It was gentle and non threatening to me and I was in London now with someone who I knew well from a long time ago. Not someone who was just a casual pick up who only knew me for a lost weekend of clubbing.

We walked and talked about life and by midnight we jumped on a bus home and kissed and hugged each other and said goodbye this was Aug 2008.

The following day Adam sat outside talking to his uncle and mentioned nothing about what had come up the night before and just commented that they had a good night in Vauxhall and after walked the river Thames.

Adam s uncle mentioned that Adam had changed and commented that Adam before in the past left London without saying much to anyone.

Adam packed his bag phoned a taxi and when it arrived said goodbye to his uncle.

Driving through the streets of London on a warm sunny afternoon Adam looked around and thought that London was thrown together with shops restaurants and building s everywhere it was full of hustle and bustle and Adam thought that he was happy to spend time in London every so often and leave it at that. He was in completely different light now and was pleased with his week and was happy to be starting his new job it kept the pressure of him at home.

After arriving at London bridge a sexy London bus driver waved at Adam while he was standing there smoking a cigarette waiting for a train outside a busy London Bridge Station. He checked his platform on the screen for Stanstead and bought a ticket from the machine and boarded his train and just sat down. When the doors closed Adam thought how there was so many people in London and thought how was anybody able commute in this every day, the train was packed.

I got more from this trip to London now than I never thought would happen in so many ways. I flew home to Dublin and started in the YMCA the following week. To deal with even more hardship in my life which I never thought was going to happen.

London brought the real me out in the open which was a very frightened young boy in a man s body who lived with his parent s in Dublin and had adopted my father s country attitude in some ways I was now living at home now almost 12 years and it was not a healthy way for a 36 year old man to be living his life. However I did not connect fully with anything or even myself and had suppressed so much in my life and now although I worked part time and walked around Dublin Town in a bubble of my own world having freedom doing so and getting older and realizing that I needed to get off the streets because my life was in a mess I started on reception in the YMCA.

6 Months Before starting in the YMCA

Adams therapist was asking him about his family and that Adam did not mention much about them. On many occasions Adam commented about how he found it difficult to connect with people and on many occasions discussed this with his therapist he'd avoid social gatherings and when his sister Patsy was planning her wedding Adam did not want to go. Adam broke down in front of his parents and told them that he was so fucked up because of sexual abuse and that he wanted to die and did not want to be around people that he did not know. His parents just looked at each other in a sad way and said nothing. Adam s dad mentioned that if it was money he was concerned about that he'd help him out and that it was a once in a lifetime gathering and that he should go. Adam was in distress and was howling in his voice that his sexual abuse had fucked up his life and he wanted to die. Adam s parents looked at each other and thought what else could they do and asked Adam was he taking his medication and maybe he needed to see his doctor and have his medication reviewed Adam told them that it was not another fucking pill he needed and that he did not want to be around strangers and feel judged.

That night Adam slept and was totally withdrawn into his own world except for his parents and friends who he was seeing on and off and was just in a state of unhappiness.

Rome arrived and Adam flew with his parents to Rome he ordered antidepressants from his doctor two weeks before so he would be on a high in Rome and the trip was a success. Adam s uncle was around and asked Adam was he alright and Adam replied yes. T J was asking Adam about his exams in college and how far did he go with them and would he return and finish what he had started. Adam replied maybe at a later date however he spent his days in the hotel in the afternoons on some of them absorbed into his own world that is the problem with sex abuse you just numb out and feel so uncomfortable around people because when you've been hurt in the past you just want to cocoon yourself in your own world.

Adam and his sister spent time in the afternoon in Rome walking about and had lunch off the Trevi fountain and chatted about her friend s and Adams too. The rest of the afternoon Adam was out by himself on the Corse and by the Spanish steps admiring the large pots of flowers about the steps and browsed around the fashion houses in Rome and up at the top of the Spanish Steps admiring the work of artists overlooking the city of Rome. The rest of the time was spent sitting in churches just sitting there absorbing the spiritual side to the peace and solitude he found there.

In the evenings there were drinks and meals out in restaurants with Patsy's friends and meeting family on Sean s side of the family. On one night there was a sing song and Adam left the hotel with two women who said come on we are going to rescue you from this and go out to see if there are any gay bars to have a drink in. So Adam asked the reception staff in the hotel did they know of any gay bars that were open and with that Adam s sister in law gave Adam a wallop over his head Adam couldn't believe her response and thought fuck this so much for understanding homosexuality and told her to fuck off and how dare she hit him like that. He was astonished by her reaction to his question to reception and was shocked by her response.

With that Adams dad arrived into the hotel reception and asked what was going on and Adam replied nothing and with that he left with the two women and ended up in the café until about 4 am. We were unable to find any bars so we ended up in an all night café in the early hours of the morning sitting having drinks. The café was art deco styled with some classic photographs of Rome and other parts of Italy which were all on the walls.

After a bottle of wine and coffees with people coming and going all through the early hours of the morning we left about 4 am and walked through the streets of Rome together and it was just starting to become bright. At the hotel reception we kissed each other good night and returned to our rooms

The following day Patsy got married and the day was a success. The church she was married in had pillars outside in the courtyard and with flowers and plants growing about and just outside on the street was the center of Rome. The courtyard was terracotta and had huge doors closing off to the outside of the Centre of Rome. Inside the church everyone was sitting and 4 of us walked up the aisle and my father led Patsy to the alter Adam turned off to the left to the alter and sat in his pew.

Patsy got married to Sean standing together in Rome with some amazing frescos above their heads with light shining through the stained glass windows.

Their day was a success. We all ended up in a restaurant and Adam sat with his sister in law there were speeches and toasts and Adam and Sally sat together in harmony talking and enjoying each other's company.

Sally told Adam that he was in a completely different space to comparison to when he was in Rome 10 years ago. When she got married to my brother.

And back then I would not have been able to get through a wedding like this 10 years ago and commented on how much I had improved she encouraged me to keep it up. I was chatting to the two women from the night before and earlier on in the restaurant we arrived to a drinks reception and we were commenting about some of the guests.

After a five course meal and many speeches and toasts and tears from Sean s dad everyone settled into a relaxing evening and ended up in an Irish bar where Adam s uncle asked Adam how was therapy going and was it helping him.

Adams mum was there and looked at Adam as if she had gone as far as she could go to help Adam and with everyone else having fun and enjoying themselves Adam felt alone and isolated and sat with the two women and chatted to them.

By two am Adam was in a dark space in his mind and one of the women commented to Adam that she worried about him. Someone else commented that he was sombre.

Adam ended up outside sitting on a Harley Davidson crying feeling sad because of his tainted life. And feeling the damage he had done to himself also feeling the time of the night where he usually ended up cruising for sex or going to a sex club and now feeling the side effects from this.

Two day s before Adam spent the day in Bourgeois park sunbathing and enjoying the bell tower in the distance with a ferret running around with a woman running after it.

There were guys cruising too and Adam ended up having sex with a guy earlier on. After having sex with this guy Adam felt alone and in his body thought here was another meaning less encounter which created a rush and left him feeling deflated and body wise damaged.

The Italian guy asked Adam where he was from and Adam replied Dublin this had become such a habit and Adam left and spent the rest of the afternoon sunbathing and later in the afternoon was approached by a guy who sat beside Adam and started talking to him. He asked Adam to remove his sunglasses and when he saw Adam s eyes replied wow.

He introduced himself as Raphael and asked Adam where he was staying and replied a hotel off the Trevi fountain and Raphael asked Adam did he like him and Adam replied yes that he thought he was nice. Raphael mentioned that he was going to buy a towel and return for the rest of the afternoon to sunbathe.

He asked Adam did he mind. Adam replied sure and later on that afternoon Adam and Raphael spent the afternoon together chatting in the sun. Raphael was thinking the same as Adam about spending an afternoon in the middle of Rome together and that Adams hotel room was free.

Adam wanted to spend the afternoon with Raphael and thought of Sean s family who seemed to be always hanging around the hotel foyer and how he could organize him to come to his room. In the end he decided against it and just enjoyed the afternoon we had together in a park in the middle of Rome.

Thinking that some of his family could come knocking on the door at anytime. Adam thought about this and that his needs were not been met emotionally and felt that he was missing out on having body contact with another person and how his body was missing out in some way since him and Mathew departed.

Even when Mathew and Adam were together after two years the nightmare of sexual abuse came up which Adam had not yet dealt with and ended up in a psychiatric hospital in Melbourne with a nervous breakdown due to drugs and alcohol abuse and also from a sex addiction. After his gang rape Adam just went out and fucked half the world and wanted to die. However maintained a loving relationship with Mathew when it was good it was fabulous and with the euphoria of drugs and booze and partying and travelling the two of us did not have time to stop that was it for Adam he did not want to stop because when he did he was faced with his harsh reality around the damage that was caused within himself and family and friends too.

So on his lazy afternoon in Rome with Raphael there was a connection which did not go any further. We parted with a hug and a kiss it was 7 pm now and Adam left to return to the hotel alone with Sean s family sitting in the foyer.

Adam sat down with them chatting and thinking if they were not there he could have spent an afternoon with Raphael he left them there and spent the rest of the early evening in his room drinking coffee and smoking. Later on he spent the night with some of Patsy's friends and had an early night.

At about midday the following day Adam was standing outside the hotel having a cigarette there was a hot guy standing outside who cruised Adam and followed him whilst walking to the central shopping area. Adam stopped and both of us caught each other's eyes. He was tall with black hair and well built Adam thought mmmmmmmm this could become interesting and followed him into a shopping center and was thinking again about his hotel room where he could have an interesting afternoon however the Italian guy which Adam followed had bought him to a toilet in a shopping center and Adam thought fuck this if we were going to have sex here and left him to it.

So Adam left after his rush and spent the rest of the afternoon in the Pantheon and around the Trevi Fountain and sitting in churches feeling so at peace with himself admiring the brilliant frescos and alters which were decorated with gorgeous flowers and which all looked so beautiful and peaceful with light shining through the stained glass windows.

Adam was delighted with his time in Rome and sex abuse was far from his mind in a city that took his mind off the shit that was coming up in therapy.

The next day after the wedding there were drinks in an Irish bar where there was play lists made from Adam and Sean. One of the tracks playing was Cheryl Lynn Got To Be Real. It was a night of exhaustion after the big day and everyone was tired and Adam said good bye to Father John who was leaving for Miami in the morning. While standing outside the wedding reception the day before Adam was talking to Father John about how that there were different Gods in the world he agreed with me and I was talking to him about my spiritual awakings in recovery there were three of them which I experienced one was with casual sex in a sauna in Dublin where I just could not have it anymore it was like the drugs don't work in the Verves song, the other two were was when I viewed an apartment in Dublin which was in bits to rent a room there was a waitress sleeping on a camp bed in the lounge area with a leak in the ceiling. Adam thought about his situation where although he was living with his parents he was not desolate after all he had been through and the rest was this book.

Adam had not had many conversations with priests before because of the bastard who abused him used to wear a priests uniform and Adam had trouble with seeing priests because of the memories which returned that disturbed him.

Father John agreed with Adam that there were many God s in the world and commented to Adam that he had a good gift in life which was that he was a good listener.

For such a long time Adam looked at priest s and hated what he saw when he looked at their uniform because it reminded him of the horrors he was exposed to when he was young.

Adam thought about Buddhism, Hindu, Catholic, Pagan and other religions. He knew he had two guardian angels looking after him. Adam asked father John to pray for him and Father John asked Adam to pray for him.

After the after drinks night in an Irish bar in Rome Adam stood outside with his parents and some friends of Patsy s we waited to hail a taxi and two arrived together racing toward s us they were over the speed limit and at about 1 am they were both driving side by side one was on the other side of the road. The taxi which got to us first cut across the other taxi which was on the right side of the road and he pulled up to us first.

He was horrible and looked like a sleaze bag. I knew that he was probably involved with the Italian mafia. However 5 of us got in and he took off we were chatting about how the wedding celebration s had come to an end and while driving through the streets of Rome we arrived outside our hotel. One of the women in the back of the taxi paid him and my Dad without realizing paid him also with that my Dad returned to the driver and was about to ask for his money back and just in another flash the driver put his foot down on the accelerator and flew off at full speed. We thought what a selfish bastard and because he knew we were tourists he decided to pull a fast one.

I knew he was dodgy and thought that we should wait for another taxi however it was late and I decided to say nothing. So with some risky driver at 1 am in Rome we were ripped off. It's not called the holy city for nothing that will also rob you just as fast. As a women mentioned to me when I returned home and was chatting to her one day.

So whilst in the hotel Foyer we all congregated around and said our good byes to each other. And wished each other well.

After Patsy s wedding Adam flew home to Dublin feeling good about himself and organized another trip spontaneously with three friends to Tenerife and was having amazing dreams about leaving his past life behind and moving into a new direction however with two of his so called friends who were continuously drinking and making a show of themselves on the plane where they drank a bottle of gin one just looked like a raving alcoholic who was completely messed up and another one who thought it was all so hilarious they got off the plane and caused a scene on the bus with everyone looking at them and Adam thought what the fuck was he doing with these two after all he was sober three years now and just the drama that was going unfold.

Adam and Mark were delighted that they were at opposite ends of the apartment complex away from them and were happy that the travel agent did not have us all together in one apartment. We checked into the complex and organized our keys and told the other two we'd see them in about two hours. Myself and Mark sat on the balcony overlooking the bars that were across the road and were delighted with our unexpected trip because Adam had thought on the train going home to drop into a travel agents near by while sitting on the dart between Salthill and Dun Laoghaire to see if there were any offers going at a special rate. He found a deal for 4 people to Tenerife for 197 euro each and organized the four of us to go.

The other two dropped by and we did our weekly shopping Granny commented on how everything was so cheap and stocked up on wines and beer she had bought a packed fry that she had in her luggage and offered myself and Mark to cook breakfast in the morning s myself and Mark declined and mentioned that it was alright that we'd organize our own breakfast. We stocked up on cereals and bread and the usual supplies of what you need when you arrive on a holiday. Myself and Mark spent the day by the pools paddling our feet and talking about the other two. We both had agreed in Dublin airport that we were going to give them a wide berth when we got back to Dublin because we were pissed off with their toxic behaviour and the nasty ness that was going on.

Granny was conscious of her spending and one night after sitting with the two of them in a bar which they just sat there drinking and drinking and doing nothing else. At one stage Adam was expecting granny to fall off her chair while she raised her arm off the bar to finish her gin and tonic and collapse on the floor however she managed to stay on the chair all night drinking her head off with her silver white hair and almost 50. They never put their hands in their pockets to buy a drink and the other one commented to Adam that fair play to him for been able to stay off the booze and stay in a bar. Because if he was not drinking he wouldn't be able to sit in a bar Adam explained to him when you first sober up its hard however after some time you eventually become used to it.

Adam tried helping the other guy on different times and in the end just stopped bothering because the state he was in was completely fucked and was living off Granny as a cash cow. Granny was so far gone that she was on the verge of no return and Adam just danced with others on the dance floor around him in the basement of the Veronica Shopping Centre which you had to enter by mazes in the basement to arrive in the club on a Thursday night.

The first night we arrived we ended up arguing in bars after drinks and myself and Mark thought that is it they can stay together for the trip and they were welcome to each other. Earlier in Dublin the other one looked at Adam and mentioned in a cunning way oh great your coming on holidays you'll be great for buying drinks. Adam just sat there thinking yeah dream on you ass whole and thought how the guy was such a user.

So the first night myself and Mark paired together and left the other two to it and in the taxi on the way home the other ass whole was screaming at Mark and causing chaos.

Granny commented to Mark that he made a show of herself in the bar and that she was thinking twice about going to another bar with Mark we all cracked up laughing.

I could not wait to get out of the taxi and the driver almost skidded into the apartment block and could not wait to get us out of the taxi the other guy got out and asked could he come in for a drink that we should have a party and we walked away and mentioned to ourselves what an ass whole.

So for the next couple of days myself and Mark spent our day s by the lagoon and having lunches together and meal s in restaurant s around where we were staying. On one day I spotted Barry walking through the apartment complex with a bag off booze all they did was sit in drinking their heads off sad really.

So after three days of separation we all ended up going out for dinner and three quarters way through the meal the other ass whole called the waiter over and asked him to take his meal away because he was not happy with the way it was cooked and the waiter asked him what was wrong with it he mentioned that it was not cooked properly and all he was looking for was a free meal and treated the waiter like shit.

Myself and Mark thought the same thought together what an ass whole and Granny mentioned why what was wrong with his meal because the three of us were happy with ours. I ended up getting mini sunstroke on the first day and had problems with my back and when I moved at the table in a certain way I shouted out fuck and Barry commented ah will you get over yourself there's nothing wrong with you so I just said to him your such a selfish bastard and that you really have not got a clue.

After this myself Granny and Mark were having dinners together and the other one was home alone with alcohol poisoning unable to leave the apartment I felt sorry for Granny because she was upset and did not know what to do. So myself and Mark welcomed him to join us for dinner and Granny just said he just needed his injection because he had bi polar and that when he returned to Dublin he was just handing him over to his family myself and Mark had heard this before and thought here we go again all this would blow over for a few weeks and then there'd be more shit to deal with.

We were on Los Cristianos for the first day and all was going alright and then we just started to argue in a bar later that night. Earlier on we were sitting in a bar having drinks and we were deciding on maybe having something to eat. We asked the waitress what was spotted dick like on the menu board and she replied that it was an English dish We all burst of laughing. Granny mentioned that we should separate for the rest of the holiday because it was better this way and after three days we had peace party in our apartment and Barry arrived and cleared us out of what booze we had what an alcoholic I thought. He turned to Adam and asked for a kiss Adam looked at him and thought forget it and changed the MP3 player to last rhythm last rhythm and we all sat on the balcony dancing and enjoying ourselves.

The other two left and myself and Mark fell asleep till the morning and spent the rest of the day after breakfast by the lagoon thinking about the other two and commented to each other how negative they were.

Later on in the afternoon I was swimming in the lagoon with waves coming over the walls and one guy commented legend and smiled and asked us where were we from and thought how beautiful it was here it was peaceful and natural Mark found it on his second day and myself and the two of us spent four days there so relaxed and happy together as friends and away from the other two. The other two arrived and said they could not wait to return to Dublin and Granny commented on how she could not wait to be in her flat with her heater and Adam thought how exciting. She mentioned that if she won the lotto it would be great and how life would be better give up work and just travel or go on a cruise. She had been on plenty of them before at home that is.

Three weeks later she won the lotto (just joking).

So on our final day we all ended up in a restaurant which Adam thought was run by ex cons who had organized between them to set it up. There was something so laid back about it and the food was great. The manager stretched in front of Adam and he noticed that Adam was checking him out. He took it as a complement and walked off in a proud way and walked in behind the bar and bought over a bottle which had the name darling on it and poured us some shots. They were a nice bunch of people and told us to relax and take it easy. Myself and Mark were there for some evening s by ourselves and were one of the last ones to leave and even though they were conscious of us been aware that they were closing the waiter told us to relax.

So after our week in Tenerife we arrived at the airport and Barry was in a state and Adam was walking around the airport buying duty free and trying to find his terminal and after running to the terminal because the flight was due to leave in 10 minutes Barry shouted Stephanie Beecham where were you and by this stage I was ready to kick the shit out of him because after passing him in the airport we looked at each other and he sensed my aggression and walked off.

So I shouted out to Granny I am having nothing to do with him in Dublin when I return in the airport. He's an ass whole. Granny turned around and said oh my god what a way to talk to someone that is awful.

We arrived home on the 20th of April 2008 which was Adam's birthday and not one of them wished me a happy birthday Adam thought this was selfish and decided that was it they could fuck off life was too short.

We flew into Dublin and that was it when we arrived at the airport baggage area we collected our suit cases and departed our separate ways. Adam had nothing much to do with them since. Except show up for Granny s 50'th birthday her so called partner showed up dressed like he was dressed for a funeral and for years she was saying everyone hates him I wonder why.

At one stage at the party Barry turned to Adam and said go on why don t you have an E and Adam thought again what a prick. After that that was the end of the foursome Granny drinks her usual amount which is into oblivion and so does her partner. When I think of her partner I think of Jazzy B from soul to soul you know you've got to get a life.

Myself and Mark fell out in Belfast one weekend after I lent him money for this trip.

When I was down and struggling with therapy he couldn't have kicked me down any further returning home from Belfast. What a superficial bitch he turned out to be.

However after Tenerife we were in touch for about a year until the Belfast episode.

Just before I started in the YMCA and after leaving the Adult store I met customer who I was introduced to by one of the guys who worked there. Alex happened to be counsellor with a government agency. We became good friends throughout our meeting s. Alex was interested in me and for some reason I thought why are you interested in me and Alex commented that I had a history with drugs and that most people were in there mundane jobs and trapping s of reality. To Adam his life up to this point was normal and did not really see the attraction that Alex had with Adam.

Alex asked Adam who really got the real Adam and to open the door and let him in. Adam thought about his life running now he was 35 and left in a state of confusion and vulnerability and did not trust anyone. Sitting there in the Irish Film Centre with Alex, Adam knew that he had to trust Alex and was willing to take the gamble.

Adam had his tarot cards done a couple of months before by a guy he used to hangout actually it was Granny with that Alex came up in them about a man who was coming into Adam s life and that he was going to help Adam.

So for two years Adam met Alex most weeks and sat there with him in different hotels and cafes in Dublin offloading everything to Alex. After a year Adam was saying that there was more and Alex replied that yes he knew. Little did Adam realize what was coming in the weeks to follow.

Adam was still living with his parents and by now did not want to connect with the real world at all and deep down he was thinking why.

However he was about to start in YMCA and god he did not realize what he was going to face over the next 12 months. The nightmares in his head were about to explode and it was only the start of it.

The first couple of weeks in work were so challenging for Adam now living in the real world dealing with people from managers to colleagues and still in therapy. Adam was withdrawn and concentrated on working. Withdrawn into his job which was so simple however Adam found it challenging because his concentration was all over the place. The Scripts song comes to mind Talk you Down when I was standing on reception in there trying to sort out my life.

Adam was disappointed in himself and how he had ended up in the YMCA he got a lot of humility there and in himself did not feel that he was worth anything. Pressure was tough psychologically for Adam and dealing with and overcoming a drug habit and sex addiction. Adam was finding it hard to relax. Adam was completely on edge and distant from everyone.

By this stage Adam was hanging out with Brad and Brad was attracted to Adam s lifestyle Adam was coming to the end of his party days thinking now that he was on a scene for such a long time and was becoming older therapy was changing his attitude now and he was not so happy go lucky. Adam explained to Brad that the gay scene is false and not to do drugs because you end up having a false emotional bonding with people who are only really connected when they are high.

Brad had only been around for two or three years and he mentioned to Adam that Adam was helping him a lot about staying away from drugs because the way Adam was now by this stage.

Flying to Croatia

Leaving to go to work was a major ordeal and doing everyday chores was challenging for Adam no one seemed to smile at Adam and lot seemed to think that Adam was scary. With what was coming up in therapy it was a lot to deal with getting all the abuse out of his head.

There were a lot of people in Dublin who did not smile at Adam and people I knew just avoided me. So much came up in the YMCA now I was off antidepressants which I had taken 6 months ago I remembered going to the chemist in Dalkey handing over a prescription just before my sisters wedding trying to hold back an explosion of tears now I was determined to find out in my mind what I had been avoiding for such a long time.

Because deep down I knew there was something but for some reason I didn't know what. It was hard connecting there I was recovering from a very bad drug sex and alcohol addiction and dealing with my body which I also let and allowed to be abused at times. There was also emotional abuse which I was going through too and it was a living nightmare. The first couple of weeks were ok however once I settled in on reception in October my world caved in.

Before my world caved in I was asked to go to Croatia with a mate of mine. Three weeks before this I flew to Croatia and with an ex of mine I met one night while I finished work outside on Aungier Street. Ciaron asked Adam one day after work was he interested in going to Croatia and Adam jumped at the chance to leave all this shit behind and managed to have a week over in Croatia away from all this shit. While I sat in the YMCA on Saturday afternoons with nothing to do I read a guide about Dubrovnik and the surrounding towns and small beaches which I was looking forward to seeing. Before this I looked at my manager one day who is a child vetting officer and saw something in her which I sensed would be good for me. Adam knew part of her job was protecting children and because Adam was abused and going through therapy he felt in time if he was able to get through this that she could understand him.

So while reading up on Croatia on reception on Saturdays that were quiet Adam could not wait to fly out to Croatia away from his situation. Whilst chatting to Romal the two of us had a good understanding of each other.

Adam suggested to Romal to shave his balls and Romal was always flirting with the girls who popped into see him. He was handsome and sexy and he was enjoying all the attention he received. The two of us would sit at reception and comment about different guy s that came in to use the gym weather they were gay or straight. We became close he was the first guy in a long time Adam had been around and because there was some sexual energy there it lightened the load from therapy. Romal mentioned to Adam that casual sex as you got older was more dangerous that you take more risks when your younger. Adam agreed.

Some weeks later Adam flew to Croatia with Ciaron. And on sitting on the plane the two of us were on a high and chatting and looking forward to our adventure. After landing we caught a taxi to the studio we were staying in we sat outside in the courtyard thinking how beautiful the scenery was and with the sun shining down on us we thought about Dublin which was grey dull and cold. We met the owners son and the two of thought he was goodlooking. He was tall with black hair and good looking. Myself and Ciaron were laughing and asked each other do we think he is gay.

After he showed us to our rooms we unpacked our bags and walked down to the beach where we sat alone. It was beautiful with amazing views of the sea with the sun glistening down and with just one man sitting on a wall at the end with some boats moored along side. Which were bobbing up and down in the water with some rocks in front of them other than this there was no one around.

We stripped off and jumped into the water and thought this is the life and Ciaron was checking out Adams body. Adam was in good shape and thought he was not having good sex and it had been some time since he enjoyed sex and a relationship with anyone. Seeing Ciaron Adam knew he was interested however Adam was not interested in Ciaron and was just happy to be with someone who he knew from his past. And pushed the rest of what was going on in Dublin out of his head.

For four days we swam snorkeled and relaxed on the beach in the sun and did a tour of Dubrovnik together and sat around in the evening chatting and having drinks on the balcony overlooking the sea. There were beautiful towns off the main road where we ended up sitting in cafes and restaurants enjoying and exploring shops and taking photographs together. In one town off the beaten track you could see how the war had affected the locals with building s burnt out in the war which was such a shame and bullet holes in deserted builings.

On the main road you had busses running every half hour from one end to the next from Dubrovnik. The town at the end was beautiful with a marina which had bars shops and restaurant s alone the side. The Croatian waiters were sexy and you could see that homosexuality was only been excepted in Croatia.

Adam knew when Ciaron was leaving that if he was out clubbing that he would have to look after himself because he was alone. The marina had some beautiful reflections from the sun setting and the atmosphere was relaxed and peaceful we were here for two night s having dinners and drinks and loved it. On Ciaron's last night we stayed up until 4 am chatting and listening to different chill out music. Sitting out on the balcony together from Adam's room.

The following morning Ciaron left feeling happy and relaxed and Adam was happy to be spending time alone by himself. He spent three days on the beach snorkeling, swimming and lying in the sun. On Saturday Adam was on a bus to Dubrovnik and arriving into the city there was an amazing view from the top of the road which looked down into Dubrovnik and out into the ocean. From there the bus ran along the main harbour where there was boats everywhere and after the bus drove from the harbour Adam got off at a shopping center where he browsed and sat in café and watched the world go by. It was really busy and there was tourists about with a relaxed vibe about the place. It was raining and Adam thought about the last night out with Ciaron and the last four days they were together. Two nights before we were sitting in the Hilton together feeling great and how we were sitting in the Hilton together chatting about this book and all I could write about. Adam used drugs as an excuse for the book and had mentioned nothing to Ciaron about sex abuse and therapy he was having in Dublin to overcome it all. The following day Ciaron flew home to Dublin. So the next day Adam ventured into Dubrovnik and after some time browsing around the park Adam walked along the coast pathway which had some cafes to the right and rocks to the sea on the left. Adam just kept walking it was a quiet Octobers Saturday afternoon with not many people about. The sea was fresh and wild with cats running about the pathway s in and out of private houses.

Two joggers passed by and one of them smiled at Adam. Adam thought it was nice for them to be staying at one of the hotels which were at the end of the walkway with hardly anybody around and how peaceful all this was. He stopped off in a café and ordered coffee and sat over the balcony looking into the ocean and thinking of noting admiring everything around him with very few people. It was great.

Later on he stopped off in the shopping center and bought food for later on. He was enjoying his roaming about and just stumbling across what he was seeing.

After waiting for a bus Adam arrived at his studio it had been raining all day slightly and now it was becoming heavier. There was a storm on the horizon the sky had changed from grey to black and the rain was pouring down outside there were clashes of thunder and flashes of lightening with some amazing flashes in the sky of fork lightening. Adam cooked a pasta dish and sat there with a coffee watching all this from the balcony and thought that his Saturday night was in safe from the storm which was happening outside.

The bottles which were left outside where smashed onto the balcony underneath and Adam opened the door and cleared the rest of what was sitting on the table. The rain was heavy and Adam was happy to be indoors and sat in that night reading a short story on a German woman which was written by Christopher Isherwood. Drinking coffees and smoking cigarettes.

The following Sunday Adam awoke to a beautiful sunny day and had coffee and cakes on the balcony and later walked to the beach and sat by the shore the beach was full of bark and the sand had been up heaved while swimming in the water there was no fish and the water was murky.

There was a family at the end of the beach sitting together and Adam spent the day sunbathing and swimming enjoying the sun. Later on he walked to the local restaurant and sat there feeling alone. He had passed some houses on the road which most had wood cut outside them and dogs sitting by the entrance of houses. The road was narrow and most of the houses were built into the hillside with pathways running along side the houses. They reminded Adam of small mazes between the houses with steps going up the higher you climbed. They bought you out onto the main road where the busses passed along with cars going from one end of Dubrovnik to the other small towns. With an amazing view overlooking the ocean.

While sitting in the restaurant Adam ordered pizza and the waitress set the table with a blue table cloth outside on the terrace overlooking the sea. After drinking a coffee and smoking a cigarette his pizza arrived and Adam had some beer. After dinner he paid the bill and took some takeaway beers and walked 15 minutes to the studio and sat watching a film. The film was about a guy who had mental health problems who lived in London with his brother who ran a restaurant. Daniel Craig was acting in it and kept Adam entertained for the rest of the evening. In the end after all his problems he moved back in with his brother. On Monday it was the last day before flying home to Dublin and Adam made the most of his day before flying home. The days just flew by having breakfast on the balcony and walking through the pathway to the beach with butterfly s flying about and lying on the beach and swimming with fish. They bought him back to his childhood in Sandy cove collecting crabs and small fish from the rocks with his fish net and thought how peaceful this part of the world was with hardly anybody around. And thinking to himself just a few hours from Dublin he could write here in winter time.

Monday night I sat in and cooked some pasta and was reading short stories from Penguin on gay life and packed my suitcase and had a shower. I slept like a baby so relaxed from 8 days of peace in Croatia. Pasko knocked on my door at 12 and drove me to the airport we were talking about Dublin and I was mentioning to him that there's a lot to do in Dublin if he was ever going to visit.

He asked me about Guinness and I explained to him that there is a Guinness store in Dublin which is worth visiting about the history of Guinness. Where after the tour, you receive a free pint in the basement of one of Dublin s oldest parts of Dublin. I also mentioned to him that Dublin is famous for its bars and that if he was ever going to go that he should travel with some friends that there is a pub on every corner.

Underneath my room Pasko was attending to making his own wine and the fruits were spicy he mentioned that he drank a lot in winter because it was a bit boring here. And in the summer he spent his time swimming and snorkeling with his friends.

After arriving at the airport I paid him and thanked him for a beautiful stay and he mentioned if I was here again to stay I still have his number.

After checking in my bags and walking through security the security guard made some comment about cocaine and I just passed through with a casual smile and collected my hand luggage and kept going.

Thinking about my drug days and how I had changed I bought some duty free and boarded a flight to Dublin with Ryan Air after having a coffee and cigarette in departures looking out from the smoking area at the last of the warm sun shine and clear blue sky and thinking of winter home in Dublin.

After arriving in Dublin after a three hour flight I collected my bags and jumped on a bus to Dalkey and arrived home. The next day I returned to work in the YMCA and thought about my trips which I took on Wednesdays to avoid what was coming up in therapy.

Gang Rape

Because the new manager had started who had changed everything and there were new rules and regulations which had to be used in other words it was not as easy. On October of 2008 my therapist was pushing me to talk about what happened on Easter Thursday night in my abusers home in Monks town.

I had pushed the matter away so many times in therapy and ended up in trances sitting there on so many occasions with my therapist and she'd ask me to come back into the room and check in with my body. In the YMCA on reception I was dealing with hundred s of people coming and going. What came up in therapy that October 2008 floored me and brought my world tumbling down. My therapist had touched on Easter Thursday night so many times and now she had me fully present in the room she asked me after half an hour into our session she asked me to explain from the start of the night what was going on. I explained what I was asked to help out with a meal to prepare with my abusers partner. For a special gathering which was to celebrate Easter Thursday I was asked to help and because I was interested in becoming a chef that the dish would be something interesting to learn.

I left my mums house and arrived at the house to Monks town where my abusers partner was preparing food and setting up the kitchen. When I arrived my abuser was in a priest's uniform and he welcomed me inside. I was bought to the kitchen where his partner was cooking an Apple and Cider dish there was pork frying in the pan and there was cider beside the hob I was interested in learning about this dish and was offered a glass of cider. I started helping with this dish and chopping some apples and drinking my abuser was outside setting up the lounge for the rest of the guests to arrive.

I explained to my therapist that he was in a great mood very enthusiastic and was dressing the dining table with flowers and silver candle holders. It was set 8 people or more what springs back to mind now is that there were two tables joined together. And while I was becoming merry in the kitchen and setting the table in the dining room I remember my abuser thanking me for been such a good help. To be honest I can not really remember doing much cooking I set up most of the dining room with plates flowers and silver cutlery and red candles.

I just remember been interested in the apple and cider pork dish and on several occasions I was tasting it. My therapist broke in at this stage and commented so I was lured to the house on Easter Thursday and asked to help with an alcohol dish giving booze and she asked what happened when everyone arrived.

I told her that because I had drank about 3 pints of cider and was excited about the dinner party and my abuser was in such good form he was almost expecting so much to happen. Anyway we sat down and I barely remember that it was about 8 in the evening and it was all now becoming a blur my therapist broke in again and asked what happened she had my full divided attention now and I could feel the blood boil up inside me now that my mind was back in the position which I had suppressed for so long. I told her that I remember my abuser sitting opposite me with other people in the room the table was dressed in flowers and with a white table cloth with high silver candles holders with red candles lighting and I was sitting there with a glass of wine and everyone was laughing and there was a lot of noise. I looked at my abuser in a blind state I think I was drugged and he spoke to me that I was in for a big surprise. I told my therapist after that I blanked out.

She asked me again what happened and after that I shouted out to her with my blood boiling all over my body that I was ganged raped and broke down into floods of tears. I always used drugs as an excuse to the outside world that that was why I was in the state I was in however it was much bigger than that for which I was dealing with in my life drugs were just a cover up. I've a vague recollection of that night in which I was passed around on the floor of that bedroom in a dark state with other men standing around me I've a distant memory of been on the floor on my knees with older men in their 40 s standing around me. It was a night mare one has which they can only remember parts of it and not much else. From what I recall it was a lot of oral sex which I was subjected to even writing this is sickening for me and I am looking out the window typing this and not even wanting to look on what is coming out on this page. It's a horrible thing for me and very nerve wracking and numbing for me to say this I hate it and am now miles away. Thinking now about the abuse I was subjected to from the age of 14 to 17 which I had to go through and then have a complete self destruct life after that for 20 years. I don t know what they did to me that night these people were evil and for some reason I think they put a curse on me in some ritual which is a dark blur for me to even go there and from what I remember I was passed around and was in a circle of wankers who totally abused me and drugged me.

There had been men on who lived in this house who had talked about trips to Thailand and they were like kids in a sweet shop all excited about going to Thailand and Adam remembers one fat fucker business man who was sleeping with a guy who was 16 and was loaded and was bringing him with him to Thailand. My abuser had asked me to move with him to England because he told me that he'd take care of me. This was always bought up to Adam. In the end Adam ran from them and has never seen any of them since. And never wants to see any of them sick fucking bastards. From 8 that evening until 1 on good Friday Adam remembers a blur of sex abuse with older men for some reason Adam remember s 8 only god knows how many there was. Adam remembers been on his knees and that s about it.

So lunchtime on good Friday Adam woke up in a bed alone in darkness he was in the middle the sheets which were dirty and there was a small dog running about the room which was called Sadie and previous occasions this dog had been in the bedroom when Adam had been abused before and was barking its fucking head off and was roared at by my abuser to shut up. He would roar at the dog in a hardened voice Sadie Sadie Sadie shut up shut up Adam remembers the harshness in his voice and the horrors of it all. It was a living night mare and Adam would have poppers shoved up his nose this bastard had long hair which was black and with a red face unshaven pushing 50 and extremely dangerous he knew all the toilets in Dublin and around the UK and would sit there after abusing Adam telling him stories about all his shit he was doing. Him and his partner met in a toilet and lived happily ever after in hell. He explained to Adam that he'd take me on these encounters and look after him while he was doing it while all this was been mentioned to Adam Adam was intoxicated and he just kept rolling one sick story after another. God this is horrible to write and my head feels ill getting all this out it is complete shit that one sick bastard groomed into a boy from the age of 14 up to the age of 17.

Recapping again to Good Friday Adam now woke up in a dirty bed alone lying diagonally across the bed and got up and opened the curtains to a sunny day. He got dressed and looked around the room.

I remember nothing else and my therapist told me that I've every reason to have blocked something like that out of my mind. Her face was white.

I was lucky to get out of it alive now that I'm typing this because my abuser was a very dangerous man and the amount of crap he filled my mind with on other times when he had me on poteen of his story s in England and Ireland travelling up and down the country cruising toilets and the disgusting horrible things he was filling my head with from the age of 14 to 17 which I ran from for the rest of my life writing this now I hope he is dead and died a horrible death or else in prison because the amount of stuff I missed out on in the life with the running I did has left me in limbo with my life I'm stronger now and don t let to many people into my life because of it.

I had to take a break there just had a cigarette the sun is shining outside on my balcony where a young boy passed by the same age I was then. Recapping again to good Friday I woke up in a dark bedroom at lunchtime alone on Good Friday the bed was dirty and the curtains were pulled my abuser was sitting outside in the lounge in a room which was very different from the night before he was in darkness which I hope he is in for the rest of his life there was a crucifix on one armchair 6 feet high and him sitting there in his priests uniform slouched in the chair opposite it. The look of horror on his face was unreal the dog was there too. The curtains were closed and all was dark in the lounge. I said what are you doing and he just grunted at Adam. I looked through the curtains and it was a beautiful day sunny and bright I left that house in a daze and left the two dogs to it. I walked down three flight s of stairs. I just remember walking to the bus stop on Bakers Corner and waited for the 46 A to Dun Laoghaire Adam was in a daze and remembers sitting upstairs on the bus looking out the window to a clear blue sunny day.

The Dart home to Dalkey was a blur and Adam arrived into his family home to his mum who was in the kitchen and she asked Adam where he had been Adam remembers saying that he was with friends and that he needed to shower. While Adam showered he can remember marks on his body like scratches and some blood which he washed off and after his shower he ended up in his room. I think I slept and can not remember anything else about this weekend. It was all a blur.

For the next 16 years I ended up out on a drink and drugs binge and just completely blotted it out of my mind. Now that I found my answer what was left to do with my life.

After exploding in therapy I could not go to work so I phoned in sick and my life fell apart. I spent three days in my room crying and my physical health was deteriorating I lost weight and became withdrawn and isolated and Christmas was approaching and with all this upset I was not looking forward to it. I had pushed so many people away and spent a lot of time by myself. I just cooked for myself and drinking cup s of coffee. Sex with anyone was completely out the window going from a promiscuous life to almost nothing I couldn't handle anyone near me I was floored and thinking to myself how the fuck was I going to deal with Christmas and work now.

The shame and shock that came up was very difficult to deal with. After that therapy session I spent about an hour upstairs in one and four crying and shocked and horrified there are blockages of this night and my therapist looked at me in horror and told me I have every reason to block it out of my head because it was a huge thing for a boy to go through and I deserved and owed it to myself. Writing this now my heart feels strong powerful Annie Lennox s why is playing at the moment.

This was last October and while I was trying to deal with a busy gym reception in the YMCA I was under a lot of pressure trying to deal with the real world and normality. By this stage there was also a sex addiction to deal with too.

The day I returned to the YMCA my manager mentioned the day I returned to work to another manager of mine that he was very independent and she commented too she was also. The only thing I could say to her was her handbag was flash and she commented yes it was. I felt like such a tramp now and broken to the core. I might have been wearing designer cloths and the ego the size of a 15 year old boy now who felt destroyed there were no more escapisms I served customers who arrived for classes with my colleges and just wanted the world to swallow me. Because I used sex as an escapism and also as a form of further abuse in my life I just felt damaged I used sex in so many ways and now it was coming back to haunt me.

Now I had met the 15 year old boy I was thinking in my mind was I gay or straight now I had reverted back to me at 15 and I walked around the YMCA with emotions flying around inside me. I was working with a security guard who I was attracted to and he was good to be around. He was the only guy I was close to in such a long time and there was sexual energy between us which was great to have.

The others were looking at me in a state of disbelief in my state of mind and one of my managers was telling me to get my act together. To be honest I could have gone in any direction with my life now that I was floored. How had my life taken such a turn I thought. I remember just after this meeting Alex and explaining to him what had happened to me about what I found out in therapy. He mentioned to me that that explains everything in my behaviour in the past and been unable to connect with someone as in having a relationship with someone. I realized there and then that s why I was promiscuous and felt a better understanding of myself now.

Adam looked at his manager and hated him he was 30 and had his own life and was confident in what he was doing he hated it all and most people around him. He was a fragile wreck and was having arguments with his manager and had conflict some days while at work. On one day his manager told Adam that he was distressed with him.

Adam had reverted back to the 14 to 17 year old boy who was been hassled by everyone around him. There were major emotions going on and each Saturday Adam spent after work in Stephen s Green crying alone with a pair of sunglasses on thinking what a life he had and was dreading Christmas because the only people who knew were his therapist and Uncle in London.

The following week after therapy my therapist told the board I was suicidal Christmas could come and go for all I cared and also I felt the same about my life to.

Sex was completely out the window and Adam could not even get close to someone. Because of what was going through in his mind.

Even when Adam saw his friends he was so unhappy and however much he was trying to put on a brave face the pain was the only thing that was present.

Adam was outraged and would go into different mood swings and saw others who were happy with their lives and younger too. The anger that came up was explosive and horrific and I just felt that I had been robbed of everything and used drugs as an excuse to cover the way I was feeling. The shame shock horror of it all was too much to bear and while trying to deal with the public and managers was becoming too much to bear.

Suicide entered Adam s head and on many other occasions was a possibility Adam had attempted it on two occasions before and now looking around at his world and feeling so unhappy and life a piece of filth just thought fuck it. I hate this life. Super Tramp is playing at the moment The Logical Song.

I was also working every Saturday and completely isolated and alone in my mind and elsewhere and on day s after work I'd sit in Stephen s Green with a coffee and just go home. It was hard facing all these feelings and I was happy to just stay in on Saturday evening s alone in my room watching television. Cocooned in my safe place.

I was also hanging out with Ciaron who was slagging me off in an innuendo way of been a tramp and also stupid. I mentioned nothing to him about what I was going through. Funny now his life is in a mess. You just never know what life is going to throw at you that includes everyone.

There was day s where I completely gone in my mind and was serving customers and not remembering 5 minutes later

I asked the same person did she want to join the gym and my manager mentioned to me Adam do you not remember that you just processed her application form. Adam looked at Jason and replied no and Jason looked at Adam and was thinking what the fuck was going on.

There were explosions of emotions where all of sudden Adam was ecstatically happy and then all of a sudden I'd have to run outside where I was breaking down and crying. Adam was thinking how was he going to come through this because life moves so fast in the real world and having all these feelings to deal with was not easy to be living with.

One colleague one night saw me outside at the fire exit in floods of tears and asked me what was going on I said that something came up from 17 years ago and that it was a huge shock and I was crying uncontrollably she replied that she did not like to see me like this and offered me a cigarette and I said nothing else this lady had been raped too and the two of us had nervous breakdowns also.

While gathering myself together I'd return to reception and continue work I was meeting the 14 to 17 year old boy and my colleague and manager would ask was I alright and I replied yes.

I met up with some friends shortly after this and was completely unhappy and withdrew and the words just were not coming out from me. And one just commented that he never met anybody like me in his life. To be honest I just wanted to fuck someone and stood out in the beer garden of Dragon feeling very hard in my life now with a friend of a friend looking at me and saying that I was something else. I did not even comment I was in a blasé attitude of I just could not give a fuck anymore and with 20 years of abuse thought to myself what was left.

317

Where was the fun in life and where was the happiness gone. I felt so severe and harsh in my reality now and felt that suicide was an option now if I was not going to come out of it all. I spent most of the night drifting through the crowd after talking to a guy who was talking to me about his interests and what made him drive he was with our group and saw in me something that was lost and also something that was still there. They had commented about sex and cruising and to each other and he shouted get over here reflecting on Adam s severity now that he was in.

After about 20 minutes Adams spirits lifted and recalled a night out in London where he had a fantastic night. And started talking about the London rave scene and commented that the bar staff put magic mushrooms in the drinks and how his night took off. We also spoke about leather bars and sex clubs in London where there's a lot more than in Dublin.

Brad was with Adam listening and laughing and the other two when leaving told Brad to look after Adam they saw something that was still not lost and said goodbye.

Later on Adam danced with Brad and drifted through the crowd not really connecting with anyone except Brad and the odd comment to certain acquaintances and that was it really. So numbed out from the gang rape and unhappy and feeling was he ever going to get his life sorted.

So the night ended with Brad and Adam in a café chatting about Adam s recovery and how Brad was doing too. Brad asked Adam was he alright and Adam replied yes thanks.

That he was thinking of the situation he was in and how he had spent most of the last 10 years doing drugs Brad told Adam that he was doing well and that he was very sorry that Adam had been sexually abused Adam mentioned nothing about his gang rape.

It took me 5 months to tell my manager who is a child vetting officer I admired her because of her work she did and how she was protecting vulnerable children in Dublin.

I could not handle children because through my therapy I was thinking of child porn not in a way that I was interested by no means but in a way that other children are at risk because of what s out there. I know because I've been through it. There was also so much about child abuse on the news at the time to do with the Catholic Church with priests who had abused alter boys. I remember an older man in the gym asking me for something and he commented that I was miles away I was staring out the window and felt that I had tranced myself into another world.

So Christmas arrived and I thought it could go just as quick for all I cared by now. I still was not connecting properly and I didn't attend the staff party because I was so fucking raw with my life and I just spent some time with my friends when they were lucky to see me which was not that often. One told me to stay away from him when I was going through all this.

Emotionally I was a wreck and by no means wanted to connect so for months I worked on reception and on different times broke down in tears running outside and coming back in to serve customers. Never really knowing when the outburst s were going to happen. I suppressed a lot of it for months and just put on a brave face using drugs as an excuse for the state I was in. There was just so much shame to deal with.

I hated myself and was suicidal people looked down on me and in a way I was looking down on myself. I hated one of my managers for putting me through the regime on reception which I had to go through in my job because I was struggling so much with in.

It was hard and at times it was so busy there were people I served and then two minutes later I'd ask them could I help you forgetting that I had served them and my manager looked at me in disbelief and so did I.

Time passed and I grew with my sex addiction too it was not all doom and gloom because I had so many drug experiences my head would go high when the crowd arrived for their gym classes. So at times I was on major highs however the lows were bad. After struggling through Christmas and enjoying parts of it I faced my family for the day. I remember standing in Dalkey village with a cigarette in one hand with people running by me happy I was feeling hurt inside with a lot of inner turmoil and thought my life was a mess and feeling so unhappy I just wanted the ground to swallow me up that was Christmas eve of 2009.

People were looking at me thinking to themselves what s up with me some I said a brave hello and others I just avoided and kept my head down in shame. My sister had been upset when she arrived home on Christmas Eve and I thought that her problems were luxury in comparison to mine and thought she should appreciate what she had with her husband who could not spent Christmas with our family. I sat there listening to all her drama and thought would she ever shut up. My life was in a mess hers was minor problem as far as I was concerned.

I mentioned nothing to my family and on Christmas day I broke down in tears because I had avoided people for such a long time within 24 hours of a day, because I was unable deal with my emotions properly. The killers were playing on the radio are we human and my mum asked me in a concerning way was I alright. I told her yes and she mentioned that everyone loves me.

Later on I was out for a walk with my sister and she mentioned to me that she love s me to bits and that I am very popular. We walked about the empty streets of Dalkey and I met a woman who I knew because I was feeling emotional I was hoping to just have a short conversation with her however my sister Patsy was talking to her which took the effort of me to go out of my way to make conversation to her because of the hurt inside. I sensed that she suspected something. Because I was upset I commented on her Egyptian ring and she mentioned that her Aunt left it to her. Other Christmas days before I used to stop and chat to her she has long blond hair and kind of on the big side. She mentioned one year that she was swimming on Vico Road in a bathing area and there were children there also I mentioned that the children probably thought that she was Misses Claus because she was the image of her just like in films.

She always was dressed really well and had herself done up with nice jewellery and usually a Christmas jumper or something which was almost like an outfit which you see on a person living in the south of France.

One year she was wearing this amazing light beige fur coat. For about three years in a row I met her on Christmas day when I was out walking in the afternoon.

We had dinner and sat around later on in the night I slept early in an emotional fucked up way. I connected with very few people that year because of my outbursts and stayed in new years eve alone sitting there watching television. Of course there were people commenting that I would not spend Christmas and that I was a miserable person. Who wouldn't be if they had to go through what I had to and then on top of that to receive emotional abuse too.

So to be honest I was happy to be returning to the YMCA to work and sort out the rest of my therapy and my mind. It was March before I told my manager who is a child vetting officer. For some reason I was starting to become close to her.

So finally I told my manager what happened it could not be avoided really I'd bottled up so much and was dying to get out of the trap which I made in my mind.

I remember one colleague mentioning to me I was like an open and closed book and that everything was locked inside my head to do with talking and expressing my self.

This scared me because I knew how important in life it is to express yourself and to be honest I never thought it would be me who would be in situation like this. I knew it was a barrier which I had to overcome.

After working 4 hours which was about as much as I could handle for any day because of what was coming up I remember been asked to work extra hours or do courses which I dreaded to do because anything over 5 hours back then just brought up so much for me.

Anyway after working after lunch I ended up in my manager's office talking about courses which would be good to do for my future.

She bought up sociology which for me was an interesting subject my manager commented on different social structures involved and how people behaved I commented oh yes this sounds interesting and that we should give it a go.

With that she mentioned sex abuse was also covered in it which at this stage I started shaking and put my arm behind my head where she looked at me and I was looking at her.

I remembered thinking I can't run any longer now and I told her that this was a delicate subject for me. With that I broke down into floods of tears.

I told her I was in one and four for therapy for sex abuse now and that I was not capable of doing a course on

Sociology. I told her what happened to me last October which came up for me and that I was trying to come to terms with myself after the after math of such a shock and traumatic experience. Also I mentioned to her that after it happened to me that I just went out to fuck the world because I ran from myself for such a long time.

She completely understood me and I understood her in her role as a child vetting officer. I explained to her that I had other intentions in my mind while I started in the YMCA about tracking my abuser down and making him pay for what he had done to me and because I was dealing with this in counselling. I was also thinking of my manager helping me in finding this person and making him pay. There were also many conversations to the rape crisis center where when I was under a lot of pressure coming to terms with all of this. Especially when I felt alone and desperate because I was not the easiest person to be around. While going through all this pain and hardship.

This was going through my mind when I started on reception so much head shit to deal with and now I was sitting in an inner city gym in a community employment manager's office facing my reality of who I really was after so many years of running from myself. I was broken in my life and however never really wanting to connect because I was so scared of how my emotions would respond in any giving situation.

My manager mentioned that I had put my trust in these people who used me and raped me and that from a young age been raped and used now I was finding it hard to trust. She mentioned to me also that the guard that I had on reception was working in not really engaging with others. My other manager was always encouraging me to engage more which I was doing at time s and at other times it was just the bare minimum.

323

She spoke also about her son who is gay and how life is hard but seems to be harder if you are gay. I cried there for about 25 minutes and we sat there talking for about an hour and 20 minutes about the Dublin gay scene.

How that when you first go out and experiment with been gay that you forget the rest of society because your now in a group of other gay people who are free to express themselves and because if your treated badly growing up has a big effect on your mind so of course in a gay club you feel free and able to forget mainstream society in the way that you connect with others who have gone through emotional abuse in their lives or even worse rape. So when the party starts it can last a long time I remember doing the party circuit half way around the world running away from myself and really enjoying it however without realizing how much I was neglecting myself in the process. I was never really anywhere long enough to have my feelings come up so bad except Australia and now in Dublin.

Which you've read about earlier so we sat there talking about my managers son and how he was experiencing his early gay life and I felt that mine had come to a brutal end. Dealing with my sex addiction too don't get me wrong I enjoyed a lot of sex but I also allowed myself to abused to because from early teenage years that was what I was exposed too. I know some people in Dublin would comment on how such a good looking guy could lower himself to this but when you've been raped for three years badly you grow up thinking that your not worth that much anyway.

I remember my therapist mentioning to me that my abuse robbed me of so much that's why I called this book Almost Robbed of Everything my sanity, self-respect, self worth and life.

She also mentioned that my sex addiction was a way for me to make myself feel better when life got too much for me.

I withdrew into sex and that because I was sexually abused and emotionally abused it was a way of coping with life and escaping from reality.

Now I was been abused in a different way emotionally and to be honest I told my manager that I spent 17 years running and deep down knowing that I could not put my finger on something which had happened in my life there were guys I really liked and had relationships with for short periods of time and I remember one saying to me that there is something missing inside me I could never put my finger on it either and because I found it hard to connect with anything in my life I was suicidal for such a long time and I told my manager when I started in the YMCA that if something doesn't give in my mind about what I could not find the answer to that I was going to take my life.

I remembered listening to news stories about others who just could not handle the pain of their abuse and ended up killing themselves. Also there was a girl in my class in school who was abused and she unfortunately took her life. It took a long time for me to connect with myself and to be honest because of my subconscious mind the way it has automatically worked now I still find it hard to connect and in a way I don t really want to. I remember a mate of mine who killed himself who I flew to Gran Canaria with one year on holidays. I remembered sitting on the plane with him and the Bee Gee s how deep is your love was playing. Just mentioned this because while talking about taking lives the Bee Gee s came on the stereo in an uncanny moment of all this. While writing about this.

I'll never forget what came up for me in the YMCA and my manager who helped me through a very hard time.

I remember looking at her in the first couple of weeks as starting and thinking that I'd have problems with her I never imagined that someone who I looked down on in some way because she did not look glamorous enough for me because I cocooned myself in a superficial world for such a long time could help me so much.

I still look at people today as sex objects because I was treated like one for such a long time and in the end I hated myself for it. Because I knew there was more to me than just a piece of meat to be picked up and dropped. I also did the same however my self-esteem was now at a low and I remember my therapist mentioned to me that it is probably like that for a reason.

Now that I sit here writing this book my heart is in touch with who I'm now becoming. I'm doing my best to look after the very hurt young boy inside now and protect myself from more abuse happening to me emotional or sexual. I've learnt now to have boundaries with my body and feel that time is healing me within. At least I'm true to myself now and still have a guard up in my life. My mind can take me to places which I'd prefer to forget however the psychological scars will be with me for some time.

The government did not help me except for a weekly disability allowance I was lucky I was living with my parents at the time. I tried to have a welfare allowance officer help me when the country was awash with money and my application was refused. Even though I was managing to pay each week out of my dole money for therapy it is just as well I was living at home.

I remember on the news about a sweet heart deal which the government decided to give only after such a long time for which survivors of abuse from the catholic were given.

They took their time the Government and Catholic Church to compensate for the ones who survived.

I remember starting in the YMCA sexually messed up because I was meeting this boy who I separated from my inside to a guy who projected to the world that I did not care anymore. My sex life was a mess and I hated myself for this and even in days of therapy I ran from one in four on days after therapy because I was so fucking scared and vulnerable inside myself. Meeting a 15 year old boy in the body of a 37 year old man it was too much to handle at times. I used to phone a friend I worked with in the adult store on certain days and he just told me to go home and relax after very bad sessions in therapy.

The adult store didn't help me from what I absorbed myself in there sub consciously not in the real world dealing with adults and me inside a boy who was desperately trying to deal with himself. You could not make any of this up and I never thought for a split second that it was me who would have to endure all this, especially not the happy go lucky guy who was around in the 1990's or at other times in my life too.

Ok I'm always dressed well and people know I've got a rich uncle who in my mind was my freedom in later on in life and to be honest all this kept me alive and going thinking what I might end up with this in the future while I was going through all this. In a way I was like a baby that's what happens when you sober up and come off drugs and deal with it all.

One night on reception there was a funeral outside beside the YMCA and snow patrol were playing on the radio if I lay here I was watching the limousine outside with a family in it and I remember now thinking back in my mind that that could be my uncle and feeling very upset now that

327

I'd changed my thinking about him I was starting to care again about me and others in my life who are important to me and I just burst into tears over it all how before I sobered up I had become so selfish that is what addictions do they make you selfish.

So I ran outside again to the steps in the YMCA in tears again thinking God would this ever end. I just remember the lyrics of the song show me a garden that's bursting into light. And thinking of the darkness I surrounded myself in and so much just came up in a short space of time. 7 months.

I'm delighted that this book has finally almost come to an end because to be honest I've wanted closure on this now for quite some time. I know it is going to give me freedom in Dublin to have this published for some reason I was unable to publish this in Dublin and I found a home for it in America. I approached publishers in Dublin and to be honest I think they thought I was mad. What a mistake you made. This book explains a lot and people think I'm bitchy because I don't let many people into my life. But no one sees the real person when there at home.

Summer of 2009 I fell in love and today we are still together. My partner bought up so much for me in my life I remember watching Edie Sedgwick's Candy Darling about her life and by the end of it I ran out of the bedroom in tears. Her life reminded me of myself so much and thinking of the risks I've taken and how I can have a decent life off drugs. There was one point in her film where she is barley literate and it reminded me of myself because how badly the drugs effected me and it scares the shit out of me if I ever started to use them again.

Therapy has come to an end and for my relationship I remember connecting with my partner and found it hard to do at first because I was living in my head for such a long time. After when we had sex I was present at times and at other times I was unable to connect which upset me because I was doing my best to live in my body now.

There were many conversations on the phone to the rape crisis center and I was trying to find a way out in my mind eventually it happened. On valentines weekend before some months before I met Tomas I was sitting in White friar's Street Church and I stood in the queue to touch St Valentines relics not really having much faith in what was happening in my life because of all the trauma I had to go through. So Tomas came along and guess when his birthday is the 14th of February.

Because I had so much meaningless sexual encounters my mind would resort back to this although now I was having a relationship with someone who meant something to me it was challenging and at times I was upset because I was almost destroyed with my chance for love and to be honest I'd become bitchy because I had not felt anything for someone in some time.

Now that I was making progress with someone there were some people who were jealous of what was happening in my life and a lot of people were sceptical of our relationship lasting which it has. Even if we are not meant to be together in the future I've learnt a valuable lesson in my life about love. Which I was robbed of for such a long time.

Even connecting sexually I was finding it difficult because I just at the end of my sex addiction I was just having sex for the sake of it. And for three or four years before I was not feeling sensations in my body which bought up a lot of anger for me because I knew that love was passing me by.

So we had an amazing summer together and I was connecting more and more with different people who I met.

Over the years I isolated myself so much and because I was scared of showing the young boy who is still inside me.

Even in the beginning I was scared of trusting anyone around me in case something else was going to happen to me either been drugged or just been used all over again. It took me a month to trust my partner and after that I was more at ease with him. I still have problems with people in power I can put people on a higher level than me because I'm still meeting the young boy inside me who I ran from for such a long time.

In some way I feel lower than others and in other situations I feel above others because of the lifestyle I've had with all the experiences mixed in.

People I know have looked down on me because of the mess I got myself into before I fell in love. And now that I'm out and about in Dublin there are people smiling at me now it's amazing that if you throw your love away how you use people and allow to use yourself too.

Emotions are tricky still because there are still moods to deal with and other times there is the highs too which I make the most of. We flew to turkey together after two months together and had an amazing week together and met a woman from the YMCA and her partner who I was working on reception with. I remembered back to when I was working with him and how my sex life was in a mess and thinking how I was destroying myself through casual sex and now 9 months later I was in a completely different situation.

We sat in a restaurant in Kusadassi chatting and drinking coffees. It's amazing how things can turn around if you are willing to put the work in and try for a better life.

After the restaurant myself and Tomas ended up in a Turkish Bath House together lying on a marble stone looking up into a white small dome with holes in it looking out to the sky with steam rising up out of it. I remembered watching Rupert Everette s documentary on the middle east of one of his escapades through Turkey in a bath house similar and thinking that now I was in somewhere similar and looked at my partner and he commented that he was really happy to meet me two months ago in Dragon in Dublin.

And the two of us smiled at each other and we felt great in our shorts lying beside each other looking through the dome with the blue holes of light shining down on us.

It was a life I could become used to on a permanent basis I thought. We spent so much time together that week in Turkey we ended up on a jeep trail through some mountains and ended up looking over to one of the Greek islands which looked beautiful.

At the end of our trail we swam in some Turkish caves with some amazing colours reflecting to the water from the rocks above it was calm and cold which was refreshing to experience something which you normally would not have been able to do.

After that we spent the afternoon on the beach together swimming in the Adriatic sea it felt like a dream come through.

Another afternoon sitting in a beach café in Turkey admiring the Adriatic sea we walked off after paying our bill with the Pet Shop Boy s song playing did you see me coming.

After Turkey I returned to the YMCA and knew that I had to leave and find something to do in my earlier career October arrived and because I was now coming up to a year of what came up last year since last October there were more emotions to deal with. What I remember thinking to my crash the year before and also watching a young baby boy come in with his parents and thinking how lovely he was. I remember looking at him crawling around on the floor with his dad and thinking how cute he was and for some reason I just got upset and I suppose I saw the child loved he was almost a year old and I remember him coming in a new born baby with his parents and I could not handle him because of what I had to deal with the year before in my shocking finding.

The year before one day his mum came in with him in a buggy and I just had to go on a break it was too much to handle in my mind because I was dealing with my nightmares of been sexually abused.

So seeing him a year later with his father I just thought how protected and loved he was and I just ran outside and burst into tears I was seeing life in a different light now and because I had fallen in love my outlook was changing. I think I cried for 10 to 15 minutes and after that I was fine.

My emotions over the next few weeks were still a mess because I was on reception a week after my outburst I was faced with a totally different challenge I was there serving customers when father and son arrived again and this time I was turned on by his dads gym body and because there were young teenage boys around I got scared because I was thinking of them in a way that I was abused and because I was their age when it happened to me. I panicked because it was just too much to handle in my emotions and I ran off reception again and got upset. I was now thinking back to my 15 year old state of mind and 12 months before and was now in floods of tears thinking god will this ever end.

The week before I called my manager who is a child vetting officer and was very upset and she asked me was I alright she told me to stay in the office and she'd be over soon we talked for about an hour about where I was at in my recovery and how that I saw children as kids who could be sexually abused because of what happened to me and now that I was seeing this young boy after a year of coming into the gym with his parents now I realized that children are protected. I never forget the caring sound coming from the tone of her voice in a concerning caring way.

We spoke about my abuser and how that if he was still alive that he could be in prison now and is probably someone s bitch I felt life saying to her that he was so fucking ugly to be someone s bitch however I kept this thought to myself.

If he was not in prison she mentioned he probably lived his life in fear always waiting for that knock on the door to come not knowing who it was going to be either the police or from someone who was also abused. I remember saying to her that Christmas was approaching and that people were going to be watching me in Dublin town and how I was going to react this Christmas because of the way I isolated myself the Christmas before.

She mentioned to me that maybe people knew that something happened to me the year before and asked me to control my outburst s because I could not deal with reception if I was going to break down and that if I was noticing something going to happen just to absorb myself into the PC on reception.

To be honest once the floodgates opened I was willing to let them out because I'd suppressed so much over the years. I remember her saying that it be a long time before I was right and I thought that this was true. However this was something I did not want to hear.

So after my second outburst I called my other manager and told him what happened to me last October and that now a year had passed and for some reason it was starting to have a bad effect on me.

I was very upset that night in work and he asked me was I able to finish my shift on reception I wasn't sure and with that he asked me was there anyone I could phone I was still upset and he bought me to an office I was still in floods of tears and I phoned the rape crisis center where I spent about 30 minutes talking to a counsellor about what had just happened to me.

I told her I was also falling in love and would this have to do with my emotions coming to the surface and she replied yes. I also asked her about children and about people who have been raped and how they see children as potential victims and she told me that this was a normal reaction to rape survivors, after about 30 minutes she calmed me down and told me that she'd be thinking of me she was opened minded because I had spoken to one other counsellor who was not as good and so I left the YMCA that night and three days later I had a meeting with my managers about my position in there and they suggested to me to work voluntary I sat there listening to them with my passive attitude thinking that working voluntary was the last thing I wanted to do and how my life had come to this.

And if I wanted to bake cakes for their Christmas sale of work that the kitchen was there for me to use.

I tested out the kitchen and baked a cake however my pride could not make me bake voluntary so I decided to take the gamble and leave what else could I loose I thought by going unemployed for some months while hopefully something else materialized. My managers told me that I could come and go as I pleased and that when my emotions came up that the office was always there to talk to a counsellor in the rape crisis center.

I decided to give the baking of cakes a miss there and somehow got through Christmas alright myself and my partner were together for most of it and I spent the rest of the time with my family and friends. It was the first Christmas tree I ever bought and we spent winter of 2009 in my first ever sober relationship I ever had. I remember my manager saying to me that I pushed so much happiness away from me and even in jobs I was in for Christmas parties that because my behaviour was so outrageous that it was best if I did not attend them. This had a subconscious effect on me now. And although some Christmases were alright there were others which were lonely and feeling out of touch with reality.

I remember dancing in a club on Camden Street with a friend I used to see and we were off our heads on e and taking speed and we both commented that we had a shite Christmas because we were taking drugs and dealing with family around this time of year was always hard for me to cope with especially when I was on drugs.

Since then I have grown into them with a more positive outlook on life I don't need anymore blows in my life now at this stage to disappoint me now that this book will be published I hope that it helps others with similar problems to change as I did and to come out the other side stronger and a bit more stable.

Because I isolated myself for such a long time I find at times when I'm around people I don't know shielded and in another world. Children can throw me still because when I'm around them I feel uneasy and I think back to my own childhood from 14 to 17 when I was viciously raped. It is hard to handle and people at the time thought I did not like children. There were other suspicions also which were going through people s mind s also.

At the time I only felt comfortable with my nephews and nieces and before I faced myself in therapy I was alright with children however when all the abuse surfaced I just pushed them away. However living in the apartment block now for over two years with children about has helped me a lot. I've been through enough now and just want to be free in life weather I set myself up in Dublin or abroad. I think I'll wait another year or two and see what happens. There's a lot of bad memories in Dublin and also a lot of good memories too.

However sunshine is a great healer. I'm well known in Dublin and a lot of people talk about me I know that.

So when I left the YMCA I felt guilty about not turning up or having a goodbye party to be honest with you I would have broke down in tears so I avoided it. I felt guilty because there is a nice bunch of people there. In March of 2010 I got myself a part time job in a café in Killiney shopping center and I moved into my first home in 14 years nearby.

Because of all the trauma I was through I'd been through I was terrified that it would not work out and I was on the verge of another nervous breakdown. I'll always carry that with me I think because when you loose your sanity it is hard to maintain stability.

Especially after coming out of a bad drug problem and sex addiction with alcohol thrown into the cycle also. The people I've met in my life now are mainly from family to foreign nationals living in Dublin and some Irish friends who I've known over the years, it's a mixture of different varieties which keep me happy. My friends I met from Slovakia were like angels in the beginning because they helped me so much in connecting again with life.

After starting in the café in Killiney I felt like the guy from shine who eventually after all this his years of abuse returned to what he originally started out doing in life after a very difficult patch which he ended up going through.

I still find it hard to express myself verbally sometimes however it's all inside my head. Which I hope will be free flowing as time goes on. My partner has mentioned to me at times that he'd probably not even be here if he had to go through half of what I had to endure.

I arrived in that café not the same as I started out first in life where I was able to take anything on board. I struggled for the first couple of weeks to keep up and it is still evolving slowly I still feel sensitive but not as raw and angry as when I faced what I had to face last October 2008 and also in 2009.

I still find it hard to express myself verbally however it's all inside my head which I hope will be free flowing as time goes on. My partner has mentioned to me at time s that he would probably not even be here if he had to go through half of what I had to endure.

I suppose I'm one of the lucky ones who managed to come through it and I hope I never have to go through anything as hard as this again in my life. I feel free to a certain degree and know now that life is starting to open up to me again in some way. I hope for anyone going through therapy this book has helped them in some way. Because I allowed myself to be used in the end of my addictions I still feel that I'm building on my self worth and will be questioning my moral s for some time to come but the scars are healing now and this book is a way of doing so.

The Closing Chapter of This Book

After some weeks in the café I was still a wreck after all I had been through and thinking about my self esteem. It was in bits after all I had been through and there was an intensity inside my head which I thought would never leave me. The same year I moved into a new apartment which was a big move for me hoping that it would all work out. The year of 2010 was hard dealing with the after math of everything.

I remember shopping in Ikea for furniture in January and picking out everything for my first real home. There were a lot of changes now. Myself and Tomas were together now and that's all that mattered to me now. So many people I knew from before had gone some I wanted to get rid of and others that I thought were friends were not friends at all. I still had my other friends in my life which stood by me through all this.

Soon after I moved in Tomas moved in too. The two of us set up our home together and is now going very well for us. I was still protecting the small boy inside me and was baking cakes for a café by myself part time from 5 to 9 in the morning. In the beginning I was still all over the place because I felt so sensitive. And some mornings I returned to the apartment and cried because I was struggling with my emotions.

Eventually I settled in and did a lot of growing. I remember one woman there who was supportive to me who understood kind of where I was coming from. She had problems in the past and the smile on her face the morning she arrived after I had been trained in was touching. However I was still having problems communicating verbally. Somehow I managed to come through so I improved in time. I worked 3 days a week and the rest of the time I concentrated on this book. Every so often I threw a party with my Slovakian friends I discovered who my true friends were when myself and Tomas got it together.

Some were jealous and one who I thought was a long term friend showed their true colours. Undermining us. Others thought we would not last. I've got to admit how my high life changed in such a short space of time. However it was all so surreal. So with time I changed and started to appreciate now what I had in my life and counted my blessings also.

It took me some time to settle into my new life and I did. The media were slagging me off and I ignored them as much as possible. The kids in the apartment complex were tricky to handle at first however I became used to them and they got used to me.

I baked them cookies for Halloween which they were happy to have.

Christmas time they were knocking on the door singing Christmas carols it was a nice surprise. So I attended the staff party in work which was good.

The media announced that all my Christmases had come at once. I've got to admit I felt very sensitive leaving the café Christmas week and wished one woman a happy Christmas. The expression on her face said it all with a loving understanding also mixed with an amount of knowing that somewhere something had gone wrong. I walked out of the café and stood at the bus stop with snow falling feeling very emotional and jumped on a bus and arrived into the apartment and burst into tears. Thinking that this was my first real Christmas at home in my own place and yes it was great. I have the photos to prove it.

After realizing the work I had done three months later I left and started a carers course which I'm happy now to leave the catering world behind me. I also travelled to Lisbon and had a nice relaxed time in Lisbon. It was funny seeing places I had been to before and how on the club scene it had all seemed to change. We were out one night in a bar and as soon as we walked in the bar man played if you could read my mind and myself and Tomas sat there I thought so many changes now. I was happy to be away because I was still going through a lot of turmoil inside my head at home in Dublin.

Free abroad what a way to go I thought. The funny thing is I had only started 4 weeks before and mentioned that when I got the job that I had booked a trip and was flying out of Dublin for 10 days. Boy Georges song Karma Chameleon is playing on my sound system as I'm writing this.

So for ten days we explored Lisbon together. We ended up in a club and the owner laughed at me when we arrived in. We stayed for the drag show. The drag Queen came out on stage singing Donna Summer's Last Dance I was thinking how much the world had changed now and I was in a different state. To when I was there before with Bob.

We stayed for about an hour and left. We were chatting to a drug dealer outside and he asked us why were we in Lisbon, and that there were better places to travel to. He was completely white and was wearing a bomber jacket in the middle of summer. He left in a taxi with his Brazilian boyfriend. I thought how much he was in the dark and how unappreciative he was in life. Thinking at the end of my drug days I was the same. And was happy now to be returning to the light after such a long time.

The rest of the time in Lisbon we spent in some botanical gardens among trees, plants, and a beautiful butter fly garden. There was some parrots flying above us and outside I was thinking about the time I spent with Bart and Jack the last time I was here and how I'd love to see them again. However in the club I met them in previously I was unable to see them.

We spent three days together the two of them were artists. In their apartment they had a photograph of one blown up in a big picture frame of Jack wearing a pair of high heels from his bum down to his feet. Taken from behind. We hung out for three days out clubbing staying in bed together hanging out in their apartment chatting to them with them explaining to me that they rented from a friend and listening to Fado music.

On our last day together we drove to the beach and spent the day sunbathing and swimming on the Lisbon coast. So myself and Tomas relaxed in Lisbon together. At the zoo and in the hotel we were entertained to a pink salmon parrot in Lisbon's zoo he seemed to take to me and we played with him for about 20 minutes. I bought Tomas to the apartment I stayed in with Bob 5 years ago. Another day we walked the hill to St George Lisbon s castle and took in some amazing views overlooking Lisbon. We ended up in a church at the end of the hill after saying a prayer and lighting a candle we left and outside was a gay cruising area. I thought this was funny to have just outside a church. There were guys walking up and down outside the church cruising each other.

Another day we jumped on a train and stopped off in a town by the coast and we walked the Atlantic Coast Road and stopped off at the rocks to take some photographs of waves crashing into the rocks below us. On our way there, there was a national park with some amazing rock plants. Later we had dinner in a restaurant. There were children there who were playing I still felt some anxiety there due to what I had gone through. I thought that my mind in Dublin was still unsettled because I was still feeling raw after the after math.

Thank god it has improved so much more now. Due to the rawness which has left me and having my own space to heal now. My friend s from Slovakia helped me so much with just been there and been friends and dealing with social gatherings because in falling into sexual addictions you loose so much self worth its also lonely too. There were times in the beginning when we hooked up and I was thinking that I did not want to be around people I suppose with emotions that were coming up which I avoided for such a long time hurt, anger love and happiness. Now things have returned to some sort of normality it is much better. I'm in touch with an old friend and realize that everyone has their emotions to deal with mine just took a little longer. I'm happy I've got 2010 behind me now. Life seems less of a struggle now. Myself and Tomas travelled to Stockholm just before Christmas and we had an amazing 5 days there in a small hotel. With temperatures freezing outside our hotel room.

We could have stayed all winter in that small hotel room in Stockholm. We ended up in a small town called Skansen on top of a hill there were Reindeer and wolves with small pink ducks swimming in a lake with snow falling on the ground taking some beautiful sights in around us. It was set in the 1800's up until the 1960's with some old houses and big open fires inside them too. In the middle of the square in

Stockholm there was people ice skating on ice with Christmas trees outside and a band playing.

I was thinking about my horrible experiences last Christmas and I was still feeling sensitive about Christmas approaching and I was happy to be away from the media in Dublin. The streets were all lit up with light s and decorations and with snow falling on the ground it was great. In the old town there were candles on the ground along outside the entrances of some shops by the old streets. We arrived into a Christmas market and there was a black guy walking through with a pink hat on he was cute and smiled at me.

It was cold outside we ended up returning to our hotel room for the rest of the evening and watched films together snuggled under our duvet and watching the snow fall outside. Other times we were out having food in restaurants. All the buildings seemed so old I suppose from Viking times.

One afternoon we took a trip to the Nobel Peace prize center and walked around the rooms which overlooked the Islands of Stockholm. Inside one room there was an artist who created mosaic from the floor to the top of the roof in Gold and Black with Egyptian art all blended in it was something else to look at how someone created this in their mind I thought was something else.

Stockholm is famous for its museums and we spent another day in the fairy castle in a park which was covered in snow. We checked out different styles of fashion dated from the 1990's up until 2010 we took some photographs of ourselves in the fashion hall thinking that we looked good. After leaving the castle outside looking up at it was something else.

After 5 days we jumped into a taxi and drove through the streets of Stockholm around 4 am to a city that was asleep. One night we were at the port waiting for a night club to open on a boat. It was late and dark and in McDonalds the counter assistant winked at me I was feeling inside that I could leave this part of my life behind now. So myself and Tomas left and returned to the hotel and watched films again under the duvet with snow falling again outside. So with the memories of Stockholm visiting the palace and looking through the guest apartments overlooking the sea and walking around the grounds of the palace with snow covered cobble stones and squares with guards standing about with heavy coats dressed in navy guarding the treasure which we saw on display we flew to Dublin and settled into Christmas.

It all worked out fine. Christmas we spent with my parents and walked about Dalkey with snow on the ground. The sky was blue with the sun setting over Killiney Hill which created a reflection in the snow as pink and walking through the streets with decorations and trees outside some houses. And through the windows it all seemed so special. We opened each others presents in the evening at home. So much had changed now and I suppose looking back I thought I'd never come through what I had to go through. I suppose time is a great healer.

2010 was a year of major changes with also a lot to dealing in the real world after going through therapy. I spent a lot of time working on this book which I have now found a good home for. Looking back the world has changed and moves so fast since I starting writing which was on and off for the best part of six years. I suppose now is the time for it all to be released. I remember my manager in the YMCA asking me to come in and see her as I was leaving. She commented to me when I sat in her office that it was not the money that bought me into the YMCA that it was the work I did on myself. She was asking me about some music she had on a play list about how to find some solution in burning a C D which I helped her with there was a problem with her pc. She deliberately set it up and with that she played a remix of KC and the Sunshine Band Please Don't Go.

We sat there listening to it and I told her I love that song. The next track she played was Black Boxes Right on Time. I remember her saying to me one day that I had to clock in when I arrived to work and told me to get my act together. The bond we created was something special. And I still think of her today after I left which was October 2009.

I drop into to see her from time to time and I remember her saying that it was a lot to go through. There s times in Dublin I think how I came through and appreciate how people helped me. I mentioned to her one time that I was thinking of leaving Dublin and she said I'd be missed. I told her I was happy in some way to have worked in the YMCA and she replied that she was happy to have me.

So since last March I left the café and I've been between jobs and now I'm exploring other options. In a way we are looked after even though at times when it becomes hard we think we are not. So many people had come and gone in my life.

The same year I flew to London to see my uncle for some reason I needed to explore London again alone. And thought about the media in Dublin giving me a hard time. So another city would take my mind off the emotions I was experiencing so off I flew. Tomas wanted me to stay even though I wanted him to come I just wanted to go over some old experiences. I arrived into London and jumped into a taxi from London Bridge and arrived into Kennington to my uncle greeting me. We sat on the balcony again overlooking central London and spoke about my aunt who passed away. He was mentioning how much he missed her and that he now wanted return to Ireland to live where he spent some of his childhood. I thought he was crazy leaving London to live in rural Ireland after spending 40 years of his life in London. What a change I thought.

So after coffee we stopped in Tesco and stocked up on food and booze and later that evening we cooked dinner and sat there with a bottle of wine. The next day I walked through Kennington feeling good about my new venture in finding a publisher for my book. I had read one of Boy Georges books and Random House who published his and was hoping that they'd do the same with mine. So I walked over Vauxhall Bridge and found Random House. I walked in and asked could I see somebody in connection to publishing a book I wrote. Feeling very optimistic the guy behind the reception told me I needed to find an agent first mate. So I left and walked to Vauxhall tube station and jumped on a tube to Piccadilly and stopped off in Boots and bought some French Connection Uk's for Tomas.

After boots I stopped off in River Island and bought a top which I wore about 5 times. Later on I walked to Brewer Street and passing through the Adult Stores I spotted a famous porn star who I thought was hot. I liked his style combats and a red muscle tee shirt. I passed by a fat guy talking to a hot guy asking him did he ever have sex where he wanted to die. I thought this was dark and thought yes there are times when you wanted to die having sex because it was so good or else so bad.

I turned onto Compton Street into a shorts shop looking at all the shorts thinking which ones would look good on me on the beach. The guy behind the counter was hot and he asked me would I like to try something on. I laughed and replied no thanks and left on a high and had a coffee outside a café on old Compton Street. The Soho scene was passing and I sat looking at muscle guys who looked like they were porn stars.

I saw an Irish guy who used to come into the adult store in Dublin with his boyfriend and the two of us smiled at each other. After my coffee I walked to Piccadilly tube station and jumped on a tube to Vauxhall. Down in the tunnels of London a lady bird flew onto my hand. I thought this was strange for such a busy city in Central London for a lady bird to land on my hand.

I walked out of Vauxhall station through Kennington and arrived into see my uncle after all he is a millionaire. We had dinner and another bottle of wine. After dinner we were on a bus to the west end to see a show called Tap Dog. With some of his friends who live in Greenwich. We met up outside the theatre and saw Australian guy s tap dancing on stage. The theatre was very elegant and designed with orange colours and chandeliers. With a lot of good looking guys on stage. After the show we left Drury Street on a high and the four of us had dinner in some fabulous theatre restaurant just around the corner. The two guys from London were together 18 years and the four of us talked about my aunt's death and where they were living in Greenwich. Their house overlooked most of London.

I remember when I was a kid my parents stayed with them and their description of how there house was so peaceful in London. That you wouldn't think you were staying in such a big city staying there. Peter mentioned to me that I should check out a club near the River Thames which had a sex party in it. I decided to party later on in Vauxhall in a club under the arches. After dinner we said goodbye and my uncle and I walked over West Minster Bridge to South Bank the view was amazing with the view of the big wheel and the Houses of Parliament with the river Thames all lit up.

We stopped off in the film center and watched a Slovakian film about a boy and his dad who was a pilot. What I noticed about this film was how the young boy seemed to be isolated and it was just him and his dad.

We left and walked along the river Thames to the Houses of Parliament. London seemed so peaceful on a Friday night we arrived into the apartment and had another drink. I sat and looked through the guide for Vauxhall for a club to go to.

I found one which seemed cool and sat there thinking I'd have another drink before I left to venture into the London Gay Scene. Later on I left and walked through Kennington and a homeless Irish Girl stopped me and asked me for a cigarette.

I gave her half my pack and said there you go. She asked me was I Irish and I replied yes. She mentioned to me that I should get myself out of London before it robbed me of my soul. I told her that she should get herself back to Ireland and see her family and that the government promised anybody that needed housing that they would help them get off the streets in 2010.

I left her about 12.30 standing outside a block of flats with a black woman who looked like she was on crack. I thought London can be a very lonely place if you have problems because it moves so fast and people now just seem to care about themselves.

I also thought about how lucky I was in my own situation at home where I was having my own problems. I walked into a club in Vauxhall and drank soda and limes for the rest of the night. The music was techno house which I noticed now had changed from the funky house music which I was into.

I felt so sensitive inside me and my body seemed stiff. I was dancing and with that a guy came over to me and said I could move it a bit he introduced himself to me. After feeling less isolated we were chatting on the dance floor together with his friends smiling over at us. He mentioned to me that he'd love to chat and asked me did I want to go outside and sit down. So we picked up our drinks and sat outside until 1 45 in the morning. Some black drug dealers approached us asking us did we want any drugs.

I was aware of my drug problem in the past and replied no thanks. Austin was more friendly and calm and mentioned that if he wanted some later he'd come back to him later.

Austin asked me to stay with him in Hampstead I replied no. Austin mentioned to me that he could sense fear in me. I suppose I was still feeling fragile after all that had come up before and also I was going out with Tomas now. He asked me why was I in London by myself and I commented about how I was looking for someone to publish my book. He asked me what it was about and I mentioned that it was about travelling and clubs. London in the 1990's and travelling through Europe, Dublin and Australia.

He told me he owned a hair salon in Soho and that I should drop by anytime to see him. He mentioned that he sensed fear inside me and I was thinking of my recent release from therapy and what I had to deal with. I mentioned nothing to him about this. He told me that I had a good heart and that on the gay scene it was hard to come across someone like this. And then he left.

I stayed on and danced the night away feeling better and relaxed. The D j played Duran Duran's the reflex. Most people were looking at me and smiling. It got me thinking that the reflex is a lonely child waiting by the park. I could relate to it and thought about the amount of times I spent cruising by myself in the past near the park. At 3 45 am I was looking at the show girls with their feathers swinging them about on the podium thinking they were transsexuals and I thought their lives looked dark. The club was not as busy as I expected it to be. One guy came up to me and told me I was a very good dancer which I thanked him for. He mentioned where his parent s were from and asked me where I was from. I told him Dublin. He was a nice guy however I knew he was involved with the London mafia. I left that night thinking if it was ten years before that I would have entertained him the world now is a lot more dangerous than before. Or else I was just looking after myself better.

I walked through Kennington alone at 4 A m thinking that my own life was dark and that I had to change my daily hours. My part time career in catering was destroying me with having to wake up at 4.30 am. And cycle through Bally brack in the middle of winter. To open up an empty café alone and one morning the alarm went off and I ran out into the middle of Killiney shopping center thinking how had my life turned to this and thinking to myself that I was usually coming home at this hour of the morning. After thinking about this walking through Kennington a devil worshipper turned out of the corner after Tesco on Kennington. He was wearing a black three quarter length coat with a silver star and I looked at him and he looked so alone in his life of darkness.

I walked past him and thought of the lonely busy street in London. Earlier on I passed Pakistani newsagents who were receiving a delivery of newspapers they opened their hatch and closed it just as fast in fear of been mugged I thought. I thought about how this world had changed with been unsafe now and dangerous. And that people just buy and sell for a living and treat each other like shit in the process. The whole world is going down it seems now.

I suppose when you've been abused to the highest order your outlook on life changes.

So I sat on the wall outside my apartment where I was staying and thought I had to change my job in Dublin. However I stayed on to prove a point over Christmas that yes I do celebrate Christmas. The last two years previously in the YMCA which was over the last two Christmases, I was unable to deal with people in a party atmosphere.

Because of the gang rape that came up in 2009. Three months later 1 left which was in March. Since then I'm currently unemployed except for writing this book. I don't care at the moment because you can be broke and happy. I remember someone saying to me not for ever though. Which I thought was funny.

I stayed in London for another three days and did nothing on Sunday except buy food and booze for some of my family who were coming over for lunch on Sunday. My aunt who I used to live with in London dropped over I commented to her that her jewellery was nice and she replied that she wore it especially for me because she knew I liked some glamour we sat on the balcony and she was asking with my cousins how was I doing with my book and I mentioned that I was unable to get past the reception in Vauxhall. We had lunch overlooking London and drinks chatting about times in Dublin and how life there was more social. I thought true.

The evening flew by so fast in time that when they left it was just one of tHose fly by Sunday afternoons with family that you haven't seen in some time who you enjoy spending time with. On Monday I was swimming in a pool off Carnaby Street someone commented in the changing area that I was a legend for the afternoon I was shopping on Oxford Street walking through Top Man I thought the design of the shop was brilliantly designed with the lighting inside with mountains of cloths on different floors with some music pumping. Two hours flew by and I noticed how my confidence was improving in London with been surrounded by so many people.

I walked to the bus stop for Kennington and stood there waiting for my bus. A nice guy was waiting there to who had just arrived and we looked at each other and smiled 2 minutes later he was on another bus that's London for you. My bus arrived and I was sitting down stairs looking through the busy London streets with so much going on and with my shopping bags noticed how many London buses were on the streets.

I got off at Kennington with my Top Man and H and M bags and passed a villain who smiled and I smiled too and the two of us seemed amused by each other. I was thinking about a recession and how I was doing alright for myself considering.

So later that night I jumped on the tube and travelled the Northern line from Kennington to Angel where I met a friend of a friend. We had drinks in a bar I was standing by the tube station in the rain where I met David and we sat in a bar with about 10 other people and talked about life in Dublin and life in London.

While I was standing out in the beer garden with a second drink some guy arrived in I have to admit he was hot and muscular kind of Jack the lad. I knew he was a criminal and he was smiling over at me we both knew there was something more to each other. Every so often we were checking each other out eventually he came over and introduced himself and joined us for a drink. He mentioned that 10 years ago this pub was packed with everyone on E and that it was overflowing with party people. He was dressed in a black bomber jacket and black jeans with a black hat on.

There was something about him which I was attracted to and by the time the three of us were chatting he asked me what was I doing in London. I told him to mind his own fucking business just joking. I mentioned that I wanted a break and I tried to approach a publisher with my book, and mentioned also that it had the potential for a musical the two of them seemed interested and asked what was it about. Without going into to many details I mentioned it was about travelling and experiences I had in different places. I mentioned nothing about abuse and glossed it over with the gay scene. We started chatting about the rave scene in the 1990's and how it was such good fun.

Now that we were older it didn't seem to have the same attraction. As the night moved on I sensed from David that he also had damaged himself through drugs. He didn't seem as confident in himself as he first appeared. There was something not right.

He mentioned to me that the book sounded like a good idea and he produced a tatty business card and told me that if I needed an accountant that I should contact this person.

I reckon he had mental health problems because his confidence was not the same as when he first arrived in. It was funny mine was improving and his was decreasing. He started talking to me about splitting up with his partner and that he was seeing his son tomorrow for the day. I could sense his loss which I myself had some sort of loss absorbing myself in clubbing too.

He was talking about clubs in Vauxhall and how he was not that interested in dancing by himself anymore. He wanted a relationship with someone. I sensed it didn't matter if it was a guy or girl.

We chatted for about 3 hours and I picked up on his loss through the drug scene. He also mentioned saunas where he ended up after night s of clubbing. I'd been there too and I told him if he could find a lover that everything would change for the better. I told him about Tomas and how I was seeing my life from a different light now.

It was funny meeting this London character on a Monday night in the middle of London. We both clicked and had an interesting conversation about life. I sensed he was living in a home because as the night moved on he mentioned he had to be in at a certain hour. I was happy with my own freedom. Even though I was experiencing tensions in my own life it was manageable to cope with though.

A lot of it was coming up in work things seemed to be better for me now. By the end of the night he left and commented that the book was a good idea. And to take care I said likewise and he mentioned it was a good night.

He thanked me for having such a good night and I watched him walk off into a cold London night walking funny with a slight hop. I thought to myself that London is such a big city and thinking about him as where he was going to in the middle of the night. There was something vulnerable inside him and I myself was feeling much stronger.

I left after my cigarette and the bar man thanked me for coming in. I walked to the night bus and a young guy asked me for a pound. I gave him a pound how generous of me I thought and he asked was I interested in buying a bottle of wine and sitting on the side of the road with him. I was thinking more of the Ritz and replied no thanks mate thinking of him in what a life. He asked me for another one I thought he was a cheeky bastard I replied no sorry.

I jumped on my bus to central London and walked into 79 Charring Cross and meet 2 guys from Dublin. One winked at me and I joined them for a drink. I used to go out with a friend of his and he asked me how long was I in London for. I mentioned that I was flying home in the morning by this stage it was 1.30 in the morning. They were staying another two days. His friend used to live above me in a house of flats in Dublin and I thought what a small world.

There was a guy with his top off dancing beside me and as it turned out he was Irish as well. There was a lot of fun between us he was very funny and also insane from whatever he was taking. I was feeling so empty inside and he commented to me that he knew how I felt. I stayed for another two drinks and to be honest I was looking forward to seeing Tomas the following day when I returned to Dublin.

Thinking how I'd done this routine in my life before and I was happy to be in a relationship that was stable. The next day I flew to Dublin and returned to Tomas. The expression on his face was beautiful and he arranged petals of flowers on a silver tray with candles in the middle and was cooking a meal.

What a welcome I thought just after I needed after feeling so empty inside the night before in central London. Leaving Charring Cross in a taxi and driving through passing homeless people on Charring Cross Road.

On returning to Dublin I noticed how there was more green grass areas in Dublin in comparison to London s concrete jungle with sea views in Dublin's more open space.

Together we sat in feeling a close bond to each other. It took me two weeks to recover from my drinking which I noticed the effect in work cycling through Ballybrack to bake for the café in the morning. My head was not in a fit state however two weeks passed and I was feeling better. I was happy that I was letting go of certain habits in my life now.

I felt so battered in work my boss was away for two weeks which I suppose I timed well. So I continued to work on this book every so often threw parties in my apartment for friends thinking that I still hadn't returned to my normal self. Last year I let go of so much and this year is so much better now and I suppose in time there is more to come. As Joan Rivers once mentioned life has a funny way of working out. What else can say.

The scars are healing all the time. It's amazing now been in a long term relationship, where the emotional shocks have disappeared. Which, however took a long time to eventually leave.

A line from my therapist who helped me (it's ok it was not my fault I was just a boy and even if I never worked again she mentioned that I survived sexual abuse)

Ended with the Village People YMCA

And song for Tomas the Beautiful South Song for Whoever I love you from the bottom of my pencil case which has the date the 28th of April on it in a cheque which also happens to be my Mums birthday. Thanks for listening to me Mum when I had to go through all this pain in therapy.

I wish anyone who's recovered from sexual abuse or who is going through sexual abuse with their nightmares the best in life now. There is light at the end of the tunnel in the land of make believe.

Take Care.

Stephen Brennan
Author.